普通高等教育规划教

机械工程专业英语

第二版

廖宇兰 主 编
李 粤 马庆芬 副主编

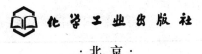

·北京·

本书共 17 个单元,内容包括机械工程基础(力学、工程材料及其处理、绘图、公差、机械原理、机械零件、热加工和成形技术等),机械加工设备与技术,计算机化制造技术和机电一体化技术(涉及数控技术、工业机器人、计算机辅助设计与制造、柔性制造和成组技术等),装配,农业机械(涉及常用的动力机械如汽油机和柴油机,常用的农业机械如拖拉机)。

本书内容的选取均为国内外报刊、杂志、教材、论著等,内容编排按照学生学习专业知识的过程循序渐进,有连贯性,英语语言由浅入深,有系统性。每个单元围绕一个主题(theme)编选课文和练习题。为方便教学,配套电子课件。

本书可作为高等工科院校学生教学用书,并可供从事机械、电子、车辆等相关专业工作的科研、工程技术人员参考。

图书在版编目(CIP)数据

机械工程专业英语/廖宇兰主编. —2 版. —北京:化学工业出版社,2016.9
普通高等教育规划教材
ISBN 978-7-122-27681-0

Ⅰ.①机⋯ Ⅱ.①廖⋯ Ⅲ.①机械工程-英语-高等学校-教材 Ⅳ.①H31

中国版本图书馆 CIP 数据核字(2016)第 171720 号

责任编辑:韩庆利　　　　　　　　　　装帧设计:关　飞
责任校对:王素芹

出版发行:化学工业出版社(北京市东城区青年湖南街 13 号　邮政编码 100011)
印　　装:高教社(天津)印务有限公司
787mm×1092mm　1/16　印张 16¼　字数 440 千字　2016 年 9 月北京第 2 版第 1 次印刷

购书咨询:010-64518888(传真:010-64519686)　　售后服务:010-64518899
网　　址:http://www.cip.com.cn
凡购买本书,如有缺损质量问题,本社销售中心负责调换。

定　价:38.00 元　　　　　　　　　　　　　　　　　　　　　　　版权所有　违者必究

前　言

本教材是结合各校目前的实际情况和教学计划安排，为机械设计制造及其自动化、机械电子工程和农业机械化及其自动化等专业而编写的。目的是在教师的指导下，通过一定的阅读量，重点培养学生阅读本专业书刊的能力。

叙述科技内容的语言和日常生活用语固然是同一种语言，但科技英语在其词汇和语言风格上毕竟有其特点。科学技术本身的多学科性要求专业英语与专业内容相互一致。因此，专业英语（Subject-Based English，简称 SBE）和科技英语（English for Special Science and Technology，简称 EST）在语言特点上虽然是一致的，但是在专业内容上（主要表现在词汇方面）其覆盖面又有其特点。同一个单词在不同的专业中往往有不同的含义。作为专业英语重点关心本专业的相关内容。目的是以英语为工具获得本专业的信息。

本教材共分五部分，共 17 个单元。第一部分为机械工程基础，包括力学、工程材料及其处理、绘图、公差、机械原理、机械零件、热加工和成形技术等。第二部分为机械加工设备与技术。第三部分为计算机化制造技术和机电一体化技术，涉及数控技术、工业机器人、计算机辅助设计与制造、柔性制造和成组技术等。第四部分为装配方面的内容。第五部分为部分农业机械方面的内容，涉及常用的动力机械如汽油机和柴油机，常用的农业机械如拖拉机。

本教材内容的选取均为国内外报刊、杂志、教材、论著和其他文选，内容编排按照本科学生学习专业知识的过程循序渐进，有连贯性，英语语言由浅入深，有系统性。每个单元围绕一个主题（theme）编选课文和练习题。因课堂学习学时有限，可有针对性地选择每单元的前面章节作为重点学习内容，其余部分可作为课后阅读材料，以获得较完整的专业英语知识。

本教材是在第一版使用的基础上针对书中的错误进行修订，同时对章节后面的习题重新编排，使习题在章节后出现的位置更加合理。相比第一版，增加了力学内容作为第二单元，其它单元以此往后类推。在计算机辅助设计与制造的章节中增加了计算机辅助设计软件如 SolidWorks 和有限元分析方法的介绍。

本书由廖宇兰担任主编，李粤、马庆芬担任副主编。编写分工为：第一部分，第 1 单元（周腾），第 2、3 单元（罗洪峰），第 4 单元（朱冬云），第 5 单元（李粤），第 6~8 单元（廖宇兰），第 9 单元（郭志忠）；第二部分，第 10 单元（王娟），第 11、12 单元（廖宇兰）；第三部分，第 13 单元（张燕），第 14 单元（周腾），第 15 单元（廖宇兰）；第四部分，第 16 单元（马庆芬）；第五部分，第 17 单元（袁成宇）；词汇附录（罗洪峰）。全书由廖宇兰统稿和校订。

本书配套电子课件，可赠送给用书的院校和老师，如果需要，可登录 www.cipedu.com.cn 下载。

对于书中存在的不足之处，望同行专家及广大读者给予批评指正。

廖宇兰
2016 年 5 月

Preface

According to the requirement for the professional English learning stage and considering the actual condition and teaching planned arrangement of most university, this teaching material is compiled for specialties such as Mechanical Manufacture and Automation, Agricultural Mechanization Automation, Mechatronic Engineering, and so on. With this book, under the guidance of teacher and through certain reading, the student will get the ability of reading his professional materials.

The language of the statement content of science and technology are same language as daily life term language, but the English of science and technology has its characteristic after all on its vocabulary and language style. As for science and technology, the subject requirement professional English and professional content are mutually consistent, and each subject has its own store of terms. Therefore, SBE should be consistent with the substance of the corresponding subject. And the English of science and technology (EST) is though consistent on language characteristic, is however on professional content (major expression in vocabulary aspect) it coverage also has its characteristic. A same word often has different meaning in different special field. Caring for the related content of own special field as professional English focal point, the main Purpose is to get the useful information of own special field by means of English.

This teaching material divides into 5 parts totally, contains 17 Units. The first part is fundamentals of mechanical engineering, includes mechanics, materials and its treatmenting and properties, mechanical drawing, engineering tolerancing, mechanism, machine parts, hot working and forming processes and so on. The second part is equipment and technology of machine manufacture. The third part is computerized manufacturing and mechatronics technologies, includes technology of numerical control, industrial robot, CAD/CAM, flexible manufacturing, group technology and so on. The fourth part is the content in the aspect of assembly. The fifth part is machinery for agriculture, concerned with the patrol engine, diesel engine, tractor and so on.

This teaching material is selected from the publications of domestic and international publishers. Its content has continuity step by step according to the process of undergraduate learning professional knowledge; English language goes from the easy to the difficult and complicated systematically. Every unit revolves around a theme to compile text and practice problem. In order to get more complete professional English knowledge, it should select the preceding chapter per unit as focal point to study because of limited class hours, others reading materials should be studied independently.

Based on the first use of teaching material, some mistakes in the book are revised and some chapters exercises are rearranged so as to get the more reasonable position. Compared to the first edition, the increasing mechanical content lay out in the second unit, the other units are in order to later. In the unit CAD/CAM/CAPP, the computer aided design soft such as SolidWorks and the the finite element method (FEM) was introduced.

Liao Yulan is chief editor, Li Yue and Ma Qingfen is Associate editor in this book. The division of labor is: The first part: The 1st unit (Zhou Teng), the 2-3rd unit (Luo Hongfeng), the 4th unit (Zhu Dongyun), the 5th unit (Li Yue), the 6-8th units (Liao Yulan), the 9th unit (Guo Zhizhong). The second part: The 10th unit (Wang Jian), the 11-12th unit (Liao Yulan). The third part: The 13th unit (Zhang Yan), The14th unit (Zhou Teng), the 15th unit (Liao Yulan). The fourth part: The 16th unit (Ma Qingfen). The fifth part: The 17th unit (Yuan Chengyu). Appendix (Luo Hongfeng). This book is compiled and checked by Liao Yulan.

There are the insufficient places and the errors and omissions in the book, expecting the experts in the same fields and the public readers can give the criticism and point out mistakes.

Liao Yulan
May 2016

CONTENTS

Part1　Fundamentals of Mechanical Engineering ·········· 1
  Unit1　Mechanical Engineering ·········· 1
    PassageⅠ　Introduction to Mechanical Engineering ·········· 1
    PassageⅡ　Introduction to Design ·········· 6
    PassageⅢ　Manufacturing ·········· 8
    PassageⅣ　The Science of Mechanics ·········· 10
  Unit2　Mechanics ·········· 14
    PassageⅠ　Introduction of Mechanics ·········· 14
    PassageⅡ　Basic Concepts of Mechanics ·········· 16
    PassageⅢ　Force ·········· 18
    PassageⅣ　Fluid Dynamics ·········· 20
  Unit3　Engineering Materials ·········· 25
    PassageⅠ　Metals and Ferrous Metals ·········· 25
    PassageⅡ　Nonmetallic Materials ·········· 28
    PassageⅢ　Powder Metallurgy ·········· 31
  Unit4　Material Treatment and Properties ·········· 35
    PassageⅠ　Heat Treatment ·········· 35
    PassageⅡ　Mechanical Properties of Metals ·········· 37
    PassageⅢ　Stress and strain ·········· 39
    PassageⅣ　Surface Treatment ·········· 41
  Unit5　Mechanical Drawing ·········· 45
    PassageⅠ　Engineering Drawing ·········· 45
    PassageⅡ　Sectional Views ·········· 48
    PassageⅢ　Machine Drawings ·········· 50
    PassageⅣ　AutoCAD ·········· 53
  Unit6　Mechanism ·········· 56
    PassageⅠ　Introduction to Mechanism ·········· 56
    PassageⅡ　Shafting ·········· 59
    PassageⅢ　Linkages ·········· 61
  Unit7　Machine Parts ·········· 65
    PassageⅠ　Fasteners ·········· 65
    PassageⅡ　Keys, Splines, and Pins ·········· 69
    PassageⅢ　Bearings ·········· 71
    PassageⅣ　Gears ·········· 73

Unit8　Mechanical Design ………………………………………………………………… 77
　　Passage I　Introduction to Mechanical Design ………………………………………… 77
　　Passage II　Machine Design ……………………………………………………………… 80
　　Passage III　Engineering Tolerancing …………………………………………………… 81
　　Passage IV　Conceptual Design ………………………………………………………… 84
Unit9　Hot Working and Forming Processes ……………………………………………… 88
　　Passage I　Casting ………………………………………………………………………… 88
　　Passage II　Welding ……………………………………………………………………… 92
　　Passage III　Forming ……………………………………………………………………… 94
　　Passage IV　Forging ……………………………………………………………………… 98

Part2　Equipment and Technology of Machine Manufacture …………………… 101

Unit10　Basic Machining Operations—Turning, Boring and Milling ………………… 101
　　Passage I　Basic Machining Operations ……………………………………………… 101
　　Passage II　Turning on Lathe centers ………………………………………………… 105
　　Passage III　Boring ……………………………………………………………………… 107
　　Passage IV　Milling ……………………………………………………………………… 108
Unit11　Broaching, Sawing, Drilling and Reaming ……………………………………… 112
　　Passage I　Broaching …………………………………………………………………… 112
　　Passage II　Sawing ……………………………………………………………………… 117
　　Passage III　Drilling ……………………………………………………………………… 118
　　Passage IV　Reaming …………………………………………………………………… 120
Unit12　Lathes and Other Machines ……………………………………………………… 124
　　Passage I　Lathes, Boring Machines and Planing Machine ………………………… 124
　　Passage II　Drill press …………………………………………………………………… 128
　　Passage III　Grinding Wheels and Grinding Machines ……………………………… 130
　　Passage IV　Milling Machines ………………………………………………………… 132

Part3　Computerized Manufacturing and Mechatronics Technologies ………… 136

Unit13　Technologies of Numerical Control and Mechatronics ………………………… 136
　　Passage I　Numerical Control of Production Equipments (I) ……………………… 136
　　Passage II　Numerical Control of Production Equipments (II) …………………… 140
　　Passage III　Industrial Robot …………………………………………………………… 146
　　Passage IV　Adaptive Control of Machine Tools …………………………………… 150
Unit14　CAD/CAM/CAPP ………………………………………………………………… 156
　　Passage I　CAD and CAM ……………………………………………………………… 156
　　Passage II　SolidWorks ………………………………………………………………… 159
　　Passage III　Finite Element Method …………………………………………………… 161
　　Passage IV　Computer Aided Process Planning (CAPP) …………………………… 165
Unit15　Advanced Technology of Manufacturing ……………………………………… 173
　　Passage I　Group Technology ………………………………………………………… 173
　　Passage II　Cellular Manufacturing …………………………………………………… 178
　　Passage III　Machine Centers ………………………………………………………… 180

PassageⅣ	Flexible Manufacturing Systems	183
PassageⅤ	Computer Integrated Manufacturing System（Ⅰ）	189
PassageⅥ	Computer Integrated Manufacturing System（Ⅱ）	193

Part4　Assembly　197
Unit16　Assembly　197
　　PassageⅠ　Introduction to Assembly　197
　　PassageⅡ　Types of Manual Assembly Methods　200
　　PassageⅢ　Automated Assembly　202
　　PassageⅣ　Assembly Machines and Systems　205

Part5　Machinery for Agriculture　210
Unit17　Engine and Tractor　210
　　PassageⅠ　How the Engine Works　210
　　PassageⅡ　The patrol Engine　216
　　PassageⅢ　Diesel Engines　217
　　PassageⅣ　The tractor　220

Glossary　224
参考文献　250

Part 1 Fundamentals of Mechanical Engineering

Unit 1 Mechanical Engineering

Passage I Introduction to Mechanical Engineering

Mechanical engineering is the branch of engineering that deals with machines and the production of power. It is particularly concerned with forces and motion.

History of Mechanical Engineering

The invention of the steam engine in the latter part of the 18th century, providing a key source of power for the Industrial Revolution, gave an enormous impetus to the development of machinery of all types. As a result a new major classification of engineering, separate from civil engineering and dealing with tools and machines, developed, receiving formal recognition in 1847 in the founding of the Institution of Mechanical Engineers in Birmingham, England.

Mechanical engineering has evolved from the practice by the mechanic of an art based largely on trial and error to the application by the professional engineer of the scientific method in research, design, and production.

The demand for increased efficiency, in the widest sense, is continually raising the quality of work expected from a mechanical engineer and requiring of him a higher degree of education and training. Not only must machines run more economically but capital costs also must be minimized.

Fields of Mechanical Engineering

Development of machines for the production of goods The high material standard of living in the developed countries owes much to the machinery made possible by mechanical engineering. The mechanical engineer continually invents machines to produce goods and develops machine tools of increasing accuracy and complexity to build the machines.

The principal lines of development of machinery have been an increase in the speed of operation to obtain high rates of production, improvement in accuracy to obtain quality and economy in the product, and minimization of operating costs. These three requirements have led to the evolution of complex control systems.

The most successful production machinery is that in which the mechanical design of the machine is closely integrated with the control system, whether the latter is mechanical or electrical in nature. A modern transfer line (conveyor) for the manufacture of automobile engines is a good example of the mechanization of a complex series of manufacturing processes. Developments are in hand to automate production machinery further, using computers to store and process the vast amount of data required for manufacturing a variety of components with a small number of versatile machine tools. One aim is a completely automated machine shop for batch production, operating on a three-shift basis but attended by a staff for only one shift per day.

Development of machines for the production of power Production machinery presupposes an ample supply of power. The steam engine provided the first practical means of generating power from heat to augment the old sources of power from muscle, wind, and water. One of first challenges to the new profession of mechanical engineering was to increase thermal efficiencies and power; this was done principally by the development of the steam turbine and associated large steam boilers. The 20th century has witnessed a continued rapid growth in the power output of turbines for driving electric generators, together with a steady increase in thermal efficiency and reduction in capital cost per kilowatt of large power stations. Finally, mechanical engineers acquired the resource of nuclear energy, whose application has demanded an exceptional standard of reliability and safety involving the solution of entirely new problems. The control systems of large power plants and complete nuclear power stations have become highly sophisticated networks of electronic, fluidic, electric, hydraulic, and mechanical components, all of these involving the province of the mechanical engineer.

The mechanical engineer is also responsible for the much smaller internal combustion engines, both reciprocating (gasoline and diesel) and rotary (gas-turbine and Wankel) engines, with their widespread transport applications. In the transportation field generally, in air and space as well as on land and sea, the mechanical engineer has created the equipment and the power plant, collaborating increasingly with the electrical engineer, especially in the development of suitable control systems.

Development of military weapons The skills applied to war by the mechanical engineer are similar to those required in civilian applications, though the purpose is to enhance destructive power rather than to raise creative efficiency. The demands of war have channelled huge resources into technical fields, however, and led to developments that have profound benefits in peace. Jet aircraft and nuclear reactors are notable examples.

Bioengineering Bioengineering is a relatively new and distinct field of mechanical engineering that includes the provision of machines to replace or augment the functions of the human body and of equipment for use in medical treatment. Artificial limbs have been developed incorporating such lifelike functions as powered motion and touch feedback. Development is rapid in the direction of artificial spare-part surgery. Sophisticated heart-lung machines and similar equipment permit operations of increasing complexity and permit the vital functions in seriously injured or diseased patients to be maintained.

Environmental control Some of the earliest efforts of mechanical engineers were aimed at controlling man's environment by pumping water to drain or irrigate land and by ventilating mines. The ubiquitous refrigerating and air-conditioning plats of the modern age are based on a reversed heat engine, where the supply of power 'pumps' heat from the cold region to the warmer exterior.

Many of the products of mechanical engineering, together with technological developments in other fields, have side effects on the environment and give rise to noise, the pollution of water and air, and the dereliction of land and scenery. The rate of production, both of goods and power, is rising so rapidly that regeneration by natural forces can no longer keep pace. A rapidly growing field for mechanical engineers and others is environmental control, comprising the development of machines and processes that will produce fewer pollutants and of new equipment and techniques that can reduce or remove the pollution already generated.

Functions of Mechanical Engineering

Four functions of the mechanical engineering, common to all the fields mentioned, be cited. The first is the understanding of and dealing with the bases of mechanical science. These include dynamics, concerning the relation between forces and motion, such as in vibration; automatic control; thermodynamics, dealing with the relations among the various forms of heat, energy, and power; fluid flow; heat transfer; lubrication; and properties of materials.

Second is the sequence of research, design, and development. This function attempts to bring about the changes necessary to meet present and future needs. Such work requires not only a clear understanding of mechanical science and an ability to analyze a complex system into its basic factors, but also the originality to synthesize and invent.

Third is production of products and power, which embraces planning, operation, and maintenance. The goal is to produce the maximum value with the minimum investment and cost while maintaining or enhancing longer term viability and reputation of the enterprise or the institution.

Fourth is the coordinating function of the mechanical engineering, including management, consulting, and, in some cases, marketing.

In all of these functions there is a long continuing trend toward the use of scientific instead of traditional or intuitive methods, an aspect of the ever-growing professionalism of mechanical engineering. Operations research, value engineering, and PABLA (problem analysis by logical approach) are typical titles of such new rationalized approaches. Creativity, however, cannot be rationalized. The ability to take the important and unexpected step that opens up new solutions remains in mechanical engineering, as elsewhere, largely a personal and spontaneous characteristic.

The Future of Mechanical Engineering

The number of mechanical engineers continues to grow as rapidly as ever, while the duration and quality of their training increases. There is a growing awareness, however, among engineers and in the community at large that the exponential increase in population and living standards is raising formidable problems in pollution of the environment and the exhaustion of natural resources; this clearly heightens the need for all of the technical professions to consider the long-term social effects of discoveries and developments. There will be an increasing demand for mechanical engineering skills to provide for man's needs while reducing to a minimum the consumption of scarce raw materials and maintaining a satisfactory environment.

Words and Expressions

mechanical engineering	机械工程（学）
key /ki:/ *n.*	键，楔
adj.	主要的，关键的
impetus /'impitəs/ *n.*	推动力，动力
trial and error	试错法
capital cost	基建费，投资费
conveyor /kən'veiə/ *n.*	输送机；运输装置，传送器
three-shift /'θri:ʃift/ *n.*	三班制
augment /ɔ:g'ment/ *vt. & vi.*	增大，增加
thermal /'θə:məl/ *n.*	热
adj.	热的，热量的
reduction /ri'dʌkʃən/ *n.*	还原
power plant	发电厂，动力装置
reciprocating /ri'siprəkeitiŋ/ *adj.*	往复的
collaborate /kə'læbəreit/ *vi.*	合作，协作
bioengineering /ˌbaiəuˌendʒi'niəriŋ/ *n.*	生物工程学
pollutant /pə'lju:tənt/ *n.*	污染物，污染物质
dynamics /dai'næmiks/ *n.*	力学，动力学
thermodynamics /'θə:məudai'næmiks/ *n.*	热力学
operations research	运筹学
value engineering	价值工程，工程经济学
PABLA	逻辑法问题分析
exponential /ˌekspəu'nenʃəl/ *n.*	指数
adj.	指数的，幂数的
formidable /'fɔ:midəbl/ *adj.*	强大的；可怕的；艰难的

Exercises

Ⅰ. Choose the best answer according to the information of the text.

1. Mechanical engineering is especially concerned with _____.
   a. stress and strains b. forces and motion
   c. electric power d. production of machines
2. _____ provided a key source of power for the Industrial Revolution.
   a. Steam engine b. The discovery of electricity
   c. Turbine d. Motors
3. In 1847 the founding of the _____ marked the formal recognition of mechanical engineering.
   a. steam engine society
   b. Institution of Mechanical Engineers in Birmingham

  c. Institution of Mechanical Engineers in London

  d. Mechanical Engineering society

 4. The fields of mechanical engineering include the following except _____.

  a. the development of machines   b. the development of military weapons

  c. the development of computers   d. environmental control

 5. Which of the following is NOT the requirements that have led to the evolution of complex control systems?

  a. the speed of operation   b. high rates of production

  c. minimization of operation cost   d. the demand for higher degree of education

 6. Which of the following is NOT included in the study of mechanical engineering functions?

  a. dynamics   b. automatic control   c. computers   d. lubrication

 7. The word 'process' in Para. 7, Line 6 means _____.

  a. series of action   b. changes

  c. deal with officially   d. perform operations in a computer

 8. Mechanical engineers collaborate more and more with _____ especially in the development of suitable control systems.

  a. electrical engineers   b. computer designers

  c. experienced technicians   d. skilled workers

 9. The demands of war have stimulated developments in mechanical field which have great benefit in peace. _____ is an example.

  a. Chemical weapons   b. Nuclear reactors

  c. Ballistic missiles   d. Cannons

 10. There is a growing awareness among modern mechanical engineers about _____.

  a. exhaustion of natural resources   b. development of military weapons

  c. pollution of the environment   d. both a and c

II. Fill in the blanks according to the information of the text.

 1. Mechanical engineering deals with _____ and _____.

 2. The mechanical design of a successful production machinery is closely integrated with _____.

 3. The demand for _____ stimulates mechanical engineers to raise the quality of work.

 4. The production of products and power includes planning _____ and _____.

 5. During the process of development mechanical engineering has undergone _____.

 6. Coordinating functions of mechanical engineers include _____, _____, even _____.

 7. The second function of mechanical engineering is about the sequence of _____, _____, and _____.

 8. The development in, mechanical engineering as well as developments in other technological fields has brought about environment problem such as _____, pollution of water, _____ of land and scenery.

 9. The high material standard of living in the developed countries owes much to _____.

 10. Production machinery presupposes _____.

Passage II Introduction to Design

The Meaning of Design

To design is to formulate a plan for the satisfaction of a human need. The particular need to be satisfied may be quite well defined from the beginning. Here are two examples in which needs are well defined:

1. How can we obtain large quantities of power cleanly, safely, and economically without using fossil fuels and without damaging the surface of the earth?

2. This gearshaft is giving trouble; there have been eight failures in the last six weeks. Do something about it.

On the other hand, the statement of a particular need to be satisfied may be so nebulous and ill defined that a considerable amount of thought and effort is necessary in order to state it clearly as a problem requiring a solution. Here are two examples:

1. Lots of people are killed in airplane accidents.

2. In big cities there are too many automobiles on the streets and highways.

This second type of design situation is characterized by the fact that neither the need nor the problem to be solved has been identified. Note, too, that the situation may contain not one problem but many.

We can classify design, too. For instance, we speak of:

1. Clothing design
2. Interior design
3. Highway design
4. Landscape design
5. Building design
6. Ship design
7. Bridge design
8. Computer-aided design
9. Heating system design
10. Machine design
11. Engineering design
12. Process design

In fact, there are an endless number, since we can classify design according to the particular article or product or according to the professional field.

In contrast to scientific or mathematical problems, design problems have no unique answers; it is absurd, for example, to request the 'correct answer' to a design problem, because there is none. In fact, a 'good' answer today may well turn out to be a 'poor' answer tomorrow, if there is a growth of knowledge during the period or if there are other structural or societal changes.

Almost everyone is involved with design in one way or another, even in daily living, because problems are posed and situations arise which must be solved. A design problem is not a hypothetical problem at all. Design has an authentic purpose—the creation of an end result by taking definite action, or the creation of something having physical reality. In engineering, the word design conveys different meanings to different persons. Some think of a designer as one who employs the drawing board to draft the details of a gear, clutch, or other machine member. Others think of design as the creation of a complex system, such as a communications network. In some areas of engineering the word design has been replaced by other terms such as systems engineering or applied decision theory. But no matter what words are used to describe the design function, in engineering it is still the process in which scientific principles and the tools of engineering—mathematics, computers, graphics, and English—are used to produce a plan which, when carried out, will satisfy a human need.

Mechanical Engineering Design

Mechanical design means the design of things and systems of a mechanical nature machines, products, structures, devices, and instruments. For the most part, mechanical design utilizes mathematics, the materials sciences, and the engineering mechanics sciences.

Mechanical engineering design includes all mechanical design, but it is a broader study, because it includes all the disciplines of mechanical engineering, such as the thermal and fluids sciences, too. Aside from the fundamental sciences that are required, the first studies in mechanical engineering design are in mechanical design.

The Phases of Design

The complete process, from start to finish, is often outlined as in Fig. 1-1. The process begins with a recognition of a need and a decision to do something about it. After many iterations, the process ends with the presentation of the plans for satisfying the need.

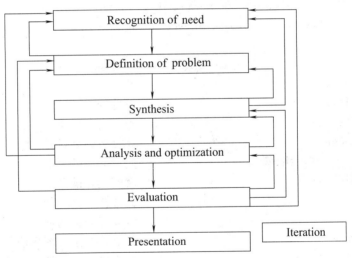

Fig. 1-1 The phases of design

Design Considerations

Sometimes the strength required of an element in a system is an important factor in the determination of the geometry and the dimensions of the element. In such a situation we say that strength is an important design consideration. When we use the expression design consideration, we are referring to some characteristic which influences the design of the element or, perhaps, the entire system. Usually quite a number of such characteristics must be considered in a given design situation. Many of the important ones are as follows:

    1. Strength   2. Reliability   3. Thermal properties
    4. Corrosion   5. Wear   6. Friction
    7. Processing   8. Utility   9. Cost

10. Safety	11. Weight	12. Life
13. Noise	14. Styling	15. Shape
16. Size	17. Flexibility	18. Control
19. Stiffness	20. Surface finish	21. Lubrication
22. Maintenance	23. Volume	24. Liability

Some of these have to do directly with the dimensions, the material, the processing, and the joining of the elements of the system. Other considerations affect the configuration of the total system.

To keep the correct perspective, however, it should be observed that in many design situations the important design considerations are such that no calculations or experiments are necessary in order to define an element or system. Students, especially, are often confounded when they run into situations in which it is virtually impossible to make a single calculation and yet an important design decision must be made. These are not extraordinary occurrences at all; they happen every day. Suppose that it is desirable from a sales standpoint—for example, in medical laboratory machinery—to create an impression of great strength and durability. Thicker parts assembled with larger-than-usual oversize bolts can be used to create a rugged-looking machine. Sometimes machines and their parts are designed purely from the standpoint of styling and nothing else. These points are made here so that you will not be misled into believing that there is a rational mathematical approach to every design decision.

Words and Expressions

gearshaft /ˈɡiəʃɑːft/ n.	齿轮轴
nebulous /ˈnebjuləs/ adj.	模糊的，朦胧的
computer-aided design	计算机辅助设计
hypothetical /ˌhaipəuˈθetikəl/ adj.	假设的，假定的
authentic /ɔːˈθentik/ adj.	真实的，确凿的
clutch /klʌtʃ/ n.	离合器，联轴器
member /ˈmembə/ n.	组成部分，构件
graphics /ˈɡræfiks/ n.	图解计算法，图形法
liability /ˌlaiəˈbiliti/ n.	易用性，倾向性，责任
configuration /kənˌfiɡjuˈreiʃən/ n.	构造，结构；配置；

Passage Ⅲ Manufacturing

Manufacturing is that enterprise concerned with converting raw material into finished products. There are three distinct phases in manufacturing. These phases are as follows: input, processing, and output.

The first phase includes all of the elements necessary to create a marketable product. First, there must be a demand or need for the product. The necessary materials must be available. Also needed are such resources as energy, time, human knowledge, and human skills. Finally, it takes capital to obtain all of the other resources.

Input resources are channeled through the various processes in Phase Two. These are the processes used to convert raw materials into finished products. A design is developed. Based on the design, various types of planning are accomplished. Plans are put into action through various production processes. The various resources and processes are managed to ensure efficiency and productivity. For example, capital resources must be carefully managed to ensure they are used prudently. Finally, the product in question is marketed.

The final phase is the output or finished product. Once the finished product has been purchased it must be transported to users. Depending on the nature of the product, installation and ongoing field support may be required. In addition, with some products, particularly those of a highly complex nature, training is necessary.

Materials and Processes in Manufacturing

Engineering materials covered herein are divided into two broad categories: metals and nonmetals. Metals are subdivided into ferrous metals, nonferrous metals, high-performance alloys, and powdered metals. Nonmetals are subdivided into plastics, elastomers, composites, and ceramics.

Production processes covered herein are divided into several broad categories including forming, forging, casting/molding, heat treatment, fastening/joining, metrology/quality control, and material removal. Each of these is subdivided into several other processes.

Stages in the Development of Manufacturing

Over the years, manufacturing processes have gone through four distinct, although overlapping, stages of development. These stages are as fellows:

Stage 1　　Manual
Stage 2　　Mechanized
Stage 3　　Automated
Stage 4　　Integrated

When people first began converting raw materials into finished products, they used manual processes. Everything was accomplished using human hands and manually operated tools. This was a very rudimentary form of fully integrated manufacturing. A person identified the need, collected materials, designed a product meet the need, produced the product, and used it. Everything from start to finish was integrated within the mind of the person who did all the work.

Then during the industrial revolution mechanized processes were introduced and humans began using machines to accomplish work previously accomplished manually. This led to work specialization which, in turn, eliminated the integrated aspect of manufacturing. In this stage of development, manufacturing workers might see only that part of an overall manufacturing operation represented by that specific piece on which they worked. There was no way to tell how their efforts fit into the larger picture or their workpiece into the finished product.

The next stage in the development of manufacturing processes involved the automation of selected processes. This amounted to computer control of machines and processes. During this phase, islands of automation began to spring up on the shop floor. Each island represented a distinct process or group of processes used in the production of a product. Although these islands of automation did tend to enhance the productivity of the individual processes within the islands, overall productivity often was unchanged. This was because the islands were sandwiched in among other processes that were not automated and were not synchronized with them.

The net result was that workpieces would move quickly and efficiently through the automated processes only to back up at manual stations and create bottlenecks. To understand this problem, think of yourself driving from stoplight to stoplight in rush hour traffic. Occasionally you find an opening and are able to rush ahead of the other cars that are creeping along, only to find yourself backed up at the next light. The net effect of your brief moment of speeding ahead is canceled out by the bottleneck at the next stoplight. Better progress would be made if you and the other drivers could synchronize your speed to the changing of the stoplights. Then all cars would move steadily and consistently along and everyone would make better progress in the long run.

This need for steady, consistent flow on the shop floor led to the development of integrated manufacturing, a process that is still emerging. In fully integrated settings, machines and processes are computer controlled and integration is accomplished through computers. In the analogy used in the previous paragraph, computers would synchronize the rate of movement of all cars with the changing of the stoplights so that everyone moved steadily and consistently along.

Words and Expressions

herein /ˌhiər'in/ adv.	于此，在这里
nonferrous /ˌnɔn'ferəs/ adj.	有色的；非铁或钢的
high-performance /ˌhaipə'fɔːməns/ n.	高性能
elastomer /i'læstəmə/ n.	弹性体，合成橡胶
composite /'kɔmpəzit/ n.	复合材料
ceramic /si'ræmik/ adj.	陶瓷的，陶器的
n.	陶瓷制品
forming /'fɔːmiŋ/ n.	成型（成形）；定型
forging /'fɔːdʒiŋ/ n.	锻造，锻件
casting /'kɑːstiŋ/ n.	铸造；铸件
molding /'məuldiŋ/ n.	翻砂；制模，压模
heat treatment	热处理
metrology /mi'trɔlədʒi/ n.	度量衡学，度量衡
quality control	质量管理，质量控制
removal /ri'muːvəl/ n.	移去，除去
rudimentary /ˌruːdi'mentəri/ adj.	初步的，基本的
shop floor	车间，工场
net result	最终结果
back up	支持，倒退
bottleneck /'bɔtlnek/ n.	瓶颈，薄弱环节；影响生产流程的因素
analogy /ə'nælədʒi/ n.	模拟

Passage IV The Science of Mechanics

That branch of scientific analysis which deals with motions, time, and forces is called mechanics and is made up of two parts, statics and dynamics. Statics deals with the analysis of stationary systems, i.e., those in which time is not a factor, and dynamics deals with systems which change with time.

As shown in Fig. 1-2, dynamics is also made up of two major disciplines, first recognized as separate entities by Euler in 1775.

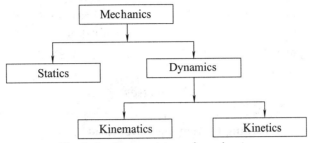

Fig. 1-2 Composition of mechanics

The investigation of the motion of a rigid body may be conveniently separated into two parts, the one geometrical, the other mechanical. In the first part, the transference of the body from a given position to any other position must be investigated without respect to the cause of the motion, and must be represented by analytical formulae, which will define the position of each point of the body. This investigation will therefore be referable solely to geometry, or rather to stereotomy.

It is clear that by the separation of this part of the question from the other, which belongs properly to Mechanics, the determination of the motion from dynamical principles will be made much easier than if the two parts were undertaken conjointly.

These two aspects of dynamics were later recognized as the distinct sciences of kinematics and kinetics, and deal with motion and the forces producing it, respectively.

The initial problem in the design of a mechanical system is therefore understanding its kinematics. Kinematics is the study of motion, quite apart from the forces which produce that motion. More particularly, kinematics is the study of position, displacement, rotation, speed, velocity, and acceleration. The study, say, of planetary or orbital motion is also a problem in kinematics.

It should be carefully noted in the above quotation that Euler based his separation of dynamics into kinematics and kinetics on the assumption that they should deal with rigid bodies. It is this very important assumption that allows the two to be treated separately. For flexible bodies, the shapes of the bodies themselves, and therefore their motions, depend on the force exerted on them. In this situation, the study of force and motion must take place simultaneously, thus significantly increasing the complexity of the analysis.

Fortunately, although all real machine parts are flexible to some degree, machines are usually designed from relatively rigid materials, keeping part deflections to a minimum. Therefore, it is common practice to assume that deflections are negligible and parts are analysis when loads are known, to design the parts so that this assumption is justified.

Words and Expressions

geometrical /dʒiə'metrikəl/ adj.　　　　　　几何的，几何学的

transference /'trænsfərəns/ n.　　　　　移动，转送
stereotomy /ˌstiəri'ɔtəmi/ n.　　　　　实体物切割术（切石法）
conjointly /'kɔndʒɔintli/ adv.　　　　　相连地，结合地
kinematics /ˌkaini'mætiks/ n.　　　　　运动学
kinetics /kai'netiks/ n.　　　　　　　　动力学
displacement /dis'pleismənt/ n.　　　　位移，移动
acceleration /æk,selə'reiʃən/ n.　　　加速度
deflection /di'flekʃən/ n.　　　　　　　偏移，挠度

Exercises

I. Choose the best answer according to what you have learnt.

1. Mostly mechanical design is involved with the following discipline of science except _____.
   a. mathematics　　　　　　　　　b. material science
   c. engineering mechanics　　　　d. computation

2. The design started with _____.
   a. a recognition of need　　　　b. drafting
   c. freehand sketching　　　　　 d. analysis

3. Mechanical engineering design covers the following except _____.
   a. thermal sciences　　　　　　 b. fluid sciences
   c. communication　　　　　　　　d. both a and b

4. The mechanics is made up of _____.
   a. statics and dynamics　　　　 b. kinematics and kinetics
   c. geometry and stereotomy　　　d. stress and strain

5. Statics deals with _____ system in which time is not a factor.
   a. stationery　　b. stationary　　c. station　　d. stational

6. The word kinematics is from the Greek word kinema which means _____.
   a. rotation　　b. acceleration　　c. motion　　d. station

7. Manufacturing comprises the following phases except _____.
   a. input　　b. output　　c. processing　　d. marketing

8. The design process ends with _____.
   a. evaluation　　　　　　　　　　b. presentation
   c. analysis　　　　　　　　　　　d. recognition of a problem

9. Manufacturing processes have undergone four distinct stages of development. Which of the following is NOT one of them?
   a. manual stage　　　　　　　　　b. mechanized stage
   c. automated stage　　　　　　　 d. flexible stage

10. Manufacturing of a product starts with _____.
    a. a demand for the product　　b. necessary material
    c. human resources　　　　　　　d. capitals

II. Fill in the blanks with phrases chosen from the list and change the form if necessary.

in the long run　　in addition　　to some degree　　amount to

aside from　　　　no matter　　　according to　　　　　　turn out
in contrast to　　spring up

1. _____ the TV，it will be fine today.
2. _____ a few faults，he is a trustworthy in the country.
3. _____ city life，time seemed to pass slowly in the country.
4. There was an earthquake and，_____ there were tidal waves.
5. _____ benevolent deception will do harm to the medicine profession.
6. His remarks _____ criticism of me.
7. We can believe his story _____ .
8. The rumor _____ to be true.
9. _____ what happens，don't be discouraged.
10. Supporting groups _____ all over the country.

III. Translate the following passage into Chinese.

Manufacturing engineers select and coordinate specific processes and equipment to be used, or supervise and manage their use. Some design special tooling that is used so that standard machines can be utilized in producing specific products. These engineers must have a broad knowledge of machine and process capabilities and of materials, so that desired operations can be done effectively and efficiently without overloading or damaging machines and without adversely affecting the materials being processed.

IV. Translate the following passage into English.

许多工程师认为他们的职责是进行产品设计，而产品是通过对材料的加工制造而生产出来的。设计工程师在材料选择、制造方法等方面起着关键作用。一个设计工程师应该比其他的人更清楚地知道他的设计需要达到什么目的。他知道他对使用载荷和使用要求所做的假设，产品必须经受的使用环境，产品应该具有的外观形貌。

Unit 2　Mechanics

Passage Ⅰ　Introduction of Mechanics

Mechanics is the oldest and the most highly developed branch of physics. As important foundation of engineering, its relevance continues to increase as its range of application grows.

The tasks of mechanics include the description and determination of the motion of bodies, as well as the investigation of the forces associated with the motion. Technical examples of such motions are the rolling wheel of a vehicle, the flow of a fluid in a duct, the flight of an airplane and the orbit of a satellite. "Motion" in a generalized sense includes the deflection of a bridge or the deformation of a structural element under the influence of a load. An important special case is the state of rest; a building, dam or television tower should be constructed in such a way that it does not move or collapse.

Mechanics is based on only a few laws of nature which have an axiomatic character. These are statements based on numerous observations and regarded as being known from experience. The conclusions drawn from these laws are also confirmed by experience. Mechanical quantities such as velocity, mass, force, momentum or energy describing the mechanical properties of a system are connected within these axioms and within the resulting theorems.

Real bodies or real technical systems with their multifaceted properties are neither considered in the basic principles nor in their applications to technical problems. Instead, models are investigated that possess the essential mechanical characteristics of the real bodies or systems. Examples of these idealizations are a rigid body or a mass point. Of course, a real body or a structural element is always deformable to a certain extent. However, they may be considered as being rigid bodies if the deformation does not play an essential role in the behaviour of the mechanical system. To investigate the path of a stone thrown by hand or the orbit of a planet in the solar system, it is usually sufficient to view these bodies as being mass points, since their dimensions are very small compared with the distances covered.

In mechanics we use mathematics as an exact language. Only mathematics enables precise formulation without reference to a certain place or a certain time and allows to describe and comprehend mechanical processes. If an engineer wants to solve a technical problem with the aid of mechanics he or she has to replace the real technical system with a model that can be analyzed mathematically by applying the basic mechanical laws. Finally, the mathematical solution has to be interpreted mechanically and evaluated technically.

Since it is essential to learn and understand the basic principles and their correct application from the beginning, the question of modelling will be mostly omitted in this text, since it requires a high degree of competence and experience. The mechanical analysis of an idealised system in which the real technical system may not always be easily recognised is, however, not simply an unrealistic game. It will familiarize students with the principles of mechanics and thus enable them to solve practical engineering problems independently.

Mechanics may be classified according to various criteria. Depending on the state of the material under consideration, one speaks of the mechanics of solids, hydrodynamics or gasdynamics. Sometimes we consider solid bodies only, which can be classified as rigid, elastic or plastic bodies. In the case of a liquid one distinguishes between a frictionless and a viscous liquid. Again, the characteristics rigid, elastic or viscous are idealizations that make the essential properties of the real material accessible to mathematical treatment.

According to the main task of mechanics, namely, the investigation of the state of rest or motion under the action of forces, mechanics may be divided into statics and dynamics. Statics (Latin: status = standing) deals with the equilibrium of bodies subjected to forces. Dynamics (Greek: dynamis = force) is subdivided into kinematics and kinetics. Kinematics (Greek: kinesis = movement) investigates the motion of bodies without referring to forces as a cause or result of the motion. This means that it deals with the geometry of the motion in time and space, whereas kinetics relates the forces involved and the motion.

Alternatively, mechanics may be divided into analytical mechanics and engineering mechanics. In analytical mechanics, the analytical methods of mathematics are applied with the aim of gaining principal insight into the laws of mechanics. Here, details of the problems are of no particular interest. Engineering mechanics concentrates on the needs of the practising engineer. The engineer has to analyse bridges, cranes, buildings, machines, vehicles or components of microsystems to determine whether they are able to sustain certain loads or perform certain movements.

The historical origin of mechanics can be traced to ancient Greece, although of course mechanical insight derived from experience had been applied to tools and devices much earlier. Several cornerstones on statics were laid by the works of Archimedes (287-212): lever and fulcrum, block and tackle, center of gravity and buoyancy. Nothing more of great importance was discovered until the time of the Renaissance. Further progress was then made by Leonardo da Vinci (1452-1519) with his observations of the equilibrium on an inclined plane, and by Simon Stevin (1548-1620) with his discovery of the law of the composition of forces. The first investigations on dynamics can be traced back to Galileo Galilei (1564-1642) who discovered the law of gravitation. The laws of planetary motion by Johannes Kepler (1571-1630) and the numerous works of Christian Huygens (1629-1695) finally led to the formulation of the laws of motion by Isaac Newton (1643-1727). At this point, tremendous advancement was initiated, which went hand in hand with the development of analysis and is associated with the Bernoulli family (17th and 18th century), Leonhard Euler (1707-1783), Jean le Rond d'Alembert (1717-1783) and Joseph Louis Lagrange (1736-1813). As a result of the progress made in analytical and numerical methods - the latter especially boosted by computer technology-mechanics today continues to enlarge its field of application and makes more complex problems accessible to exact analysis. Mechanics also has its place in branches of sciences such as medicine, biology and the social sciences through the application of modelling and mathematical analysis.

Words and Expressions

mechanics /mi'kæniks/ n.	力学
principle /'prinsəpəl/ n.	原则，准则
equilibrium /ˌikwi'libriəm/ n.	平衡
analytical mechanics	分析力学
engineering mechanics	工程力学
analysis /ə'nælisis/ n.	分析，分解；[数]解析；验定

Exercises

Ⅰ. Translate the following passage into Chinese.

Mechanics is based on only a few laws of nature which have an axiomatic character. These are statements based on numerous observations and regarded as being known from experience. The conclusions drawn from these laws are also confirmed by experience. Mechanical quantities such as velocity, mass, force, momentum or energy describing the mechanical properties of a system are connected within these axioms and within the resulting theorems.

Ⅱ. Translate the following passage into English.

力学是一门独立的基础学科，是有关力、运动和介质（固体、液体、气体和等离子体），宏、细、微观力学性质的学科，研究以机械运动为主，及其同物理、化学、生物运动耦合的现象。力学是一门基础学科，同时又是一门技术学科。它研究能量和力以及它们与固体、液体及气体的平衡、变形或运动的关系。力学可区分为静力学、运动学和动力学三部分，静力学研究力的平衡或物体的静止问题；运动学只考虑物体怎样运动，不讨论它与所受力的关系；动力学讨论物体运动和所受力的关系。

Passage Ⅱ Basic Concepts of Mechanics

The following concepts and definitions are basic to the study of mechanics, and they should be understood at the outset. Space is the geometric region occupied by bodies whose positions are described by linear and angular measurements relative to a coordinate system. For three-dimensional problems, three independent coordinates are needed. For two-dimensional problems, only two coordinates are required.

Time is the measure of the succession of events and is a basic quantity in dynamics. Time is not directly involved in the analysis of statics problems.

Mass is a measure of the inertia of a body, which is its resistance to a change of velocity. Mass can also be thought of as the quantity of matter in a body. The mass of a body affects the gravitational attraction force between it and other bodies. This force appears in many applications in statics. Force is the action of one body on another. A force tends to move a body in the direction of its action. The action of a force is characterized by its magnitude, by the direction of its action, and by its point of application.

A particle is a body of negligible dimensions. In the mathematical sense, a particle is a body whose dimensions are considered to be near zero so that we may analyze it as a mass concentrated at a point. We often choose a particle as a differential element of a body. We may treat a body as a particle when its dimensions are irrelevant to the description of its position or the action of forces applied to it.

Rigid body

A body is considered rigid when the change in distance between any two of its points is negligible for the purpose at hand. For instance, the calculation of the tension in the cable which supports the boom of a mobile crane under load is essentially unaffected by the small internal deformations in the structural members of the boom. For the purpose, then, of determining the external forces which act on the boom, we may treat it as a rigid body. Statics deals primarily with the calculation of external forces which act on rigid bodies in equilibrium. Determination of the internal deformations belongs to the study of the mechanics of deformable bodies, which normally follows statics in the curriculum.

Scalars and Vectors

We use two kinds of quantities in mechanics—scalars and vectors. Scalar quantities are those with which only a magnitude is associated. Examples of scalar quantities are time, volume, density, speed, energy, and mass. Vector quantities, on the other hand, possess direction as well as magnitude, and must obey the parallelogram law of addition as described later in this article. Examples of vector quantities are displacement, velocity, acceleration, force, moment, and momentum. Speed is a scalar. It is the magnitude of velocity, which is a vector. Thus velocity is specified by a direction as well as a speed.

Vectors representing physical quantities can be classified as free, sliding, or fixed. A free vector is one whose action is not confined to or associated with a unique line in space. For example, if a body moves without rotation, then the movement or displacement of any point in the body may be taken as a vector. This vector describes equally well the direction and magnitude of the displacement of every point in the body. Thus, we may represent the displacement of such a body by a free vector.

A sliding vector has a unique line of action in space but not a unique point of application. For example, when an external force acts on a rigid body, the force can be applied at any point along its line of action without changing its effect on the body as a whole, and thus it is a sliding vector.

A fixed vector is one for which a unique point of application is specified. The action of a force on a deformable or non rigid body must be specified by a fixed vector at the point of application of the force. In this instance the forces and deformations within the body depend on the point of application of the force, as well as on its magnitude and line of action.

Units

In mechanics we use four fundamental quantities called dimensions. These are length, mass, force, and time. The units used to measure these quantities cannot all be chosen independently because they must be consistent with Newton's second law. Although there are a number of different systems of units, only the two systems most commonly used in science and technology will be used sometimes.

Dimensions

In mechanics the three basic physical quantities length, time and mass are considered. Force is another important element that is considered; however, from a physical point of view, force is a derived quantity. All other mechanical quantities, such as velocity, momentum or energy can be expressed by these four quantities. The geometrical space where mechanical processes take place is three dimensional. However, as a simplification the discussion is limited sometimes to two-dimensional or, in some cases, one-dimensional problems.

Words and Expressions

succession /sək'sɛʃən/ n.　　　　　　　自然演替；一系列，接连
resistance /ri'zistəns/ n.　　　　　　　阻力；抵抗；抗力
sliding / 'slaidiŋ/ adj.　　　　　　　　滑行的，变化的
deformable /di'fɔ:məbəl / adj.　　　　可变形的
fundamental /ˌfʌndə'mentl / adj.　　　基本的
dimensional /di'menʃənl / n. & adj.　　…维的；尺寸的

Exercises

I. Translate the following passage into Chinese.

Mass is a measure of the inertia of a body, which is its resistance to a change of velocity. Mass can also be thought of as the quantity of matter in a body. The mass of a body affects the gravitational attraction force between it and other bodies. This force appears in many applications in statics. Force is the action of one body on another. A force tends to move a body in the direction of its action. The action of a force is characterized by its magnitude, by the direction of its action, and by its point of application.

II. Translate the following passage into English.

质点就是有质量但不存在体积或形状的点，是物理学的一个理想化模型。在物体的大小和形状不起作用，或者所起的作用并不显著而可以忽略不计时，我们近似地把该物体看作是一个只具有质量而其体积、形状可以忽略不计的理想物体，用来代替物体的有质量的点称为质点。

Passage III　Force

Before dealing with a group or system of forces, it is necessary to examine the properties of a single force in some detail. A force has been defined in the last unit as an action of one body on another. In dynamics we will see that a force is defined as an action which tends to cause acceleration of a body. A force is a vector quantity, because its effect depends on the direction as well as on the magnitude of the action. Thus, forces may be combined according to the parallelogram law of vector addition.

Force Classification

Forces are classified as either contact or body forces. A contact force is produced by direct physical contact; an example is the force exerted on a body by a supporting surface. On the other hand, a body force is generated by virtue of the position of a body within a force field such as a gravitational, electric, or magnetic field. An example of a body force is your weight.

Forces may be further classified as either concentrated or distributed. Every contact force is actually applied over a finite area and is therefore really a distributed force. However, when the dimensions of the area are very small compared with the other dimensions of the body, we may consider the force to be concentrated at a point with negligible loss of accuracy. Force can be distributed over an area, as in the case of mechanical contact, over a volume when a body force such as weight is acting, or over a line, as in the case of the weight of a suspended cable.

The weight of a body is the force of gravitational attraction distributed over its volume and may be taken as a concentrated force acting through the center of gravity. The position of the center of gravity is frequently obvious if the body is symmetric. If the position is not obvious, then a separate calculation will be necessary to locate the center of gravity.

We can measure a force either by comparison with other known forces, using a mechanical balance, or by the calibrated movement of an elastic element. All such comparisons or calibrations have as their basis a primary standard. The standard unit of force in SI units is the newton (N) and in the U. S. customary system is the pound (lb).

Newton's Laws

Sir Isaac Newton was the first to state correctly the basic laws governing the motion of a particle and to demonstrate their validity. Slightly reworded with modern terminology, these laws are:

Law Ⅰ. A particle remains at rest or continues to move with uniform velocity (in a straight line with a constant speed) if there is no unbalanced force acting on it.

Law Ⅱ. The acceleration of a particle is proportional to the vector sum of forces acting on it, and is in the direction of this vector sum.

Law Ⅲ. The forces of action and reaction between interacting bodies are equal in magnitude, opposite in direction, and collinear (they lie on the same line).

Newton's first law contains the principle of the equilibrium of forces, which is the main topic of concern in statics. This law is actually a consequence of the second law, since there is no acceleration when the force is zero, and the particle either is at rest or is moving with a uniform velocity. The first law adds nothing new to the description of motion but is included here because it was part of Newton's classical statements.

The third law is basic to our understanding of force. It states that forces always occur in pairs of equal and opposite forces. Thus, the downward force exerted on the desk by the pencil is accompanied by an upward force of equal magnitude exerted on the pencil by the desk. This principle holds for all forces, variable or constant, regardless of their source, and holds at every instant of time during which the forces are applied. Lack of careful attention to this basic law is the cause of frequent error by the beginner.

In the analysis of bodies under the action of forces, it is absolutely necessary to be clear about which force of each action-reaction pair is being considered. It is necessary first of all to isolate the body under consideration and then to consider only the one force of the pair which acts on the body in question.

Words and Expressions

concentrated /'kɑːnsntreitid/ *adj.*	集中的
distributed /di'stribjuːtid/ *adj.*	分散的
balance /'bæləns/ *n.*	平衡
terminology /tɜːrmə'nɑːlədʒi/ *n.*	专门名词；术语，术语学；用辞
magnitude /'mæɡnituːd/ *n.*	量级；巨大，广大；重大，重要
uniform /'juːnifɔːrm/ *adj.*	一样的；规格一致的
reaction /ri'ækʃən/ *n.*	反应；反作用力

Exercises

Ⅰ. Translate the following passage into Chinese.

Forces may be further classified as either concentrated or distributed. Every contact force is actually applied over a finite area and is therefore really a distributed force. However, when the dimensions of the area are very small compared with the other dimensions of the body, we may consider the force to be concentrated at a point with negligible loss of accuracy. Force can be distributed over an area, as in the case of mechanical contact, over a volume when a body force such as weight is acting, or over a line, as in the case of the weight of a suspended cable.

Ⅱ. Translate the following passage into English.

在物理学中，力是任何导致自由物体历经速度、方向或外形的变化的影响。力也可以借由直觉的概念来描述，例如推力或拉力，这可以导致一个有质量的物体改变速度（包括从静止状态开始运动）或改变其方向。一个力包括大小和方向，这使力是一个矢量。牛顿第二定律，可以公式化地来陈述一个有定质量的物体将会和作用在其身上的合力成比例的加速，这个近似将在接近光速时失效。

Passage Ⅳ Fluid Dynamics

A fluid is defined as a substance that deforms continuously whilst acted upon by any force tangential to the area on which it acts. Such a force is termed a shear force, and the ratio of the shear force to the area on which it acts is known as the shear stress. Hence when a fluid is at rest neither shear forces nor do shear stresses exist in it. A solid, on the other hand, can resist a shear force while at rest. In a solid, the shear force may cause some initial displacement of one layer over another, but the material does not continue to move indefinitely and a position of stable equilibrium is reached. In a fluid, however, shear forces are possible only while relative movement between layers is taking place. A fluid is further distinguished from a solid in that a given amount of it owes its shape at any time to that of the vessel containing it, or to forces that in some way restrain its movement.

The distinction between solids and fluids is usually clear, but there are some substances not easily classified. Some fluids, for example, do not flow easily: thick tar or pitch may at times appear to behave like a solid. A block of such a substance may be placed on the ground, and, although its flow would take place very slowly, over a period of time-perhaps several days-it would spread over the ground by the action of gravity. On the other hand, certain solids may be made to 'flow' when a sufficiently large force is applied; these are known as plastic solids. Nevertheless, these examples are rather exceptional and outside the scope of mainstream fluid mechanics.

The essential difference between solids and fluids remains. Any fluid, no matter how thick or viscous it is, flows under the action of a net shear force. A solid, however, no matter how plastic it is, does not flow unless the net shear force on it exceeds a certain value. For forces less than this value the layers of the solid move over one another only by a certain amount. The more the layers are displaced from their original relative positions, the greater are the internal forces within the material that resist the displacement. Thus, if a steady external force is applied, a state will be reached in which the internal forces resisting the movement of one layer over another come into balance with the external applied force and so no further movement occurs. If the applied force is then removed, the resisting forces within the material will tend to restore the solid body to its original shape.

In a fluid, however, the forces opposing the movement of one layer over another exist only while the movement is taking place, and so static equilibrium between applied force and resistance to shear never occurs. Deformation of the fluid takes place continuously so long as a shear force is applied. But if this applied force is removed the shearing movement subsides and, as there are then no forces tending to return the particles of fluid to their original relative positions, the fluid keeps its new shape.

Liquid

Fluids may be sub-divided into liquids and gases. A fixed amount of a liquid has a definite volume which varies only slightly with temperature and pressure. If the capacity of the containing vessel is greater than this definite volume, the liquid occupies only part of the container, and it forms an interface separating it from its own vapour, the atmosphere or any other gas present.

Gas A fixed amount of a gas, by itself in a closed container, will always expand until its volume equals that of the container. Only then can it be in equilibrium. In the analysis of the behaviour of fluids an important difference between liquids and gases is that, whereas under ordinary conditions liquids are so difficult to compress that they may for most purposes be regarded as incompressible, gases may be compressed much more readily. Where conditions are such that an amount of gas undergoes a negligible change of volume, its behaviour is similar to that of a liquid and it may then be regarded as incompressible.

If, however, the change in volume is not negligible, the compressibility of the gas must be taken into account in examining its behaviour.

A second important difference between liquids and gases is that liquids have much greater densities than gases. As a consequence, when considering forces and pressures that occur in fluid mechanics, the weight of a liquid has an important role to play. Conversely, effects due to weight can usually be ignored when gases are considered.

Molecular structure

The different characteristics of solids, liquids and gases result from differences in their <u>molecular</u> structure. All substances consist of vast numbers of molecules separated by empty space. The molecules have an attraction for one another, but when the distance between them becomes very small (of the order of the diameter of a molecule) there is a force of repulsion between them which prevents them all gathering together as a solid lump. The molecules are in continual movement, and when two molecules come very close to one another the force of repulsion pushes them vigorously apart, just as though they had collided like two billiard balls. In solids and liquids the molecules are much closer together than in a gas. A given volume of a solid or a liquid therefore contains a much larger number of molecules than an equal volume of a gas, so solids and liquids have a greater density (i. e. mass divided by volume) .

In a solid, the movement of individual molecules is slight-just a <u>vibration</u> of small amplitude-and they do not readily move relative to one another. In a liquid the movement of the molecules is greater, but they continually attract and repel one another so that they move in curved, wavy paths rather than in straight lines. The force of attraction between the molecules is sufficient to keep the liquid together in a definite volume although, because the molecules can move past one another, the substance is not rigid. In a gas the molecular movement is very much greater; the number of molecules in a given space is much less, and so any molecule travels a much greater distance before meeting another. The forces of attraction between molecules - being inversely proportional to the square of the distance between them-are, in general, negligible and so molecules are free to travel away from one another until they are stopped by a solid or liquid boundary.

The activity of the molecules increases as the temperature of the substance is raised. Indeed, the temperature of a substance may be regarded as a measure of the average kinetic energy of the molecules.

When an external force is applied to a substance the molecules tend to move relative to one another. A solid may be deformed to some extent as the molecules change position, but the strong forces between molecules remain, and they bring the solid back to its original shape when the external force is removed. Only when the external force is very large is one molecule wrenched away from its neighbours; removal of the external force does not then result in a return to the original shape, and the substance is said to have been deformed beyond its elastic limit. In a liquid, although the forces of attraction between molecules cause it to hold together, the molecules can move past one another and find new neighbours. Thus a force applied to an unconfined liquid causes the molecules to slip past one another until the force is removed. If a liquid is in a confined space and is compressed it exhibits elastic properties like a solid in compression. Because of the close spacing of the molecules, however, the resistance to compression is great. A gas, on the other hand, with its molecules much farther apart, offers much less resistance to compression.

The continuum

An absolutely complete analysis of the behaviour of a fluid would have to account for the action of each individual molecule. In most engineering applications, however, interest centres on the average conditions of velocity, pressure, temperature, density and so on. Therefore, instead of the actual conglomeration of separate molecules, we regard the fluid as a continuum that is a continuous distribution of matter with no empty space. This assumption is normally justifiable because the number of molecules involved in the situation is so vast and the distances between them are so small. The assumption fails, of course, when these conditions are not satisfied as, for example, in a gas at extremely low pressure. The average distance between molecules may then be appreciable in comparison with the smallest significant length in the fluid boundaries. However, as this situation is well outside the range of normal engineering work, we shall in this book regard a fluid as a continuum. Although it is often necessary to postulate a small element or particle of fluid, this is supposed large enough to contain very many molecules.

The properties of a fluid, although molecular in origin, may be adequately accounted for in their overall effect by ascribing to the continuum such attributes as temperature, pressure, viscosity and so on. Quantities such as velocity, acceleration and the properties of the fluid are assumed to vary continuously (or remain constant) from one point to another in the fluid. The new field of nanotechnology is concerned with the design and fabrication of products at the molecular level, but this topic is outside the scope in most time.

Mechanics of fluids

The mechanics of fluids is the field of study in which the fundamental principles of general mechanics are applied to liquids and gases. These principles are those of the conservation of matter, the conservation of energy and Newton's laws of motion. In extending the study to compressible fluids, we also need to consider the laws of thermodynamics. By the use of these principles, we are not only able to explain observed phenomena, but also to predict the behaviour of fluids under specified conditions. The study of the mechanics of fluids can be further sub-divided. For fluids at rest the study is known as fluid statics, whereas if the fluid is in motion, the study is called fluid dynamics.

Words and Expressions

fluid dynamics	流体动力学
shear stress	切向应力
vessel /ˈvɛsel/ n.	容器；船，飞船；血管
molecular /məˈlɛkjələ/ adj.	分子的
vibration /vaiˈbreʃən/ n.	振动
phenomena /fiˈnɑmənə/ n.	现象

Exercises

Ⅰ. Translate the following passage into Chinese.

The mechanics of fluids is the field of study in which the fundamental principles of general mechanics are applied to liquids and gases. These principles are those of the conservation of matter, the conservation of energy and Newton's laws of motion. In extending the study to compressible fluids, we also need to consider the laws of thermodynamics. By the use of these principles, we are not only able to explain observed phenomena, but also to predict the behavior of fluids under specified conditions. The study of the mechanics of fluids can be further sub-divided. For fluids at rest the study is known as fluid statics, whereas if the fluid is in motion, the study is called fluid dynamics.

II. Translate the following passage into English.

液体是物质的四个基本状态之一（其它状态有固体、气体、等离子体），没有确定的形状，但有一定体积，具有移动与转动等运动性。液体是由经分子间作用力结合在一起的微小振动粒子（例如原子和分子）组成。水是地球上最常见的液体。和气体一样，液体可以流动，可以容纳于各种形状的容器。有些液体不易被压缩，而有些则可以被压缩。和气体不同的是，液体不能扩散布满整个容器，而是有相对固定的密度。

Unit 3 Engineering Materials

Passage I Metals and Ferrous Metals

Metals are divided into two general types—ferrous and nonferrous. Ferrous metals are those which contain iron. Nonferrous metals are those which do not contain iron. However, some nonferrous metals may contain a small amount of iron as an <u>impurity</u>.

Steel and cast iron are the most common ferrous metals in general use. Steel is an alloy containing chiefly iron, carbon, and certain other elements in varying amounts. A wide range of physical properties may be obtained in steel by controlling the amount of carbon and other alloying elements and by subjecting the steel to various heat treatments.

Plain carbon steels usually contain, besides iron and carbon, small amounts of <u>silicon</u>, <u>sulphur</u>, <u>phosphorus</u>, and <u>manganese</u>. Alloy steels are formed by the addition of one or more of the following elements: <u>nickel</u>, <u>chromium</u>, <u>molybdenum</u>, <u>vanadium</u>, <u>tungsten</u>, manganese, silicon, and small amounts of other alloying elements.

Carbon is by far the most important alloying element in steel. It is the amount of carbon present which largely determines the maximum hardness obtainable. The higher the carbon content, the higher the <u>tensile strength</u> and the greater the hardness to which the steel may be heat-treated.

Low-carbon steels are usually used for low-strength parts requiring a great deal of forming. Medium-carbon steels are used for forgings and other applications where increased strength and a certain amount of <u>ductility</u> are necessary. High-carbon steels are used for high-strength parts such as springs, tools, and dies. The following list is a classification of ferrous materials according to their carbon content.

Ferrous Material	Carbon	Content
<u>Wrought iron</u>	Trace to	0.08%
Low-carbon steel	0.04 to	0.30%
Medium-carbon steel	0.30 to	0.60%
High-carbon steel	0.60 to	1.70%
Cast iron	1.70 to	4.50%

Alloy steels have special properties determined by the mixture and the amount of other metals added. To the <u>metallurgist</u> who works in metal mining and manufacturing, steels containing very small quantities of elements other than carbon, phosphorus, sulphur, and silicon are known as alloy steels. Each alloy steel has a personality of its own. A car is made of about 100 different kinds of alloy steel.

Some of the common alloying elements are described below:

Manganese Manganese helps to reduce certain undesirable effects of sulphur by combining with the sulphur. It also combines with carbon to increase hardness and toughness. Manganese possesses the property of aiding in increasing the depth of hardness penetration. It also improves the forging qualities by reducing brittleness at rolling and forging temperatures.

Silicon Silicon does not normally occur in steels in excess of 3.00 percent. A small amount of silicon improves ductility. It is used largely to increase impact resistance when combined with other alloys.

Sulphur Sulphur is generally regarded as detrimental to the hot working of steel and to the impact properties of steel treated to high tensile strength. However, sulphur is an invaluable aid to machining, and steels are often resulphurized to as high as 0.30 percent to gain advantage of this property.

Phosphorus Phosphorus has an undesirable effect on steel in that it imparts brittleness. There is some evidence that a small amount of phosphorus, less than 0.05 percent, increases tensile strength.

Nickel Nickel dissolves easily in molten steel. It is present in the common nickel steels in a proportion of 0.40 percent up to 5.00 percent. The addition of nickel increases strength, yield point, hardness, and ductility. It also increases the depth of hardening. Nickel steels are less susceptible to warping and scaling than most other steels. Nickel increases corrosion resistance and is one of the major constituents of the 'stainless' or corrosion-resisting steels.

Chromium Addition of chromium imparts hardness, strength, wear resistance, heat resistance, and corrosion resistance to steels.

Molybdenum Molybdenum, even in extremely small amounts, has considerable effect as an alloying element on the physical properties of steels. Molybdenum increases elastic limit, impact strength, wear resistance, and fatigue strength. Molybdenum steels are readily heat-treated, forged and machined.

Vanadium Vanadium is usually used in amounts of less than 0.25 percent. As an alloying agent, vanadium improves fatigue strength, ultimate strength, yield point, toughness, and resistance to impact and vibration. Chromium-vanadium steels have good ductility and high strength.

Tungsten Tungsten is used largely with chromium as a high-speed tool steel which contains 14.00 to 18.00 percent tungsten and 2.00 to 4.00 percent chromium. This steel possesses the characteristic of being able to retain a sharp cutting-edge even though heated to redness in cutting.

Tool-and-die Steels Tool-and-die steels are a large group of steels used when careful heat-treating must be done. These steels are used for parts such as chisels, hammers, screwdrivers, springs, and tools and dies used to cut and form metals.

Tool steels with certain alloying elements are designed for specific uses. The most common kinds of tool steels include high-speed tool steels, hot work tool steels, cold work tool steels and special-purpose tool steels.

Rolled Steel Rolled steel, which includes bar, rod, and structural steels, is produced by rolling the steel into shape. Hot-rolled steels are formed into shape while the metal is red-hot. The metal passes through a series of rollers, each a little closer to the next one. As the steel passes through the last rollers, hot water is sprayed over it, forming a bluish scale. This steel is fairly uniform in quality and is used for many different kinds of parts. Hot-rolled bars of the best quality are used to produce cold-finished steels. Cold-finished steels are used when great accuracy, better surface finish, and certain mechanical properties are needed. There are several ways of producing cold-finished bars. The most common results in what is called cold-worked steel. After the scale from the hot-rolled bars is removed, one of two techniques is employed. (1) The bars are cold-drawn, that is, drawn through dies a few thousandths smaller than the original bar. (2) The steel is cold-rolled, that is, rolled cold to the exact size.

Drill Rod Drill rod is a grade of high-carbon tool steel or high-speed steel. It is finished by grinding and polishing so that the outside is smooth and very accurate in size. You can identify drill rod by its shiny surface, which is much smoother than any of the other steels used in the shop. Drill-rod bars are generally made in 3-ft lengths and come in round, hexagonal, and square shapes. Drill rod is more expensive than most other steels.

Cast Iron Cast iron is used for the heavy parts of many machines. It is the most common material for making castings. Cast iron is low in cost and wears well. It is very brittle, however, and cannot be hammered or formed. It contains 2 to 4 percent carbon. The basic kinds of cast iron are white iron, gray iron, and malleable iron. Malleable iron is a particular kind of cast iron, made more malleable by an annealing procedure. Malleable-iron castings are not so brittle or hard. They can stand a great deal of hammering. Many plumbing fixtures are made of malleable iron. Nodular iron is a kind of cast iron that is even better for withstanding shocks, blows, and jerks.

Words and Expressions

impurity /im'pjuəriti/ n.	不纯；杂质
silicon /'silikən/ n.	硅；硅元素
sulphur /'sʌlfə/ n.	硫，硫磺
phosphorus /'fɔsfərəs/ n.	磷
manganese /'mæŋgəni:z/ n.	锰
nickel /'nikl/ n.	镍
chromium /'krəumjəm/ n.	铬
molybdenum /mə'libdinəm/ n.	钼
vanadium /və'neidjəm/ n.	钒
tungsten /'tʌŋstn/ n.	钨
tensile strength	抗拉强度，抗张强度
ductility /dʌk'tiliti/ n.	延展性；顺从
die /dai/ n.	模，冲模
wrought /rɔ:t/ adj.	可锻的
wrought iron	熟铁
metallurgist /me'tælədʒist/ n.	冶金家
brittleness /'britlnis/ n.	脆度
detrimental /ˌdetri'mentl/ adj.	有害的
impart /im'pɑ:t/ vt.	给予
hardening /'hɑ:dəniŋ/ n.	淬火，硬化
susceptible /sə'septəbl/ adj.	易受影响的，易感动的
warping /'wɔ:piŋ/ n.	翘曲，歪扭变形

fatigue strength	疲劳强度
tool-and-die /ˈtuːlənˈdai/ n.	工具和模具
chisel /ˈtʃizl/ n.	凿子
red-hot /ˌredˈhɔt/ adj.	炽热的，最新的
polishing /ˈpɔliʃiŋ/ n.	磨光，抛光
malleable /ˈmæliəbl/ adj.	有延展性的，可锻的
annealing /æˈniːliŋ/ n.	退火
plumbing /ˈplʌmiŋ/ n.	铅管系统，水管装置
nodular iron	球墨铸铁
jerk /dʒəːk/ n.	急拉，急推，弯扭

Passage II   Nonmetallic Materials

Nonmetallic is a broad category. It comprises organic materials of nature origin like wood, leather, and natural rubber. It includes materials such as plastics and paper which are manufactured at least in part from natural substances. It also includes inorganic (mineral) materials like glass, ceramics, and concrete. Fig. 3-1 illustrates the generic relationship of common nonmetallic materials.

General Properties of Nonmetallic Materials

Nonmetallic materials have varied properties, and few characteristics are applicable to all of them. Two that are almost universal are low electrical heat conductivity. With the exception of carbon, nonmetallic materials, when dry, are nonconductors.

Nonmetallic materials are usually less tough and less strong than metals, except that the inorganic materials normally have very high compressive strengths. The inorganic materials also have superior high-temperature properties. Resistance to corrosion is a common property with many nonmetallics. Ease of fabrication is a property shared by polymers, wood, and some other organic materials.

Polymers: Plastics and Elastomers

A plastic is an organic polymer available in some resin form or a form derived from the basicpolymerized resin. These forms include liquids and pastes for embedding, coating, and adhesive bonding. They also encompass molded, laminated, or formed shapes including sheet, film, and larger bulk shapes. While there are numerous minor classifications for polymers, depending upon how one wishes to categorize them, nearly all can be placed in one of two major classifications. These two major plastic-material classes are thermosetting materials (or thermosets) and thermoplastic materials, as shown in Fig. 3-1. Although Fig. 3-1 shows elastomers separately (and they are a separate application group), elastomers, too, are either thermoplastic or thermosetting, depending on their chemical nature.

As the name implies, thermosetting plastics, or thermosets, are cured, set, or hardened into a permanent shape. This curing is an irreversible chemical reaction known as cross-linking, which usually occurs under heat. For some thermosetting materials, however, curing is initiated or completed at room temperature. Even then, however, it is often the heat of the reac-

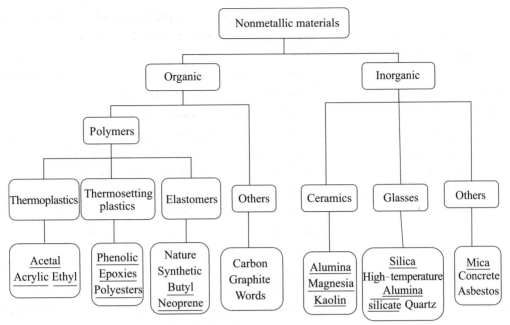

Fig. 3-1 Generic relationship of common nonmetallic materials

tion, or the exotherm, which actually cures the plastic material. Such is the case, for instance, with room-temperature-curing epoxy, polyester, or urethane compounds.

Thermoplastics differ from thermosets in that they do not cure or set under heat. They merely soften, when heated, to a flowable state in which under pressure they can be forced or transferred from a heated cavity into a cool mold. Upon cooling in a mold, thermoplastics harden and take the shape of the mold. Since thermoplastics do not cure or set, they can be remelted and rehardened by cooling many times. Thermal aging, brought about by repeated exposure to the high temperatures required for melting, causes eventual degradation of the material and so limits the number of reheat cycles.

The term 'elastomers' includes the complete, spectrum of elastic or rubberlike polymers which are sometimes randomly referred to as rubbers, synthetic rubbers, or elastomers. More properly, however, rubber is a natural material, and synthetic rubbers are polymers which have been synthesized to reproduce consistently the best properties of natural rubber. Since such a large number of rubberlike polymers exist, the broad term 'elastomer' is most fitting and most commonly used.

Other Organic Materials

Carbon and Graphite Carbon is a very common element and the key constituent of all organic materials. In the uncombined pure state, it exists as diamond or graphite. In a less pure state, it exists as charcoal, coal, or coke (amorphous carbon). Both amorphous carbon and graphite are produced in structural shapes when the particles are bonded together with elemental carbon.

Carbon and graphite exhibit properties similar to those of ceramics with two major exceptions. They are electrically and thermally conductive. The ceramiclike properties include greater compressive than tensile strength, a lack of malleability and ductility, and a resistance to high temperatures and corrosive environments. The usable temperature limits for carbon and graphite are on the order of 2,400℃ and even higher. Strength is actually higher at elevated than at room temperatures. Specific electrical resistance ranges from a low of 0.004Ω-in (graphite) to 0.0022Ω-in (carbon).

The production of carbon and graphite components involves two processes: (1) molding or extrusion followed by oven baking; (2) machining. High pressures and consequently significant die or mold costs are involved in the first method, which therefore is economically advantageous only for large-quantity production. Machining is more suitable for limited or moderate quantities.

Carbon and graphite components have mechanical, metallurgical, chemical, electrical, and nuclear applications. Typical uses include electrodes for the production of metals and chemicals in electric-arc furnaces, lighting electrodes, brushes for electric motors, electrodes in electrolytic cells, crucibles, molds for metal casting, resistance-furnace parts, and rocket components when high-temperature and thermal-shock resistance are important.

Carbon and graphite are available in round, square, and rectangular sections. Round bars commonly stocked range from 3 to 1,100mm in diameter and from 300 to 2800mm in length. Rectangular bars range from 13 by 100 by 400mm long to 600 by 750mm by 4.5m long.

Graphite is favored over carbon for applications requiring extensive machining. Graphite machines fairly well, and tolerances comparable with those of rough machining of metals can be achieved. Carbon members are recommended if only cut off or other minimum machining is required.

Wood has a number of desirable properties. It machines and fastens easily; it is attractive, it has a high strength-to-weight ratio; when dry, it has good electrical-, heat-, and noise-insulating properties; it is long-lasting in dry environments; and it accepts preservative treatment readily. On the negative side are its directional-strength characteristics (because of its grain), its large dimensional change and tendency to warp with changes in moisture content, its susceptibility to rot in moist environments, and its poor abrasion resistance.

Ceramics and Glasses

Ceramics and glasses are nonorganic, nonmetallic materials made by fusing clays and other 'earthy' materials which usually contain silicon and oxygen in various compositions with other materials.

Ceramics are hard, strong, brittle, and heat- and corrosion-resistant and are electrical insulators. They are used when these properties are important, particularly heat and corrosion resistance and electrical nonconductivity. Glass is used when transparency is important in addition to these other properties.

Words and Expressions

compressive strength	抗压强度，耐压强度
polymer /'pɔlimə/ n.	聚合物
resin /'rezin/ n.	树脂
polymerize /'pɔləmraiz/ v.	（使）聚合
encompass /in'kʌmpəs/ vt.	围绕，拥有
laminated /'læmineitid/ adj.	薄板状的，层压的
thermosetting /ˌθə:məu'setiŋ/ n.	热硬化，加热固化

thermoset /ˈθəːməuset/	n.	热固性塑料
	adj.	热固性的
thermoplastic /ˈθəːməuˈplæstik/	adj.	热塑性的
	n.	热塑性塑料
acetal /ˈæsitæl/	n.	乙缩醛
acrylic /əˈkrilik/	n.	丙烯酸
ethyl /ˈeθil/	n.	乙基
phenolic /fiˈnɔlik/	n.	酚醛
epoxy /eˈpɔksi/	n.	环氧树脂
	adj.	环氧的
polyester /ˈpɔlistə/	n.	聚酯
butyl /ˈbjuːtil/	n.	丁基,丁基橡胶
neoprene /ˈniːəupriːn/	n.	氯丁橡胶
alumina /əˈluːminə/	n.	矾土
magnesia /mægˈniːʃə/	n.	氧化镁
kaolin /ˈkeiəlin/	n.	高岭土
silica /ˈsilikə/	n.	硅石,硅土
alumina silicate		水合硅酸铝
mica /ˈmaikə/	n.	云母
asbestos /æzˈbestɔs/	n.	石棉
cure /kjuə/	v.	硬化
cross-linking /ˈkrɔsˈliŋkiŋ/	n.	交联
exotherm /ˌeksouˈθəːm/	n.	放热量
urethane /ˈjuəriˌθein/	n.	氨基甲酸乙酯
cavity /ˈkæviti/	n.	空腔,模槽
spectrum /ˈspektrəm/	n.	光谱,波谱
charcoal /ˈtʃɑːkəul/	n.	木炭
coke /kəuk/	n.	焦炭
amorphous /əˈmɔːfəs/	adj.	无定形的,非晶体的
graphite /ˈgræfait/	n.	石墨
conductive /kənˈdʌktiv/	adj.	传导的,导电的
malleability /ˌmæliəˈbiliti/	n.	有延展性,柔顺
extrusion /eksˈtruːʒən/	n.	挤压加工,挤压件
metallurgical /ˌmetəˈləːdʒikəl/	adj.	冶金学的,冶金的
electrolytic /iˌlektrəuˈlitik/	adj.	电解的,由电解产生的
grain /grein/	n.	晶粒
susceptibility /səˌseptəˈbiliti/	n.	敏感度,灵敏度
abrasion /əˈbreiʒən/	n.	磨损,磨蚀

Passage Ⅲ Powder Metallurgy

Powder metallurgy is a process for making a wide range of components and shapes from a variety of metals and alloys in the form of powder. The process is automated and uses pressure and heat to form precision metal parts into net or near net shapes, requiring a minimum amount of secondary finishing. Modern powder metallurgy began in the early 1900s when incandescent lamp filaments were fabricated from tungsten powder. Other important products followed, such as cemented tungsten carbide cutting tools, friction materials, and self-lubricating bearings.

Metal Powders

The most common metals available in powder form are iron, tin, nickel, copper, aluminum, and titanium, and refractory metals such as tungsten, molybdenum, tantalum, and niobium (columbium). Prealloyed powders such as low-alloy steels, bronze, brass, and stainless steel are produced in which each particle is itself an alloy. Also available in powder form are nickel-cobalt-base superalloys and tool steels.

Significant research and development effort has been devoted to designing processes for producing metal powders. Powder particles are not merely ground-up chips or scraps of metal. They are highly engineered materials of specific shapes and sizes. Metal powders range from 0.1 to 1,000 μm size with shapes that are spherical, acicular, irregular, dendritic, flake, angular, or fragmented. Particle shape has a direct influence on the density, surface area, permeability, and flow characteristics of a powder.

Porosity of the powder particle varies with the method of production and influences the density of the particle and the final product. While size, shape, density, and structure are the major physical characteristics, chemical characteristics are also important. Commercial powders are available in many grades of purity. Usually, the base metal has a minimum purity of 97.5% and for most applications ranges from 98.5 to 99.5% or higher.

Powder Production

Metal powders are produced by three major methods: physical, chemical, and mechanical.

Physical The most important physical method of metal powder production is atomization, in which a stream of molten metal is broken up into droplets that freeze into powder particles. In most atomizing processes, a stream of liquid, usually water, or a gas impinges upon the liquid metal stream to break it into droplets. Iron and steel, aluminum, copper, stainless steel, brass, tin, bronze, zinc, and high-alloy powders are made this way.

Chemical Chemical methods of powder production are those in which a metal powder is produced by chemical decomposition of a compound of the metal. Oxide in the form of finely divided solid powder particles may be reduced. Typical are the reduction of tungsten oxide to tungsten powder and of copper oxide to copper powder with hydrogen, and the reduction of iron oxide to iron powder with carbon monoxide. The deposition of a metal by an electric current from an electrolyte containing a metal salt (for example, the electrodeposition of copper powder from an aqueous copper sulfate solution) can be treated as a special kind of reduction process.

Mechanical Certain metal powders can also be produced by mechanical comminution. Materials include iron, iron-aluminum alloys, and ferrosilicon and ferrophosphorus powders.

Words and Expressions

powder metallurgy	粉末冶金，粉末冶金学
metallurgy /me'tælədʒi/ n.	冶金学，冶金术
incandescent /ˌinkæn'desnt/ adj.	遇热发光的，白炽的
filament /'filəmənt/ n.	细丝，丝状体
carbide /'ka:baid/ n.	碳化物，硬质合金
titanium /tai'teinjəm/ n.	钛
refractory /ri'fræktəri/ adj.	耐熔的；耐火的
n.	耐火材料
tantalum /'tæntələm/ n.	钽
niobium /nai'əubiəm/ n.	铌
columbium /kə'lʌmbiəm/ n.	铌
prealloy /pri'ælʌi/ n.	预合金
nickel-cobalt-base /'nikl,kəubɔ:lt'beis/ n.	镍钴基
superalloy /ˌsju:pə'ælɔi/ n.	超合金，超耐热合金
chip /tʃip/ n.	碎片
acicular /ə'sikjulə/ adj.	针状的，针尖状的
dendritic /den'dritik/ adj.	树枝状的；多枝的
permeability /ˌpə:miə'biliti/ n.	渗透性
porosity /pɔ:'rɔsiti/ n.	多孔性，有孔性
atomization /ˌætəmai'zeiʃən/ n.	雾化，粉化
droplet /'drɔpli:t/ n.	小滴，液滴
impinge /im'pindʒ/ n.	碰撞，冲击；v. 撞击
decomposition /ˌdi:kɔmpə'ziʃən/ n.	分解，腐烂
oxide /'ɔksaid/ n.	氧化物
deposition /ˌdepə'ziʃn/ n.	沉积，淀积
electrolyte /i'lektrəulait/ n.	电解液，电解质
aqueous /'eikwiəs/ adj.	水的，含水的
ferrosilicon /ˌferəu'silikən/ n.	硅铁
ferrophosphorus /ˌferəu'fɔsfərəs/ n.	铁磷合金

Exercises

Ⅰ. Fill in the blanks with appropriate words.

1. The two major plastic-material classes are _____ materials and _____ materials.
2. Carbon is the key _____ of all organic materials.
3. Carbon and graphite are electrically and thermally _____ .
4. The production of carbon and graphite involves two processes: _____ and _____ .
5. Carbon and graphite components have mechanical, _____ , chemical, electrical and _____ applications.
6. Nonmetallic comprises _____ materials, materials such as _____ and paper materials.

7. Ceramics are hard, strong, _____ and heat _____ resistant and are electrical _____.

8. Metal powders are produced by three major methods: _____, _____, and _____.

9. Particles in metal powders has a direct influence on the _____, _____ area, _____ and flow characteristics.

10. Organic matrix resins are typically _____, _____, and thermoplastics.

Ⅱ. Choose the best answer for each of the following.

1. _____ dose not use composites?
   a. Skis   b. Fishing rod   c. Sailboats   d. Knife

2. The earliest composites perhaps were produced by the _____.
   a. Egyptians   b. Italians   c. Chinese   d. Americans

3. Modern powder metallurgy begun in the early _____ when incandescent lamp filaments were fabricated.
   a. 1960s   b. 1950s   c. 1970s   d. 1900s

4. With the exception of _____, nonmetallic materials when dry, are nonconductors.
   a. carbon   b. plastic   c. wood   d. leather

5. For some thermosetting materials, curing is initiated or completed at _____ temperature.
   a. high   b. room   c. low   d. below zero

6. Thermoplastics differ from thermosetting materials in that they do not _____ under heat.
   a. warp   b. cure   c. melt   d. deflect

7. _____ of the powder particle influences the density of the particle and the final product.
   a. Shape   b. Amount   c. Porosity   d. Nature

8. The most important physical method of metal powder production is _____.
   a. atomization   b. heating   c. electrify   d. squeezing

9. The inorganic materials normally have very high _____.
   a. brittleness   b. tensile strength   c. compressive strength   d. ductility

10. Polymers, wood and some other organic materials share a common property, that is _____.
    a. ease of fabrication   b. compressive strength
    c. resistance to corrosion   d. depth of hardness penetration

Ⅲ. Translate the following passage into Chinese.

The earth contains a large number of metals which are useful to man. One of the most important of these is iron. Modern industry needs considerable quantities of this metal, either in the form of iron or in the form of steel. A certain number of non-ferrous metals, including aluminium and zinc, are also important but even today the majority of our engineering products are of iron or steel.

Ⅳ. Translate the following passage into English.

从特点来看，金属不透明，有韧性，是热和电的良导体。金属分为黑色金属和有色金属。前者含铁，后者不含铁。某些元素加进钢中能够改善钢的性能。例如：加铬后能耐腐蚀，加钨后可增加强度。铝、铜、合金、黄铜等是常用的有色金属。

Unit 4 Material Treatment and Properties

Passage I Heat Treatment

Heat treatment is a term applied to a variety of procedures for changing the characteristics of metal by heating and cooling. By proper heat treatment, it is possible to obtain certain characteristics in metal such as hardness, tensile strength (ability to resist stretching), and ductility. Heat treatment can be a simple process requiring few tools. In industry, it is a highly scientific and complicated procedure requiring much equipment.

Many of the projects or products made in the machine shop have little or no value until they are heat-treated. This article includes only the most elementary information about the heat treatment of steel. Heat treatment can also be done on many of the nonferrous metals such as aluminium, copper and brass. The procedures are different, however, and will not be considered here.

The procedures of heat treatment of steel include hardening, tempering, annealing, and case hardening.

Hardening Hardening is a process of heating and cooling steel to increase its hardness and tensile strength, to reduce its ductility, and to obtain a fine grain structure. The procedure includes heating the metal above its critical point or temperature, followed by rapid cooling. As steel is heated, a physical and chemical change takes place between the iron and carbon. The critical point, or critical temperature, is the point at which the steel has the most desirable characteristics. When steel reaches this temperature—somewhere between 1,400 and 1,600 °F—the change is ideal to make for a hard, strong material if it is cooled quickly. If the metal cools slow-

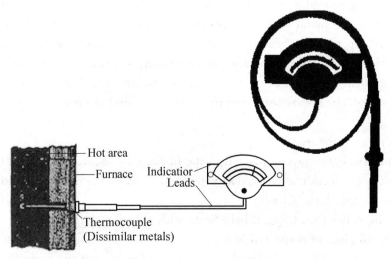

Fig. 4-1 A pyrometer accurately tells the temperature in the furnace

ly, it changes back to its original state. By plunging the hot metal into water, oil, or <u>brine</u> (quenching), the desirable characteristics are retained. The metal is very hard and strong and less <u>ductile</u> than before.

Heating is done in a furnace fired by gas, oil, or electricity. A device called a <u>pyrometer</u> is attached to the furnace. This accurately registers the exact temperature in the furnace (Fig. 4-1). The temperature of the metal can also be determined by observing its colour. You can make use of the colours when heat-treating simple metal parts and tools. Colours are not very accurate, however. Even the expert heat-treater will be off as much as 20°F from the true temperature.

The hardening procedure is:

1. Light the furnace, and allow it to come to the right temperature.
2. Place the metal in the furnace, and heat it to the critical temperature. For carbon tool steel, allow about 20 to 30 minutes per inch of thickness for coming up to heat. Allow about 10 to 15 minutes per inch of thickness for soaking at hardening temperature.
3. Select the correct cooling solution. Some steels can be cooled in water, and others must be cooled in oil or brine. Water is the most widely used material for quenching carbon steels because it is inexpensive and effective. Brine is usually made by adding about 9 percent of common salt to the water. Brine helps to produce a more uniform hardness. The brine cools the parts all over more quickly. Oil is used for a somewhat slower speed of quenching. Most oils used for quenching are mineral oils.
4. Remove the hot metal with <u>tongs</u>, and plunge it into the cooling solution. <u>Agitate</u> so that the metal cools quickly and evenly. If it is a thin piece (like a knife or blade), cut the cooling solution with the object so it won't warp. If one side cools faster than the other, there will be some warping.
5. A properly hardened piece of steel will be hard and brittle and have high tensile strength. It will also have internal strain. If left in this state, these internal strains could cause the metal to crack.

Tempering Tempering is a process of reducing the degree of hardness and strength and increasing the toughness. It removes the brittleness from a hardened piece. It is a process that follows the hardening procedure and makes the metal as hard and tough as possible. Tempering is done by reheating the metal to low or moderate temperature, followed by quenching or by cooling in air. As the metal is heated for tempering, it changes in colour. These colour are called <u>temper</u> colours. you can watch these colours to know when the correct heat is reached. A more accurate method, of course, is to watch the pyrometer. Many parts and projects are completely tempered. Others are tempered in one section, and the rest remains in the hardened state.

The tempering procedure is:

1. To temper the entire piece, place it in the furnace. Reheat to the correct temperature to produce the hardness and toughness you want. Remove the metal and cool it quickly.
2. To temper small cutting tools:
a. Harden the entire tool. Clean off the scale with <u>abrasive cloth</u>.
b. Heat a scrap piece of metal red hot.
c. Place the tool on the metal with the point extending beyond the hot piece of metal.
d. Watch the temper colours. When the correct colour reaches the point of the tool

quench it.

Annealing   Annealing is the process of softening steel to relieve internal strain. This makes the steel easier to machine. The metal is heated above the critical temperature and cooled slowly. The most common method is to place the steel in the furnace and heat it thoroughly. Then turn off the furnace, allowing the metal to cool slowly. Another method is to pack the metal in clay, heat it to the critical temperature, remove it from the furnace, and allow it to cool slowly.

Case hardening   Case hardening is a process of hardening the outer surface or case of ferrous metal. By adding a small amount of carbon to the case of the low-carbon steel, it can be heat-treated to make the case hard. At the same time the centre, or core, remains soft and ductile.

There are many methods of case hardening. In industry, molten <u>cyanide</u> is used (this is called <u>cyaniding</u>). Another industrial method is <u>carburizing</u>. This is a case-hardening procedure in which carbon is added to steel from the surface inward by one of the following methods: pack method, gas method, or liquid-salt method.

This process can be done on such items as hammer heads, piston pins, and other items that must stand a good deal of shock and wear. It can never be used on anything that must be sharpened by grinding.

Words and Expressions

tempering /ˈtempəriŋ/ n.		回火
case hardening		表面淬火，表面硬化
brine /brain/ n.		盐水
quenching /ˈkwentʃiŋ/ n.		淬火，骤冷
ductile /ˈdʌktail/ adj.		可延展的，易于塑造的
pyrometer /paiˈrɔmitə/ n.		高温计
tong /tɔŋ/ n.		夹钳，抓手
agitate /ˈædʒiteit/ v.		摇晃，搅动
temper /ˈtempə/ v.		回火，调和，调节
abrasive cloth		砂布
cyanide /ˈsaiənaid/ n.		氰化物
cyaniding /ˈsaiənaidiŋ/ n.		氰化法，氰化处理
carburizing /ˈkɑːbjuraiziŋ/ n.		渗碳，碳化

Passage II   Mechanical Properties of Metals

Mechanical properties are measures of how materials behave under applied loads. Another way of saying this is how strong is a metal when it comes in contact with one or more forces. If you know the strength properties of a metal, you can build a structure that is safe and sound. Hence strength is the ability of a metal to withstand loads (forces) without breaking down.

Strength properties are commonly referred to as tensile strength, <u>bending strength</u>, compressive strength, <u>torsional strength</u>, <u>shear strength</u>, fatigue strength and <u>impact strength</u>.

1. **Stress** is the internal resistance a material offers to being deformed and is measured in

terms of the applied load.

2. **Strain** is the deformation that results from a stress and is expressed in terns of the amount of deformation per centimeter.

3. **Elasticity** is the ability of a metal to return to its original shape after being elongated or distorted, when the forces are released. A <u>rubber band</u> is a good example of what is meant by elasticity. If the rubber is stretched, it will return to its original shape after you let it go. However, if the rubber is pulled beyond a certain point, it will break. Metals with elastic properties react in the same way.

4. **Elastic limit** is the last point at which a material may be stretched and still return to its undeformed condition upon release of the stress.

5. <u>**Modulus of elasticity**</u> is the ratio of stress to strain within the elastic limit. The less a material deforms under a given stress the higher the modulus of elasticity. By checking the modulus of elasticity the comparative stiffness of different materials can readily be ascertained. Rigidity or stiffness is very important for many machine and structural applications.

6. **Tensile strength** is that property which resists forces acting to pull the metal apart. It is one of the more important factors in the evaluation of a metal.

7. **Compressive strength** is the ability of a material to resist being crushed. Compression is the opposite of tension with respect to the direction of the applied load. Most metals have high tensile strength and high compressive strength. However, brittle materials such as cast iron have high compressive strength but only a moderate tensile strength.

8. **Bending strength** is that quality which resists forces from causing a member to bend or <u>deflect</u> in the direction in which the load is applied. Actually a bending stress is a combination of tensile and compressive stresses.

9. **Torsional strength** is the ability of a metal to withstand forces that cause a member to twist.

10. **Shear strength** refers to how well a member can withstand two equal forces acting in opposite directions.

11. **Fatigue strength** is the property of a material to resist various kinds of rapidly alternating stresses. For example, a piston rod or an axle undergoes complete reversal of stresses from tension to compression. Bending a piece of wire back and forth until it breaks is another example of fatigue strength.

12. **Impact strength** is the ability of a metal to resist loads that are applied suddenly and often at high velocity. The higher the impact strength of a metal the greater the energy required to break it. Impact strength may be seriously affected by <u>welding</u> since it is one of the most structure sensitive properties.

13. **Ductility** refers to the ability of metal to stretch, bend, or twist without breaking or cracking. A metal having high ductility, such as copper or soft iron, will fail or break gradually as the load on it is increased. A metal of low ductility, such as cast iron, fails suddenly by cracking when subjected to a heavy load.

14. **Hardness** is that property in steel which resists indentation or penetration. Hardness is usually expressed in terms of the area of an indentation made by a special ball under a standard load, or the depth of a special indenter under a specific load.

15. **Cryogenic properties** of metals represent behavior characteristics under stress in environments of very low temperatures. In addition to being sensitive to crystal structure and processing, metals are also sensitive to low and high temperatures. Some alloys which perform satisfactorily at room temperatures may fail completely at low or high temperatures. The changes from ductile to brittle failure occurs rather suddenly at low temperatures.

Words and Expressions

bending strength	抗弯强度
torsional strength	抗扭强度
shear strength	抗剪强度
impact strength	冲击强度，冲击韧性
rubber band	橡胶圈，橡皮筋
modulus /'mɔdjuləs/ n.	模数，模量
deflect /di'flekt/ v.	（使）偏斜，（使）偏转
welding /'weldiŋ/ n.	焊接
cryogenic /ˌkraiə'dʒenik/ adj.	低温学的

Passage Ⅲ Stress and strain

Stress and strain are not the same but are related in that either one will produce the other. Consider the simple example of a manila rope used to tow an automobile. The pull on the rope causes a stress or force in the rope fibers. After the pull, or stress, on the rope is relaxed, the rope has been permanently stretched owing to this stress. The increase in length is a deformation or strain. The warping that always accompanies fusion welding is a strain and clearly indicates that there are stresses in the metal after welding.

Stresses are calculated in pounds per square inch (psi) just like pressures. The stress in psi is equal to the load P divided by the area supporting the load:

$$S = \frac{P}{A}$$

There are three possible types of stresses (Fig. 4-2):

1. compression (crushing)

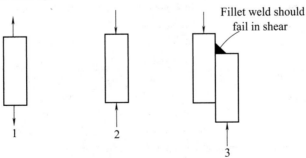

Fig. 4-2 Types of stresses
1. Tension (Pull) 2. Compression (Crushing) 3. Shear (Cutting)

2. tension (pull)
3. shear (cutting)

All materials when loaded or stressed will deform, shorten, or stretch. This change in dimension or shape under a load is occasionally large enough to be visible, as in the case of rubber bands and metal springs, but for metal structural members carrying the loads for which they were designed, the deformations are only a few microinches. Being very stiff metals will strain very little under large stresses. Now it is generally understood that if a materials is stressed, it will also strain or deform, but it must be borne in mind that the reverse applies also, that is, if a metal is strained, it will also be stressed. Basically, strain is the cause of stress.

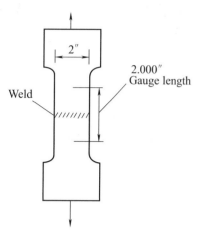

Fig. 4-3 Weld test sample

To demonstrate the relationship between stress and strain, we shall analyze a tension test performed on a weld sample. The weld is a double butt weld with full penetration on 1/2-in plate, and a sample 2 in. wide is cut out of the plate for testing the strength of the weld. Although it is not a requirement of all weld tests, we shall note the elongation in a gauge length of 2.0000 in. which includes the weld area. Such elongations are measured by strain gauges. The sample is dimensioned in Fig. 4-3.

The large dial on the testing machine indicates the tension load applied to the weld test sample. The cross-sectional area of the test sample is 2 in. by 1/2 in. which equals 1 sq in., and with this cross section the load and the stress are the same. A strain indicator will indicate the elongation over the 2.0000 in. gauge length. The elongation per inch of length is a more useful piece of information; this merely requires that the readings on the strain indicator be divided by 2. This is the actual unit strain—the definition of unit strain is the elongation in inches per inch of original length.

The weld test specimen is held in the grips of the testing machine, and a steadily increasing load is applied to it in tension. Periodically, readings are taken of load and elongation in 2.00000 in. Suppose the results of the test are those given in the following tabulation:

Stress-Strain Readings for a Weld Test Sample

Load, lb	Stress, psi	Elongation, in 2.0000 in.	Unit strain in./in.
1,000	1,000	0.000066	0.000033
2,000	2,000	0.000133	0.000066
4,000	4,000	0.000266	0.000133
6,000	6,000	0.000400	0.000200
10,000	10,000	0.000666	0.000333
20,000	20,000	0.001333	0.000666
30,000	30,000	0.002000	0.001000
42,000	42,000	0.0028	0.0014
42,000	42,000	0.040	0.020
44,000	44,000	0.060	0.030

50,000	50,000	0.170	0.085
60,000	60,000	0.264	0.132
63,000	63,000	0.280	0.140 Rupture

Scrutiny of the tabulated results discloses much information about the weld sample. First, very large stresses produce only minute strains: 15 tons per sq in. produce a strain of only 1/10% or 1/1000% in. per in. of length. Second, there appear to be two strain regions. For low stresses, up to 42,000 psi, the strain is proportional to the stress. For the higher stresses, the strain no longer proportional to the stress, and in this region the metal stretches considerably, or yields. The stress separating these two kinds of strain behavior is termed the yield stress, which for this sample is 42,000 psi. The region below the yield stress is the elastic region, and the elastic strain is that part of the strain which disappears when the load is removed. A steel spring, for example, works on elastic strain. Beyond the yield stress, the strain is plastic, meaning that it is permanent and remains after the stress is removed.

We can now properly explain the terms brittle and ductile. A brittle material is any material which shows very little or no plastic strain, and a ductile material develops a long plastic region when stressed. Plasticity is an important requirement of structural materials because plastic deformation gives a warning that the material is being stressed close to its ultimate strength. Brittle materials, having no plastic deformation, give no warming of failure. The weld test sample analyzed above increased in length by 14% before it broke: the total elastic strain was only 0.14%, or one-hundredth as much as the plastic strain. By and large, soft and weak materials behave plastically, and hard and strong materials show little plastic behavior. This is true of steels in particular: the soft or 'mild' steels may elongate plastically 25% to 35%.

Words and Expressions

manila /mə'nilə/ n.	马尼拉麻
microinch /'maikrəuintʃ/ n.	百万分之一英寸，微英寸
elongation /ˌiːlɔŋ'geiʃən/ n.	伸长，拉伸
unit strain	单位应变
specimen /'spesimin/ n.	范例，标本，样品，样本，待试验物
tabulation /ˌtæbju'leiʃən/ n.	制表，造册
rupture /'rʌptʃə/ n.	断裂，破裂
scrutiny /'skruːtini/ n.	研究，推敲
disclose /dis'kləuz/ v.	揭露，披露，泄露
yield stress	屈服应力

Passage Ⅳ Surface Treatment

Nearly all metals and alloys in common use, and especially iron and steel, are attacked by substances in the air and are eaten away by corrosion unless protected by a layer of grease, paint, chemical or another less corrodible metal. The most serious form of corrosion, though not the most common is an 'intercrystalline' corrosion, where the corroding substance acts between the crystals of which the metals are composed. Surface treatment aims at preventing this substance from reaching the crystals.

A simple coating of oil or grease, being soft, is easily damaged so that the air can find a way in. But a really tough and sticky grease such as lanolin, obtained from sheep's wool, can be a very useful way of keeping iron and steel articles free from rust for periods of temporary storage.

Large structures are generally treated with several coats of paint. If the metal surface is shiny, it is difficult for the paint to get a good grip; so the metal is given a chemical treatment first, by dipping it into a solution of phosphoric acid and other salts which attack the metal and produce a thin coating of phosphate crystals, making a rough surface which helps the paint to stick. If the paint is accidentally scratched later, the coating beneath helps to stop the rust spreading from the scratch mark and causing severe damage.

An important way of protecting metal surfaces is electroplating—that is, depositing on the metal by electric current a very thin film of a non-rusting metal. A familiar example is chromium plate—a very thin film of chromium metal applied over a coating of bright or polished nickel. When a bright and shiny surface is not so important, zinc, cadmium, tin, or an alloy of tin and zinc are generally used.

The surface must be absolutely clean so that the thin metal coating can stick on firmly; even the grease from a finger mark is enough to spoil the treatment. Grease or oil is first removed with paraffin or a similar solvent; then a boiling alkali solution such as washing soda is used to remove the last traces of grease; and finally the metal is 'pickled'—soaked in dilute acid to take off any rust.

Iron or steel articles can be coated more thickly by being dipped into a bath of melted zinc or tin. Coating with zinc in this called 'galvanizing'. Tinning is the process used in the making of tinplate. To give a zinc coating to small iron or steel articles such as nuts and bolts the articles are put into a box full of zinc dust and heated in a furnace; the zinc then combines with the surface of the iron or steel to form an alloy. This process is known as 'sherardizing'. In a similar process, 'chromizing', chromium is used instead of zinc, giving an alloy coating similar to stainless steel.

A coating which is used on steel articles is vitreous enamel, sometimes called porcelain enamel. This enamelling, not to be confused with hard gloss paint, often called enamel, produces a smooth, shiny surface, nearly as hard as glass and difficult to scratch. Vitreous enamelling needs a very clean metal surface. Steel can be easily cleaned by acid 'pickling', but this is not possible for cast iron, which is cleaned by a process called shot blasting. Small, broken pieces of hardened steel shot are thrown forcibly against the article to be cleaned so that their sharp edges knock and scrape off all the rust and dirt. The bits of shot are blown across the surface of the article by a blast of compressed air or are spun round in a wheel so that they are flung out across the surface. Sand was used to serve this purpose instead of steel shot, but the dust from the sand damaged the workers' lungs.

One protective process known as 'anodizing' can be applied only to aluminium and certain of its alloys. In some ways the process is similar to electroplating, in that the article is immersed in a solution and an electric current is passed through it; but the direction of the flow of the current is reversed. The oxygen gas produced by the current converts the surface of the aluminium into a tough film of aluminium oxide. When the article is put into service the oxygen in the air cannot attack it further, as it already has a thin oxide coating all over it. This process cannot be applied to iron or steel, as the oxide coating do not adhere well and are porous, so that air can get through them and still attack the metal underneath.

Surface treatments can be given to iron, steel, and other metals by immersing them in chemicals which produce an oxide coating—usually black, dark blue, or brown. The familiar blue colour of a <u>gun barrel</u> is produced by such a process. These coating do not give great protection as they are usually somewhat porous, but they can be made more effective if they are oiled.

Words and Expressions

intercrystalline /ˌintəˈkristəlain/ adj.	晶（粒）间的，沿晶界的
surface treatment	表面处理
lanolin /ˈlænəlin/ n.	羊毛脂
phosphoric acid	磷酸
phosphate /ˈfɔsfeit/ n.	磷酸盐，磷酸酯
scratch /skrætʃ/ n.	刻痕，划痕
stop /stɔp/ n.	挡块
electroplating /iˈlektrəupleitiŋ/ n.	电镀，电镀法
cadmium /ˈkædmiəm/ n.	镉
paraffin /ˈpærəfin/ n.	石蜡，烷烃
dilute /daiˈljuːt/ v.	冲淡，变淡，变弱，稀释
tin /tin/ n.	锡，马口铁
sherardizing /ˈʃerədaiziŋ/ n.	渗锌法
chromizing /ˈkrəumaiziŋ/ n.	渗铬，铬化
vitreous /ˈvitriəs/ adj.	玻璃状的，透明的
vitreous enamel	釉瓷，搪瓷
porcelain /ˈpɔːslin/ adj.	瓷制的，精美的
n.	瓷器
porcelain enamel	搪瓷
enamelling /iˈnæməliŋ/ n.	上珐琅，上釉
shot /ʃɔt/ n.	丸，砂
blasting /ˈblɑːstiŋ/ n.	喷丸处理，喷砂处理
shot blasting	喷砂清理
gun barrel	枪筒，炮筒

Exercises

I. Choose the appropriate words to complete the following sentences and change the form if necessary.

1. corrosion   corrosive   corrodible   corrode
   a. The metal has _____ away because of rust.
   b. Clean off any _____ before applying the paint.
   c. Rust and acids are _____ .

2. treatment   treatable   treat
   a. It is possible to _____ sewage so that it can be used as fertilizer.
   b. This is an effective _____ for dry rot.
   c. A _____ illness or injury can be helped with drugs or an operation.
3. adherent   adhesion   adhesive   adhere
   a. Paste is used to make one surface _____ to another.
   b. The movement is gaining more and more _____ .
   c. Something that is _____ is able to stick firmly to something else.
4. convert   converter   conversion   convertible
   a. _____ to gas central heating will save you a lot of money.
   b. This is part of the process of _____ iron into steel.
   c. A _____ is a machine that changes the form of things, especially one that makes steel from melted iron.
5. compress   compression   compressive   compressor   compressible
   a. The machine _____ old cars into blocks of scrap metal.
   b. _____ strength is the ability of a material to resist being crushed.
   c. A _____ is a machine or part of a machine that compresses air or other gases.

II. Translate the following passage into Chinese.

The properties of materials arise from their internal structures. If the engineer wants a specific set of properties, he must choose his materials appropriately so that they have suitable structures. Should the internal structure of a material be changed during processing of service, there are corresponding changes in properties.

III. Translate the following passage into English.

低碳钢由于含碳量低，因此在经受这种热处理时，材质不可能变硬。若欲在低碳钢制成的零件表面获得硬的表面层，就需要进行表面硬化处理。氰化是一种表面硬化方法。氰化时，将工件置入氰化钠的溶液中5～30min。工件经过这一处理后，再将其淬入水或油中，于是形成了厚度为0.254～0.381mm的十分硬的表面层。

Unit5 Mechanical Drawing

Passage I Engineering Drawing

Engineering drawing is a graphical language used by engineers and other technical personnel associated with the engineering profession. The purpose of engineering drawing is to convey graphically the ideas and information necessary for the construction or analysis of machines, structures, or systems.

In colleges and universities, engineering drawing is usually treated in courses with titles like Engineering Graphics. Sometimes these courses include other topics, such as computer graphics and nomography.

The basis for much engineering drawing is orthographic representation (projection). Objects are depicted by front, top, side, auxiliary, or oblique views, or combinations of these. The complexity of an object determines the number of views shown. At times, pictorial views are also shown.

Engineering drawings often include such features as various types of lines, dimensions, lettered notes, sectional views, and symbols. They may be in the form of carefully planned and checked mechanical drawings, or they may be freehand sketches. sketches. Usually a sketch precedes the mechanical drawing. Final drawings are usually made on tracing paper, cloth or Mylar film, so that many copies can be made quickly and cheaply by such processes as, blueprinting, ammonia-developed (diazo) printing, or lithography.

Section Drawings

Many objects have complicated interior detail which cannot be clearly shown by means of front, top, side, or pictorial views. Section views enable the engineer or detailer to show the interior detail in such cases. Features of section drawings are cutting-plane symbols, which show where imaginary cutting planes are passed to produce the sections, and section-lining (sometimes called cross-hatching), which appears in the section view on all portions that have been in contact with the cutting plane. When only a part of the object is to be shown in section, conventional representation such as a revolved, rotated, or broken-out section is used. Details such as flat surfaces, knurls, and threads are treated conventionally, which facilitates the making and reading of engineering drawings by experienced personnel. Thus, certain engineering drawings will be combinations of top and front views, section and rotated views, and partial or pictorial views.

Dimensioning

In addition to describing the shape of objects, many drawings must show dimensions, so that workers can build the structure or fabricate parts that will fit together. This is accomplished by placing the required values along dimension lines (usually outside the outlines of the object) and by giving additional information in the form of notes which are referenced to the parts in question by angled lines called leaders. In drawings of large structures the major unit is the foot, and in drawings of small objects the unit is the inch. In metric dimensioning, the basic unit may be the meter, the centimeter, or the millimeter, depending upon the size of the object or structure.

Working types of drawings may differ in styles of dimensioning, lettering (inclined lowercase, vertical uppercase, and so on), positioning of the numbers (aligned, or unidirectional—a style in which all numbers are lettered horizontally), and in the type of fraction used (common fractions or decimal fractions). If special precision is required, an upper and a lower allowable limit are shown. Such tolerance, or limit, dimensioning is necessary for the manufacture of interchangeable mating parts, but unnecessarily close tolerances are very expensive.

Layout Drawings

Layout drawings of different types are used in different manufacturing fields for various purposes. One is the plant layout drawing, in which the outline of the building, work areas, aisles, and individual items of equipment are all drawn to scale. Another type is the aircraft, or master, layout, which is drawn on glass cloth or on steel or aluminum sheets. The object is drawn to full size with extreme accuracy. The completed drawing is photographed with great precision, and a glass negative made. From this negative, photo templates are made on photosensitized metal in various sizes and for different purposes, thereby eliminating the need for many conventional detail drawings. Another type of layout, or preliminary assembly, drawing is the design layout, which establishes the position and clearance of parts of an assembly.

Assembly Drawings

A set of working drawings usually includes detail drawings of all parts and an assembly drawing of the complete unit. Assembly drawings vary somewhat in character according to their use, as: design assemblies or layouts; working drawing assemblies; general assemblies; installation assemblies; and check assemblies. A typical general assembly may include judicious use of sectioning and identification of each part with a numbered balloon. Accompanying such a drawing is a parts list, in which each part is listed by number and briefly described; the number of pieces required is stated and other pertinent information given. Parts lists are best placed on separate sheets and typewritten to avoid time-consuming and costly hand lettering.

Schematic Drawings

Schematic or diagrammatic drawings make use of standard symbols and single lines between symbols which indicate the direction of flow. In piping and electrical schematic diagrams, symbols recommended by the American National Standards Institute (ANSI), other agencies, or the Department of Defense (DOD) are used. The fixtures or components are not labeled in most schematics because readers usually know what the symbols represent.

Additional information is often lettered on schematic drawing, for example, the identification of each replaceable electrical component. Etched-circuit drawing has revolutionized the wiring of electronic components. By means of such drawing, the wiring of an electronic circuit is photographed on a copper-clad board, and unwanted areas are etched away. On electrical and other types of flow diagrams, all single lines (often with arrows showing direction of flow) are drawn horizontally or vertically; there are few exceptions. In some flow diagrams, rectangular enclosures are used for all items. Lettering is usually placed within the enclosures.

Structural Drawings

Structural drawings include design and working drawings for structures such as build-lings, bridges, dams, tanks, and highways. Such drawings form the basis of legal contracts. Structural drawings embody the same principles as do other engineering drawings, but use terminology and dimensioning techniques different from those shown in previous illustrations.

Words and Expressions

engineering drawing	工程制图，工程图
nomography /nəuˈmɔgrəfi/ n.	图解构成术
orthographic representation	正视表示法
oblique /əˈbliːk/ adj.	倾斜的；间接的
pictorial view	插图，示图
sectional view	剖视图，截面图
mechanical drawing	机械图，机械制图
tracing paper	描图纸，透明纸
Mylar film	聚酯薄膜
blueprint /ˈbluːprint/ n.	蓝图，设计图
vt.	制成蓝图
ammonia /əˈməunjə/ n.	氨水
diazo /daiˈæzəu/ adj.	重氮基的
lithography /liˈɔgrəfi/ n.	平版印刷术
section-lining /ˈsekʃənlainiŋ/ n.	剖面线法
cross-hatching /ˈkrɔsˈhætʃiŋ/ n.	交叉影线；用交叉线画成的阴影
fabricate /ˈfæbrikeit/ vt.	构成，制作
fraction /ˈfrækʃən/ n.	分数，分式
negative /ˈnegətiv/ n.	负片，底片
template /ˈtempleit/ n.	样板，模板
photosensitize /ˌfəutəˈsensitaiz/ vt.	使感光；使具有感光性
detail drawing	细部图
assembly drawing	总图，装配图，组装图
judicious /dʒuˈdiʃəs/ adj.	明智的，有见识的；审慎的
schematic drawing	简图，示意图
American National Standards Institute	美国国家标准协会
fixture /ˈfikstʃə/ n.	装置，夹具，卡具，定位器
etched-circuit /ˈetʃidˈsəːkit/ n.	腐蚀印制电路

structural drawing　　　　　　　　　　　　　　结构图，构造图

Exercises

Answer the following questions according to the information of the text.
1. What's engineering drawing?
2. Why do we make engineering drawing?
3. What do engineering drawings often include?
4. What may be the form of engineering drawings?
5. What's the advantage of section drawings?
6. What are the features of section drawings?
7. How can people accomplish dimensional drawings?
8. What are the layout drawings mentioned in the passage?
9. How many types do the assembly drawing have?
10. What's the characteristic of schematic drawings?

Passage Ⅱ　Sectional Views

Although the invisible features of a simple object usually may be described on an exterior view by the use of <u>hidden lines</u>, it is unwise to depend on a <u>perplexing</u> mass of such lines to describe adequately the interior of a complicated object or an assembled mechanism. Whenever a representation becomes so confused that it is difficult to read, it is customary to make one or more of the views 'in section'. A view, 'in section' is one obtained by imagining the object to have been cut by a cutting plane, the front portion being removed to reveal clearly the interior features. Fig. 5-1 illustrates the use of an imaginary cutting plane. At this point it should be understood that a portion is shown removed only in a sectional view, not in any of the other views (Fig. 5-1).

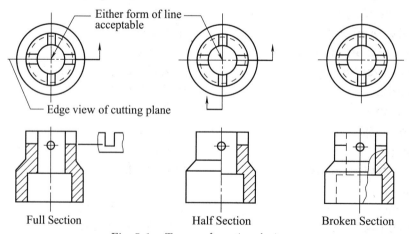

Fig. 5-1　Types of sectional views

When the cutting plane cuts an object lengthwise, the section obtained is commonly called a <u>longitudinal section</u>; when crosswise, it is called a cross section. It is designated as being either a <u>full section</u>, a <u>half section</u>, or a <u>broken section</u>. If the plane cuts entirely across the object, the section represented is known as a full section. If it cuts only halfway across a symmetrical object, the section is a half section. A broken section is a partial one, which is used when less than a half section is needed (Fig. 5-1).

On a completed sectional view, fine section lines are drawn across the surface cut by the imaginary plane, to emphasize the contour of the interior.

Full Section

Since a cutting plane that cuts a full section passes entirely through an object, the resulting view will appear as illustrated in Fig. 5-1. Although the plane usually passes along the main axis, it may be offset to reveal important features.

A full-sectional view, showing an object's characteristic shape, usually replaces an exterior front view; however, one of the other principal views, side or top, may be converted to a sectional view if some interior feature thus can be shown to better advantage or if such a view is needed in addition to a sectioned front view.

The procedure in making a full-sectional view is simple, in that the sectional view is an orthographic one. The imaginary cut face of the object simply is shown as it would appear to an observer looking directly at it from a point an infinite distance away. In any sectional view, it is considered good practice to omit all invisible lines unless such lines are necessary to clarify the representation. Even then they should be used sparingly.

Half Section

The cutting plane for a half section removes one-quarter of an object. The plane cuts halfway through to the axis or center line so that half the finished sectional view appears in section and half appears as an external view (Fig. 5-1). This type of sectional view is used when a view is needed showing both the exterior and interior construction of a symmetrical object. Good practice dictates that hidden lines be omitted from both halves of the view unless they are absolutely necessary for dimensioning purposes or for explaining the construction. Although the use of a solid object line to separate the two halves of a half section has been approved by the Society of Automotive Engineers and has been accepted by the American National Standards Institute, many draftsmen prefer to use a center line. They reason that the removal of a quarter of the object is theoretical and imaginary, and that an actual edge, which would be implied by a solid line, does not exist. The center line is taken as denoting a theoretical edge.

Broken Section

A broken or partial section is used mainly to expose the interior of objects so constructed that less than a half section is required for a satisfactory description. The object theoretically is cut by a cutting plane and the front portion is removed by breaking it away. The 'breaking away' gives an irregular boundary line to the section.

Words and Expressions

hidden line	隐线，虚线
perplexing /pə'pleksiŋ/ adj.	复杂的，令人困惑的

longitudinal section	纵剖面
full section	全剖面
half section	半剖面
broken section	局部剖视
symmetrical /si'metrikəl/ *adj.*	对称的；均匀的
contour /'kɔntuə/ *n.*	轮廓，形状；断面
sparingly /'spɛəriŋjli/ *adv.*	节俭地，保守地
external view	外视图
Society of Automotive Engineers	汽车工程师协会
draftsman /'drɑ:ftsmən/ *n.*	制图员

Passage Ⅲ Machine Drawings

There are two recognized classes of machine drawings: detail drawings and assembly drawings.

Detail Drawing

A detail drawing should give complete information for the manufacture of a part, describing with adequate dimensions the part's size. Finished surfaces should be indicated and all necessary shop operations shown. The title should give the material of which the part is to be made and should state the number of the parts that are required for the production of an assembled unit of which the part is a member.

Since a machinist will ordinarily make one part at a time, it is advisable to detail each piece, regardless of its size, on a separate individual sheet. In some shops, however, custom dictates that related parts be grouped on the same sheet, particularly when the parts form a unit in themselves. Other concerns sometimes group small parts of the same material together thus: castings on one sheet, forgings on another, special fasteners on still another, and so on.

Making a Detail Drawing

With a design layout or original sketches as a guide, the procedure for making a detail drawing is as follows:

1. Select the views, remembering that, aside from the view showing the characteristic shape of the object, there should be as many additional views as are necessary to complete the shape description. These may be sectional views that reveal a complicated interior construction, or auxiliary views of surfaces not fully described in any of the principal views.

2. Decide on a scale that will allow, without crowding, a balanced arrangement of all necessary views and the location of dimensions and notes. Although very small parts should be drawn double-size or larger, to show detail and to allow for dimensions, a full-size scale should be used when possible. In general, the same scale should be used for pieces of the same size.

3. Draw the main center lines and block in the general outline of the views with light, sharp 6H pencil lines.

4. Draw main circles and arcs in finished weight.

5. Starting with the characteristic view, work back and forth from view to view until the shape of the object is completed. Lines whose definite location and length are known may be drawn in their finished weight.

6. Put in fillets and rounds.

7. Complete the view by darkening the object lines.

8. Draw extension and dimension lines.

9. Add arrowheads, dimensions, and notes.

10. Complete the title.

11. Check the entire drawing carefully.

One-View Drawings

Many parts, such as shafts, bolts, studs, and washers, may require only one properly dimensioned view. In the case of each of these parts, a note can imply the complete shape of the piece without sacrificing clearness. Most engineering departments, however, deem it better practice to show two views.

Detail Titles

Every detail drawing must give information not conveyed by the notes and dimensions, such as the name of the part, part number, material, number required, and so on. The method of recording and the location of this information on the drawing varies somewhat in different drafting rooms. It may be lettered either in the record strip or directly below the views.

If all surfaces on a part are machined, finish marks are omitted and a title note, 'FINISH ALL OVER', is added to the detail title.

Title Blocks and Record Strips

The purpose of a title or record strip is to present in an orderly manner the name of the machine, name of the manufacturer, date, scale, drawing number, and other drafting-room information.

Every commercial drafting room has developed its own standard title forms, whose features depend on the processes of manufacture, the peculiarities of the plant organization, and the established customs of particular types of manufacturing. In large organizations, the blank form, along with the borderline, is printed on standard sizes of tracing paper and/or Mylar.

A record strip is a form of title extending almost the entire distance across the bottom of the sheet. In addition to the usual title information, it may contain a section for recording revisions, changes, and so on, with the dates on which they were adopted.

Contents of the Title

The title on a machine drawing generally contains the following information:

1. Name of the part.

2. Name of the machine or structure. (This is given in the main title and is usually followed by one of two words: details or assembly.)

3. Name and location of the manufacturing firm.

4. Name and address of the purchasing firm, if the structure has been designed for a particular company.

5. Scale.

6. Date. (Often spaces are provided for the date of completion of each operation in the preparation of the drawing. If only one date is given, it is usually the date of completion of the drawing.)

7. Initials or name of the draftsman who made the pencil drawing.

8. Initials of the checker.

9. Initials or signature of the chief draftsman, chief engineer, or another in authority who approved the drawing.

10. Initials of the tracer (if drawing has been traced).

11. Drawing number. This generally serves as a filing number and may furnish information in code form. Letters and numbers may be so combined to indicate departments, plants, model, type, order number, filing number, and so on. The drawing number is sometimes repeated in the upper-left-hand corner (in an upside-down position), so that the drawing may be quickly identified if it should become reversed in the file.

Some titles furnish information such as material, part number, pattern number, finish, treatment, estimated weight, superseded drawing number, and so on.

Assembly Drawings

A drawing that shows the parts of a machine or machine unit assembled in their relative working positions is an assembly drawing. There are several types of such drawings: design assembly drawings, working assembly drawings, unit assembly drawings, installation diagrams, and so on.

Working Assembly Drawings

A working assembly drawing, showing each piece completely dimensioned, is sometimes made for a simple mechanism or unit of related parts. No additional detail drawings of parts are required.

Subassembly (Unit) Drawings

A unit assembly is an assembly drawing of a group of related parts that form a unit in a more complicated machine. Such a drawing would be made for the tail stock of a lathe, the clutch of an automobile, or the carburetor of an airplane. A set of assembly drawings thus takes the place of a complete assembly of a complex machine.

Words and Expressions

full-size /ˌfulˈsaiz/ *n.*		实际大小
clearness /ˈkliənis/ *n.*		清晰度，明白
record strip		记录员
tracer /ˈtreisə/ *n.*		描图员

supersede /ˌsjuːpəˈsiːd/ *vt.*		代替，紧接着…而到来
tail stock		尾架，顶尖座
lathe /leɪð/ *n.*		车床
vt.		用车床加工
carburetor /ˈkɑːbjuretə/ *n.*		化油器

Passage Ⅳ   AutoCAD

Description

AutoCAD is a PC-based 2D and 3D mechanical design and drafting <u>package</u>. Geometric shapes and figures are created and modified for engineering drawing. A <u>reduced instruction set processor</u> (RISC), with a limited number of instructions, is built into the processor, reducing the response time to run some applications on the AutoCAD development system (ADS). <u>Crosshairs</u> and a mouse are used to locate geometric shapes within the work area. An X-Y construction plane is used for the 2D mode that uses a three-point origin placed by the user, known as the User Coordinate System (UCS).

Command Structure

To support many applications, AutoCAD has an open architecture for easy customization of menus. The main menu is the screen menu, which includes the drawing editor, configuration, <u>plot</u>, file utility, and operating parameters menus. A <u>dialogue box</u> appears when selected items are chosen from the <u>pull-down</u> menus to assist the user. The following are examples of screen editor commands.

  1. Set-up types of measurements or limits to the drawing area.
  2. Blocks allow drawings to be, grouped for insertion in other parts of the drawing.
  3. Display commands refresh, redraw, or automatically redraw the screen and changes the viewing area.
  4. Draw creates and modifies geometric shapes and adds text.
  5. Edit allows modification of the actual drawing geometry using trim, move, rotate, and extend commands.
  6. <u>Inquiry</u> shows the location of a point or angle, evaluates areas, and gives database information.
  7. <u>Layer</u> changes the visibility, color, and line type of a layer.
  8. Settings controls the grid spacing, axis, size of the target box, and color.

Other special menus are the utility or directory files, 3D for 3D drawings, and <u>autoshade</u> to show shading or a shadowing from a chosen line of light.

Discussion

The AutoCAD commands are path dependent, e.g., the undo command will remove the screen image and any previous drawing layers up to an earlier drawing level. Other features are AutoLISP and ADS. AutoLISP is an AutoCAD program that enhances the AutoCAD drawing and editing commands. For example, reference coordinates can be created and 2D spirals, holes, or slots in a 3D surface can be programmed and saved, AutoLISP is an interpretive system, with instructions being read, interpreted, validated, and then executed in sequence.

Description of ADS

ADS is an AutoCAD development system using a C language base interface into the core and an independent C compiler. The AutoCAD core holds the basic instruction set of the AutoCAD platform, maintains the database, and allows access to the data, using AutoCAD geometry commands, functions, and C options. Limited animation is available.

Solid modeling and wire frames are created using simple Boolean rules to add or subtract geometric shapes to a drawing shape, e. g., a pipe is created by using two cylinders to obtain an inside and outside diameter (ID, OD). These types of 2D forms are used to generate solids or extruded solids of revolution.

Words and Expressions

package /'pækidʒ/ n.	程序包；组件；成套设备
reduced instruction set processor	简化指令集处理器
crosshair /'krɔshɛə/ n.	横标线，十字线
plot /plɔt/ n.	曲线；图表
dialogue box	对话框
pull-down /'puldaun/ n.	下拉
inquiry /in'kwaiəri/ n.	查询
layer /'leiə/ n.	层
autoshade /'ɔːtouʃeid/ n.	自动遮蔽
validate /'vælideit/ vt.	使生效，确认
solid modeling	实体造型
Boolean rule	布尔定律
extrude /eks'truːd/ vt.	挤压，模压

Exercises

Ⅰ. Choose the appropriate words to complete the sentences and change the form if necessary.

1. customer   customary   customarily   custom
   a. It has become the _____ for our family to go to the seaside in summer.
   b. Is it _____ for guests at hotels in your country to tip the waiters?
   c. Mr. White has lost some of his best _____ .

2. adequately   adequacy   adequate
   a. Are you getting an _____ wage for the work you're doing?
   b. He often doubts his _____ as a husband and father.
   c. Are you _____ insured?

3. imaginary   imagine   imaginative   imagination   imaginable
   a. Can you _____ life without electricity and other modern conveniences?
   b. We had the greatest difficulty _____ getting here in time.

c. Her talk captured the _____ of the whole class.
4. assistant   assistance   assist
   a. Two men are _____ the police in their enquiries.
   b. I can't move this piano without _____ .
   c. My _____ will operate the tape recorder.
5. clarified   clarification   clarity   clarify
   a. The report aims to _____ how these conclusions were reached.
   b. Churchill's _____ of vision impressed all who knew him.
   c. The _____ butter was very tasty.

Ⅱ. Translate the following passage into English.

一个有能力的工程师不应该害怕在提出自己的方案时遭到失败的可能性。事实上，偶然的失败肯定会发生的，因为每一个真正有创造性的设想似乎总是有失败或批评伴随着它。从一次失败中可以学到很多东西，只有那些愿意冒失败危险的人才能够取得最大的收获。总之，真正的失败是根本不提任何方案。

Unit6   Mechanism

Passage I   Introduction to Mechanism

Mechanisms may be categorized in several different ways to emphasize their similarities and differences. One such grouping divides mechanisms into <u>planar</u>, <u>spherical</u>, and <u>spatial</u> categories. All three groups have many things in common; the criterion which distinguishes the groups, however, is to be found in the characteristics of the motions of the links.

A planar mechanism is one in which all particles describe plane curves in space and all these curves lie in parallel planes; i. e., the loci of all points are plane curves parallel to a single common plane. This characteristic makes it possible to represent the locus of any chosen point of a planar mechanism in its true size and shape on a single drawing or figure. The motion transformation of any such mechanism is called <u>coplanar</u>. The plane <u>four-bar linkage</u>, the <u>plate cam</u> and <u>follower</u>, and the <u>slider-crank mechanism</u> are familiar examples of planar mechanisms. The vast majority of mechanisms in use today are planar.

Planar mechanisms utilizing only lower pairs are called planar linkages; they may include only revolute and <u>prismatic pairs</u>. Although a planar pair might theoretically be included, this would impose no constraint and thus be equivalent to an opening in the kinematic chain. Planar motion also requires that the axes of all prismatic pairs and all revolute axes be normal to the plane of motion.

A spherical mechanism is one in which each link has some point which remains stationary as the linkage moves and in which the stationary points of all links lie at a common location; i. e., the locus of each point is a curve contained in a spherical surface, and the spherical surfaces defined by several arbitrarily chosen points are all <u>concentric</u>. The motions of all particles can therefore be completely described by their radial projections, or 'shadows', on the surface of a sphere with properly chosen center. Hooke's universal joint is perhaps the most familiar example of a spherical mechanism.

Spherical linkages are constituted entirely of revolute pairs. A spheric pair would produce no additional constraints and would thus be equivalent to an opening in the chain, while all other lower pairs have nonspheric motion. In spheric linkages, the axes of all revolute pairs must intersect at a point.

Spatial mechanisms, on the other hand, include no restrictions on the relative motions of the particles. The motion transformation is not necessarily coplanar, nor must it be concentric. A spatial mechanism may have particles with loci of <u>double curvature</u>. Any linkage which contains a screw pair, for example, is a spatial mechanism, since the relative motion within a <u>screw pair</u> is helical.

Thus, the overwhelming large category of planar mechanisms and the category of spherical mechanisms are only special cases, or subsets, of the all-inclusive category spatial mechanisms. They occur as a consequence of special geometry in the particular orientations of their pair axes.

If planar and spherical mechanisms are only special cases of spatial mechanisms, why is it desirable to identify them separately? Because of the particular geometric conditions which identify these types, many simplifications are possible in their design and analysis. As pointed out earlier, it is possible to observe the motions of all particles of a planar mechanism in true size and shape from a single direction. In other words, all motions can be represented graphically in a single view. Thus, graphical techniques are well suited to their solution. Since spatial mechanisms do not all have this fortunate geometry, visualization becomes more difficult and more powerful techniques must be developed for their analysis.

Since the vast majority of mechanisms in use today are planar, one might question the need of the more complicated mathematical techniques used for spatial mechanisms. There are a number of reasons why more powerful methods are of value even though the simpler graphical techniques have been mastered.

1. They provide new, alternative methods which will solve the problems in a different way. Thus they provide a means of checking results. Certain problems by their nature may also be more amenable to one method than another.

2. Methods which are analytical in nature are better suited to solution by calculator or digital computer than graphical techniques.

3. Even though the majority of useful mechanisms are planar and well suited to graphical solution, the few remaining must also be analyzed, and techniques should be known for analyzing them.

4. One reason that planar linkages are so common is that good methods of analysis for the more general spatial linkages have not been available until quite recently. Without methods for their analysis, their design and use has not been common, even though they may be inherently better suited in certain applications.

5. We will discover that spatial linkages are much more common in practice than their formal description indicates.

Consider a four-bar linkage. It has four links connected by four pins whose axes are parallel. This 'parallelism' is a mathematical hypothesis; it is not a reality. The axes as produced in a shop-in any shop, no matter how good-will only be approximately parallel. If they are far out of parallel, there will be binding in no uncertain terms, and the mechanism will only move because the 'rigid' links flex and twist, producing loads in the bearings. If the axes are nearly parallel, the mechanism operates because of the looseness of the running fits of the bearings or flexibility of the links. A common way of compensating for small nonparallelism is to connect the links with self-aligning bearings, actually spherical joints allowing three-dimensional rotation. Such a 'planar' linkage is thus a low-grade spatial linkage.

Words and Expressions

planar /ˈpleinə/ adj.	平面的，二维的
spherical /ˈsferikəl/ adj.	球面的；球形的
spatial /ˈspeiʃəl/ adj.	空间的，立体的
coplanar /kəuˈpleinə/ adj.	共面的，同一平面的
four-bar linkage	四连杆机构

plate cam	平板凹轮
follower /ˈfɔləuə/ n.	从动机构；从动轮
slider-crank /ˌslaidəˈkræŋk/ n.	滑块曲柄
slider-crank mechanism	滑块曲柄机构
prismatic pair	棱形副
concentric /kɔnˈsentrik/ adj.	同心的，同轴的
double curvature	双曲面；双曲率
screw pair	螺旋副
inherently /inˈhiərəntli/ adv.	本能的，自然的，本质上的
nonparallelism /ˌnɔnˈpærəlelizm/ n.	不平行度

Exercises

Choose the best answer for each the following according to the text.

1. It is based on the _____ that mechanisms are divided into planar, spherical and spatial categories.
   a. characteristics of the motion of the links
   b. ways to emphasize their similarities and differences
   c. different categories
   d. criterion of grouping

2. A planar mechanism is called _____ if it only involves lower pairs.
   a. coplanar   b. locus of points   c. planar linkage   d. paralleled planes

3. Which of the following is NOT true about a planar mechanism?
   a. Plane curves are parallel to a common plane.
   b. The locus of any point can be described in its true size and shape.
   c. Planar linkages usually include revolving and prismatic pairs.
   d. The characteristic of a planar mechanism is the motion transformation.

4. The spherical surfaces of a spherical mechanism must be _____.
   a. arbitrary   b. stationary   c. concentric   d. projecting

5. A linkage with a _____ pair must be _____ mechanism.
   a. lower…spherical   b. screw…spatial
   c. screw…planar   d. revolve…spatial

6. Which of the following is NOT true about a spherical mechanism?
   a. In spherical mechanism each link has some point which remains stationary.
   b. The locus of each point is a curve.
   c. The stationary point of all links lie at a common location.
   d. The spherical surfaces needn't be concentric.

7. In spherical linkages, the axes of all revolute pairs must _____ at a point.
   a. parallel   b. intersect   c. revolve   d. interact

8. The necessity of the more complicated mathematical techniques used for spatial mechanism includes the following except that _____.
   a. they provide new, attractive methods which will solve the problems in a different way
   b. methods which are analytical in nature are better

c. spatial linkages are the most common in practice

  d. there still remains some to be analyzed except great majority of planar and spherical mechanism and techniques should be known to analyze them

9. The word 'projection' in Para. 4. Line 6 means _____ .

  a. drawing lines throwing a point, line, figure, etc. and reproducing it on a surface

  b. plan

  c. estimation of future situation

  d. thing that juts from a surface

10. The word 'normal' in Para. 3. Line 5 means _____ .

  a. in accordance with what is usual   b. free from mental or emotional disorder

  c. vertical   d. in accordance with what is typical

Passage II Shafting

Shafting is the machine element that supports a roller and wheel so that they can perform their basic functions of rotation. Shafting, made from round metal bars of various lengths and machined to dimension the surface, is used in a great variety of shapes and applications. Because shafts carry loads and transmit power, they are subject to the stresses and strains of operating machine parts. Standardized procedures have been evolved for determining the material characteristics and size requirements for safe and economical construction and operation.

Types

Most shafting is rigid and carries bending loads without appreciable deflection. Some shafting is highly flexible, it is used to transmit motion around corners.

Solid shafting The normal form of shafting is a solid bar. Solid shafting is obtainable commercially in round bar stock up to 15cm in diameter; it is produced by hot-rolling and cold-drawing or by machine-finishing with diameters in increments of 6mm or less. For larger sizes, special rolling procedures are required, and for extremely large shafts, billets are forged to the proper shape. Particularly in solid shafting, the shaft is stepped to allow greater strength in the middle portion with minimum diameter on the ends at the bearings. The steps allow shoulders for positioning the various parts pressed onto the shaft during the rotor assembly.

Hollow shifting To minimize weights, solid shafting is bored out or drilled, or hollow pipes and tubing are used. Hollow shafts also allow internal support or permit other shafting to operate through the interior. The main shaft between the air compressor and the gas turbine in a jet aircraft engine is hollow to permit an internal speed reduction shaft with the minimum requirement of space and weight. A hollow shaft, to have the same strength in bending and torsion, has a larger diameter than a solid shaft, but its weight is less. The center of large shafts made from ingots are often bored out to remove imperfections and also to allow visual inspection for forging cracks.

Functions

Shafts used in special ways are given specific names, although fundamentally all applications involve transmission of torque.

Axle The primary shafting connection between a wheel and a housing is an axle. It may simply be the extension of a round member from each side of the rear of a wagon, and on the end of each the hub of a wagon wheel rotates. Similarly, railroad car axles are large, round bars of steel spanning between the car wheels, supporting the car frame with bearings on the axle outside the wheels. Axles normally carry only transverse loads, as in the examples above, but occasionally, as in rear automobile housings, they also transmit torsion loads.

Spindle A short shaft is a spindle. It may be slender or tapered. A spindle is capable of rotation or of having a body rotate upon it. The term originated from the round tapering stick on a spinning wheel on which the thread is twisted.

Head A short stub shaft mounted, as part of a motor or engine or extending directly therefrom is a head shaft. An example is the power takeoff shaft on a tractor.

Countershaft A secondary shaft that is driven by a main shaft and from which power is supplied to a machine part is called a countershaft. Often the countershaft is driven by gears, and thus rotates counter to the direction of the main shaft. Countershafts are used in gear transmissions to obtain speed and torque changes in transmitting power from one shaft to another.

Jackshaft A countershaft, especially when used as an auxiliary shaft between two other shafts, is termed a jackshaft.

Line shafting One or more pieces of shafting joined by couplings is used to transmit power from, for example, an engine to a remotely located machine. A single engine can drive many lines of shafting which, in turn, connect in multiple fashion to process equipment machines. Belts operate on pulleys to transmit the torque from one line to another and from the shafting to the machines. Clutches and couplings control the transfer of power from the shafting.

The delivery of power to the machines in a shop has generally been converted from line shafting to individual electric motor drives for each machine. Thus, in a modern processing plant, line shafting is obsolete.

Words and Expressions

shafting /ˈʃɑːftɪŋ/ n.　　　　　　　　传动轴，轴系
hot-rolling /ˌhɔtˈrəulɪŋ/ n.　　　　　热轧，加热压光
cold-drawing /ˌkəuldˈdrɔːɪŋ/ n.　　　冷拔，冷拉
machine-finishing /məˈʃiːnˈfɪnɪʃɪŋ/ n.　机械精加工，机械抛光
increment /ˈɪnkrɪmənt/ n.　　　　　　增加
shoulder /ˈʃəuldə/ n.　　　　　　　　肩，凹肩
tubing /ˈtjuːbɪŋ/ n.　　　　　　　　　管，管材
compressor /kəmˈpresə/ n.　　　　　　压气机，压缩器
ingot /ˈɪŋɡɔt/ n.　　　　　　　　　　锭，钢锭
axle /ˈæksl/ n.　　　　　　　　　　　车轴，轮轴
spindle /ˈspɪndl/ n.　　　　　　　　　轴，主轴
stub /stʌb/ n.　　　　　　　　　　　 轴端
countershaft /ˈkauntəʃɑːft/ n.　　　 （机械中的）副轴，间轴
jackshaft /ˈdʒækʃɑːft/ n.　　　　　　中间轴

line shafting   轴系

Passage Ⅲ Linkages

A linkage may be defined as an assemblage of solid bodies, or links, in which each link is connected to at least two others by pin connections (hinges) or sliding joints. To satisfy this definition, a linkage must form an endless, or closed, chain or a series of closed chains. It is obvious that a chain with many links will behave differently from one with few. This raises the vitally important question regarding the suitability of a given linkage for the transmission of motion in a machine. This suitability depends on the number of links and the number of joints.

Degrees of Freedom

A three-bar linkage (containing three bars linked together) is obviously a rigid frame; no relative motion between the links is possible. To describe the relative positions of the links in a four-bar linkage it is necessary only to know the angle between any two of the links. This linkage is said to have one degree of freedom. Two angles are required to specify the relative positions of the links in a five-bar linkage; it has two degrees of freedom.

Linkages with one degree of freedom have constrained motion; i.e., all points on all of the links have paths on the other links that are fixed and determinate. The paths are most easily obtained or visualized by assuming that, the link on which the paths are required is fixed, and then moving the other links in a manner compatible with the constraints.

Four-Bar Mechanisms

When one of the members of a constrained linkage is fixed, the linkage becomes a mechanism capable of performing a useful mechanical function in a machine. On pin-connected linkages the input (driver) and output (follower) links are usually pivotally connected to the fixed link; the connecting links (couplers) are usually neither inputs nor outputs. Since any of the links can be fixed, if the links are of different lengths, four mechanisms, each with a different input-output relationship, can be obtained with a four-bar linkage. These four mechanisms are said to be inversions of the basic linkage.

Slider-Crank Inversions

When one of the pin connections in a four-bar linkage is replaced by a sliding joint, a number of useful mechanisms can be obtained from the resulting-linkage. In Fig. 6-1 (top) the connection between links 1 and 4 is a sliding joint that permits block 4 to slide in the slot in link 1. It would make no difference, kinematically, if link 1 were sliding in a hole or slot in link 4.

If link 1 in Fig. 6-1 (top) is fixed, the resulting slider-crank mechanism is shown in Fig. 6-1 (center). This is the mechanism of a reciprocating engine. The block 4 represents the piston; link 1, shown shaded, is the block that contains the crankshaft bearing at A and the cylinder; link 2 is the crankshaft and link 3 the connecting rod. The crankpin bearing is at B, the wrist pin bearing at C. The stroke of the piston in twice AB, the throw of the crank.

The slider-crank mechanism provides means for converting the translatory motion of the

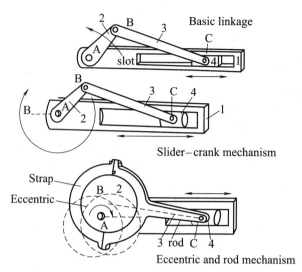

Fig. 6-1 Types of linkages

pistons in a reciprocating engine into rotary motion of the crankshaft, or the rotary motion of the crankshaft in a pump into a translatory motion of the pistons. In Fig. 6-1 (center), when B is in position B', the connecting rod would interfere with the crank if both were in the same plane. This problem is solved in engines and pumps by offsetting the crankpin bearing from the crankshaft bearing. By using an eccentric-and-rod mechanism in place of a crank, no <u>offsetting</u> is necessary and very small throws can be obtained.

In Fig. 6-1 (bottom) the crankpin bearing at B has become a large circular disk <u>pivoted</u> at A with an eccentricity or throw AB. The connecting rod has become the <u>eccentric</u> rod with a strap that encircles and slides on the eccentric. The mechanisms in the center and bottom drawings of Fig. 6-1 are kinematically equivalent.

By fixing links 2, 3, and 4 instead of link 1, three other inversions of the linkage in Fig. 6-1 (top) are obtained.

Words and Expressions

linkage /ˈliŋkidʒ/ n.   连杆机构，连接
assemblage /əˈsemblidʒ/ n.   集合
hinge /hindʒ/ n.   铰接，铰链
inversion /inˈvəːʃən/ n.   颠倒，转换
crankshaft /ˈkræŋkʃɑːft/ n.   曲柄轴
crankpin /ˈkræŋkpin/ n.   曲柄销
stroke /strəuk/ n.   冲程，行程；一笔，一画
translatory /ˈtrænslətəri/ adj.   平移的，平动的
offsetting /ˈɔːfsetiŋ/ n.   偏心距，位移，偏移
pivot /ˈpivət/ n.   枢轴，支点
eccentric /ikˈsentrik/ adj.   偏心的；
         n.   偏心轮

Exercises

I. Choose the best answer for each of the following.

1. The advantages of belt drive are the following except that they _____ .
   a. are economical
   b. cause little noise
   c. are strong
   d. are simple

2. The disadvantages of belts are the following except that _____ .
   a. speed is limited to usually 35 meters second
   b. noise and vibration are damped out
   c. operating temperatures are usually restricted
   d. power transmission is limited

3. _____ served as the basic belt drive from the beginning of the industrial revolution.
   a. Flat belts   b. V-belt   c. Film belt   d. Timing belt

4. Which of the following statements about flat belts is NOT true?
   a. They can transmit large amount of power at high speed.
   b. Flat belts are generally used in power delivery applications.
   c. Large power and high speed belt drives are cumbersome.
   d. Flat belts are widest used where high speed motive is the main concern.

5. Which of the following statements about V-belt is true?
   a. They are the basic power-transmission belt.
   b. They provide the least combination of traction operating speed, bearing load and service life.
   c. V-belts are far superior to flat belts.
   d. V-belts require smaller pulleys than flat belts.

6. _____ is often classified as a variety of flat belt.
   a. Timing belt   b. V-belt   c. Film belt   d. Multiple belt

7. Which of the following statements about timing belts is NOT true?
   a. They provide constant speed drive.
   b. They are lubrication free.
   c. They require the most tension of all belt drives.
   d. They are among the most efficient.

8. Shafts are subject to _____ of operating machine parts because they carry loads and transmit power.
   a. stress and strains   b. pressure   c. pulling   d. drawing

9. In modern processing plant, _____ is out of date.
   a. spindle   b. line shafting   c. jackshaft   d. head

10. The suitability of a given linkage for the transmission of motion in a machine depends on the _____ of links and joints.
    a. size   b. speed   c. number   d. material

II. Translate the following passage into Chinese.

Cam system, where a uniform motion of an input member is converted into a non-uniform motion of the output member. The output motion may be either shaft rotation, slider translation, or other follower motions created by direct contact between the input cam shape and the follower. The kinematics design of cams involves the analytical or graphical specification of the cam surface shape required to drive the follower with a motion that is a prescribed function the input motion.

Ⅲ. **Translate the following passage into English**

机构的运动设计通常是设计一台完整机器的第一步。在考虑力的作用时，应该考虑动力学、轴承载荷、应力、润滑等一系列问题。在所考虑的问题的范围扩大之后，机构设计就变成了机械设计。作为机器的一个组成部分，机构的作用是在刚体之间传递或转换运动。通常的基本机构有 3 种。它们是齿轮机构、凸轮机构、平面和空间连杆机构。

Unit 7 Machine Parts

Passage I Fasteners

'Fasteners' is a general term including such widely separated and varied materials as nails, screws, nuts and bolts, locknuts and washers, retaining rings, rivets, and adhesives, to mention but a few.

Fasteners are of many different types. Some fasteners, like nuts, bolts and washers, have been in use for years. Other fasteners, such as rivnuts and retaining rings, are fairly new in the field. A large number of different fasteners are used in most products.

Fasteners can be divided into two classifications: those that do not permanently join the pieces, and those that do. Included in the first category are such fasteners as nuts and bolts, lock washers, locknuts, and retaining rings. The second classification includes such fasteners as rivets, metal stitching, and adhesives.

Nuts, Bolts, and Screws

Nuts, bolts, and screws are undoubtedly the commonest means of joining materials. Since they are so widely used, it is essential that these fasteners attain maximum effectiveness at the lowest possible cost. Bolts are, in reality, carefully engineered products with a practically infinite use over a wide range of services.

An ordinary nut loosens when the forces of vibration overcome those of friction. In a nut and lock washer combination, the lock washer supplies an independent locking feature preventing the nut from loosening. The lock washer is useful only when the bolt might loosen because of a relative change between the length of the bolt and the parts assembled by it. This change in the length of the bolt can be caused by a number of factors-creep in the bolt, loss of resilience, difference in thermal expansion between the bolt and the bolted members, or wear. In the above static cases, the expanding lock washer holds the nut under axial load and keeps the assembly tight. When relative changes are caused by vibration forces, the lock washer is not nearly as effective.

The slotted nut and cotter pin provides an assembly that locks. Since the diameter of the pin is smaller than the hole in the bolt and the slot in the nut, the nut can back off under vibration until these clearances are reduced and the cotter pin jams the assembly. Another method of locking is the use of a self-locking nut for which the top threads are manufactured at a reduced pitch diameter. During assembly, they clamp the threads of the bolt and produce greater frictional forces than an ordinary nut does. Another type of locknut that has received considerable attention is the nonmetallic-insert type. The elastic locking medium in this nut is independent of bolt loading, and seals the bolt threads against external moisture or leakage of internal pressure or liquids. The primary limitation in the use of this type nut is the inability of the insert to maintain its elasticity and locking characteristics at elevated temperatures.

When dissimilar materials, such as sheet metal and plastics or wood are to be joined, or when one side of the work is blind and the application of nuts to bolts becomes practically impossible, self-tapping and drive screws are available. They are used to fasten nearly everything from sheet metal and castings to plastics, fabrics, and leather.

Lead holes are necessary for the application of self-tapping or drive screws. Self-tapping screws have specially designed threads suitable to their applications. There are cutting threads and forming threads. For varied applications, they are available in all the standard head forms, either slotted or with a recess. Drive screws are usually self-tapping and are driven with a hammer. The holding power is greater than that of a nail and in many cases they may be backed out with a screw driver.

A special type of screw is the self-piercing screw. This is often used for attaching wood panels to light structural parts without having to drill lead holes. The screw is hammered through the wood to the metal and is then turned down with a screw driver.

For fastening metallic elements, machine screws, setscrews, and cap screws frequently are used. Machine screws are usually threaded the full length of the shaft, and are applied with a screwdriver. Cap screws have square, hexagonal, or knurled heads, and are threaded for only part of the shank. Setscrews are threaded for the length of the shaft and may be either headed or headless. The headless setscrew is usually fluted or provided with a slot or hexagonal socket for driving. Setscrews are used to secure machine tools or some machine element in a precise setting. Many types of points are provided on these screws for various applications.

Rivets

Rivets are permanent fasteners. They depend on deformation of their structure for their holding action. Rivets are usually stronger than the thread-type fastener and are more economical on a first-cost basis. Rivets are driven either hot or cold, depending upon the mechanical properties of the rivet material. Aluminum rivets, for instance, are cold-driven, since cold working improves the strength of aluminum. Most large rivets are hot-driven, however.

A hammer and bucking bar are used for heading rivets. The bar is held against the head of the inserted rivet, while the hammer heads the other end. Squeeze heading usually replaces hammer and bucking-bar methods. In this method, the rivet is inserted and brought between the jaws of a compression tool, which does the setting by mechanical, hydraulic, or pneumatic pressure. Where production runs are larger, riveting machines are used, exerting pressure on the rivet to head it rather than heading it by hammering. Improperly formed heads fail quickly when placed under stress.

Riveting is the commonest method of assembling aircraft. A medium bomber requires 160000 rivets and a heavy bomber requires 400000 rivets. Some of the forms of rivets are solid rivets with chamfered shanks, tubular or hollow rivets, semitubular rivets, swaged rivets, split rivets, and blind rivets. Solid rivets are used where great strength is required. Tubular rivets are used in the fastening of leather braces. Split rivets are used frequently in the making of suitcases. The materials used in making rivets are aluminum alloys, Monel metal, brass, and steel. Aluminum rivets make possible the maximum saving in weight, and are also quite resistant to corrosion. Anodic coating of aluminum improves the resistance of the rivets to corrosion and also provides a better surface for painting. Steel rivets are stronger than aluminum rivets and offer certain advantages in ease of driving from the standpoint of equipment required; however, their use is limited to those applications in which the structure can be protected adequately against corrosion by painting. Some of the types of rivet heads are button, mushroom, brazier, universal, flat, <u>tinners</u>, and <u>oval</u>. <u>Brazier</u> and mushroom heads are used for interior work. The flat head is used for streamlined pieces.

Words and Expressions

fastener /ˈfɑːsnə/ n.	固定器,紧固零件
bolt /bəult/ n.	螺栓,螺钉
washer /ˈwɔʃə/ n.	垫圈
rivnut /ˈraivnʌt/ n.	螺纹铆钉
locknut /ˈlɔknʌt/ n.	防松螺母
retaining ring	挡圈,卡环,固定环
rivet /ˈrivit/ n.	铆钉
vt.	铆;铆接
adhesive /ədˈhiːsiv/ n.	黏合剂;
adj.	带黏性的,胶黏
lock washer	锁紧垫圈,止动垫圈,防松垫圈
resilience /riˈziliəns/ n.	弹性,弹力
slotted nut	有槽螺母,开槽 螺母
cotter pin	开口销,扁销,开尾销
clearance /ˈkliərəns/ n.	间隙,游隙
self-locking nut	自锁螺母,防松螺母
thread /θrəd/ n.	螺纹;线
pitch diameter	节径,节圆直径,中径
self-tapping /ˌselfˈtæpiŋ/ adj.	自动攻螺纹的
drive screw	传动螺杆
recess /riˈses/ n.	凹进部分,退刀槽
self-piercing /ˌselfˈpiəsiŋ/ adj.	自开孔的
setscrew /ˈsetskruː/ n.	固定螺钉,止动螺钉,定位螺钉
cap screw	帽螺钉
hexagonal /hekˈsæɡənəl/ adj.	六边形的,六角形的
knurl /nəːl/ n.	刻痕,滚花
shank /ʃæŋk/ n.	柄,刀柄,钎尾
flute /fluːt/ n.	沟槽
socket /ˈsɔkit/ n.	承物的凹处
deformation /ˌdiːfɔːˈmeiʃən/ n.	变形,形变
bucking bar	打钉杆,铆钉顶棒
pneumatic /njuˈmætik/ adj.	气体的,气体力学的
stress /stres/ n.	应力,应力状态
chamfered /ˈtʃæmfəd/ adj.	倒角的

tubular /ˈtju(ː)bjulə/ adj.　　　　　管状的，空心的
swage /sweidʒ/ vt.　　　　　　　　锻造，顶锻
split rivet　　　　　　　　　　　　开口铆钉
blind rivet　　　　　　　　　　　　埋头铆钉，盲铆钉，空心铆钉
Monel metal　　　　　　　　　　　　蒙乃尔合金，铜镍合金
anodic coating　　　　　　　　　　阳极镀层，阳极保护层
tinner /ˈtinə/ n.　　　　　　　　　白铁工，锡工
oval /ˈəuvəl/ adj.　　　　　　　　卵形的，椭圆的
　　　　　　　　n.　　　　　　　　椭圆形
brazier head　　　　　　　　　　　扁头

Exercises

Choose the best answer according to the text.

1. Which of the following can't be grouped to fasteners?
   a. screws　　　b. nuts　　　c. bolts　　　d. keys
2. Which of the following is a relatively new kind of fastener?
   a. rivnuts　　　b. washers　　　c. nuts　　　d. bolts
3. The change in the length of the blot which can loose the bolt can be caused by the following factors except _____ .
   a. creep in the bolt　　　b. loss of resilience
   c. rust of the bolt　　　d. wear
4. _____ is often used to attach wood panels to light structural parts without having to drill lead holes.
   a. Self-piercing screw　　　b. Self-tapping screw
   c. Drive screw　　　d. Nut
5. _____ are used to fasten almost everything from metal and castings to plastics, fabrics and leather.
   a. Self-tapping screws　　　b. Drive screws
   c. Self-piercing screws　　　d. Both A and B
6. When we want to fasten metallic element we can use the following except _____ .
   a. machine screws　　　b. setscrews　　　c. cap screws　　　d. drive screws
7. _____ are often applied with a screwdriver.
   a. Rivets　　　b. Machine screws
   c. Setscrews　　　d. Drive screws
8. _____ have square, hexagonal heads.
   a. Cap screws　　　b. Locknuts　　　c. Setscrews　　　d. Bolts
9. _____ are used to secure machine tools in a precise setting.
   a. Cap screws　　　b. Machine screws
   c. Setscrews　　　d. Drive screws
10. Rivets belong to one group of fasteners which _____ .
    a. can join the pieces permanently　　　b. can only join the pieces for some time
    c. are stronger　　　d. are weaker

Passage II Keys, Splines, and Pins

When power is being transmitted from a machine member such as a coupling, a clutch, a gear, a flywheel, or a pulley to the shaft on which it is mounted, means must be provided for preventing relative motion between the shaft and the member. On helical and bevel gears, relative movement along the shaft caused by the thrust (axial) loads is prevented by a step in the shaft or by having the gear contact the bearing directly or through a tubular spacer. When axial loads are incidental and of small magnitude, the members are kept from sliding along the shaft by means of a set screw. The primary purpose of keys, splines, and pins is to prevent relative rotary movement.

A commonly used type of key has a square cross section (Fig. 7-1 (a)) and is sunk half in the shaft and half in the hub of the other member. If the key is made of steel of the same strength as the shaft and has a width and depth equal to one fourth of the shaft diameter then it will have the same torque capacity as the solid shaft if its length is 1.57 times that of the shaft diameter. Another common type of key has a rectangular cross section with a depth to width ratio of 0.75. Both of these keys may either be straight or tapered in depth. The straight keys fit snugly on the sides of the keyways only, the tapered keys on all sides. Gib-head keys are tapered keys with a projection on one end to facilitate removal.

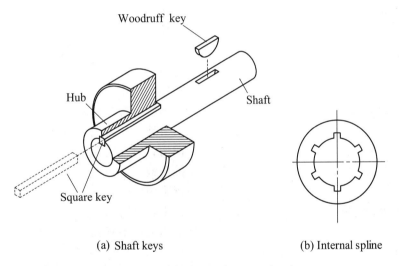

(a) Shaft keys (b) Internal spline

Fig. 7-1 Shaft keys and internal spline

Woodruff keys are widely used on machine tools and motor vehicles. The key is a segment of a disk and fits in a keyway in the shaft that is cut with a special milling cutter. Though the extra depth of these keys weakens the shaft considerably, it prevents any tendency of the key to rotate or move axially. Woodruff keys are particularly suitable for tapering shaft ends.

Because they weaken the shaft less, keys with straight or tapered circular cross sections are sometimes used in place of square and rectangular keys, but the keyways, half in the shaft and half in the hub, must be cut with a drill after assembly, and interchangeability of parts is practically impossible. When a large gear blank is made by shrinking a high-strength rim on a cheaper cast center, circular keys, snugly fitted, are frequently used to ensure a permanent connection.

Splines (Fig. 7-1 (b)) are permanent keys integral with the shaft, fitting in keyways cut in the hub. The dimensions of splined fittings are standardized for both permanent (press) fits and sliding fits. The teeth have either straight or involute profiles; the latter are stronger, more easily measured, and have a self-centering action when twisted.

Tapered circular pins can be used to restrain shaft-mounted members from both axial and rotary movement. The pin fits snugly in a reamed tapered hole that is perpendicular to the shaft axis and either radial or tangential to the shaft surface. A number of straight pins that grip by deforming elastically or plastically when driven into straight holes are commercially available.

All the keys and pins that have been described are standard driving devices. In some cases they are inadequate, and unorthodox means must be employed.

Words and Expressions

spline /splain/ n.	花键，止转楔
coupling /'kʌpliŋ/ n.	连接；连接器
flywheel /'flaihwi:l/ n.	飞轮
pulley /'puli/ n.	滑轮
bevel gear	伞齿轮
hub /hʌb/ n.	轮毂
torque /tɔ:k/ n.	扭矩，转矩
tapered /'teipəd/ adj.	带梢的；有锥度的
snugly /'snʌgli/ adv.	贴身地；隐藏地；尚可地
keyway /'ki:wei/ n.	键沟；扁形钥孔
tapered key	锥形键
gib-head key	弯头键
projection /prə'dʒekʃən/ n.	投影，投射
woodruff key	半圆键，半月键
milling /'miliŋ/ n.	铣削
cutter /'kʌtə/ n.	刀具
drill /dril/ vt.	钻
n.	钻头
interchangeability /'intə:,tʃeindʒə'biliti/ n.	互换性
rim /rim/ n.	边缘；轮缘
fitting /'fitiŋ/ n.	安装，装配
involute /'invəlu:t/ n.	渐开线，切展线
ream /ri:m/ vt.	铰大（…的）口径
tangential /tæn'dʒenʃel/ adj.	相切的，切线的
unorthodox /ʌn'ɔ:θədɔks/ adj.	非正式的，不正统的

Passage III Bearings

A bearing can be defined as a member specifically designed to support moving machine components. The most common bearing application is the support of a rotating shaft that is transmitting power from one location to another. Since there is always relative motion between a bearing and its mating surface, friction is involved. In many instances, such as the design of pulleys, brakes, and clutches, friction is desirable. However, in the case of bearings, the reduction of friction is one of the prime considerations: friction results in loss of power, the generation of heat, and increased wear of mating surfaces.

Journal and antifriction bearings are the two general types of bearings in existence. Journal bearings operate with sliding contact, whereas antifriction bearings operate under predominantly rolling contact. The amount of sliding friction in journal bearings depends on the surface finishes, materials, sliding velocities, and type of lubricant used. The principal motion-retarding effect in antifriction bearings is called rolling resistance rather than rolling friction. This is so because the resistance to motion is essentially due to the deformation of the rolling elements and, hence, is not a sliding phenomenon.

To reduce the problems associated with sliding friction in journal bearings, a lubricant is used in conjunction with compatible mating materials. When selecting the lubricant and mating materials, one must take into account bearing pressures, temperatures, and rubbing velocities. The principal function of the lubricant in sliding contact bearings is to prevent physical contact between the rubbing surfaces. Thus the maintenance of an oil film under varying loads, speeds, and temperatures is the prime consideration in sliding contact bearings.

Journal Bearings

A journal bearing, in its simplest form, is a cylindrical bushing made of a suitable material and containing properly machined inside and outside diameters. The journal is usually the part of a shaft or pin that rotates inside the bearing. Fig. 7-2 shows such a bearing, which is also commonly called a sleeve bearing. Notice the oil hole that leads to an axial oil groove. Such a bearing is designed to provide lubrication to reduce friction.

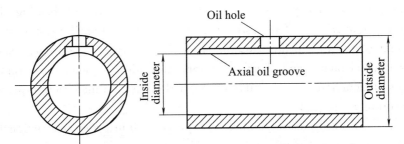

Fig. 7-2 Sleeve bearing with provision for lubrication

The bore (inside diameter) of a journal bearing is machined to accept a rotating shaft, as shown in Fig. 7-3 (a). The bearing outside diameter is supported in a properly machined bore of a fixed housing. An oil cup is shown attached to one side of the housing, where a passageway leads to the oil hole of the bushing. Notice that the axial oil groove in the bushing does not extend all the way to the ends of the bearing. This prevents undue loss of oil from the bearing. Moreover, notice the annular groove in the bushing in Fig. 7-3 (a); such grooves ensure more complete distribution of the lubricant. Since there will normally be a load R coming into the bearing, a normal force N and friction force F will exist between the shaft and bushing, as shown in Fig. 7-3 (b).

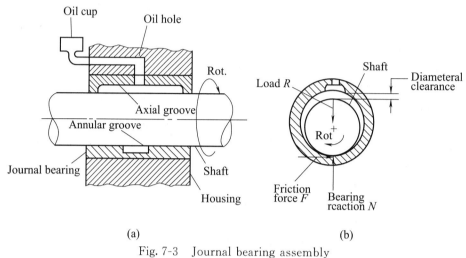

Fig. 7-3 Journal bearing assembly

Even though bearings are usually lubricated, there is friction and some wear. With time, the friction will result in wearing down of the bushing bore. Proper selection of bearing materials is an important design consideration.

Antifriction Bearings

Antifriction bearings operate with rolling elements (either balls or rollers), and hence rolling resistance, rather than sliding friction, predominates. The cause of rolling resistance is the deformation of mating surfaces of the rolling element and the raceway on which it rolls. The three basic types of antifriction bearings are ball bearings, roller bearings, needle bearings. Ball and roller bearings can be designed to absorb thrust loads in addition to radial loads, whereas needle bearings are limited to radial load applications only.

One of the principal advantages of antifriction (rolling contact) bearings is the almost complete elimination of friction. Therefore, the main function of antifriction bearing lubricants is to help prevent corrosion and dirt contamination. Since some friction does exist, especially between the rolling elements and their separator, the lubricant also must remove the heat caused by this sliding action. As a result, although there is minimal friction present, a lubricant is still absolutely essential.

Fatigue, which is the cause of failure of a properly lubricated antifriction bearing, is a stress-reversal phenomenon that takes place on the contacting surfaces of the raceways and rolling elements. Hence the life of an antifriction bearing is measured by the number of shaft revolutions that occur prior to fatigue failure. The greater the bearing load, the shorter will be the life of the bearing in revolutions. Also, the greater the shaft speed, the shorter will be the bearing life. Since fatigue is a statistical occurrence, the percent probability of failure also must be considered.

It is essential to know the advantages and disadvantages of the various types of bearings, as well as their salient features. For example, ball and roller bearings can be of the <u>self-aligning</u> type to <u>accommodate</u> shaft <u>misalignment</u> and deflections. In addition, shields and seals are available to protect bearings from foreign <u>contaminants</u>. Some antifriction bearings contain a permanently sealed lubricant that is administered by the manufacturer and lasts for the life of the bearing.

Words and Expressions

brake /breik/ n.	刹车,压弯机
journal bearing	滑动轴承
predominantly /pri'dɔminəntli/ adv.	主要地,显著地
surface finish	表面粗糙度
film /film/ n.	薄膜
cylindrical /'silindrikəl/ adj.	圆筒形的,圆柱的
bushing /'buʃiŋ/ n.	轴衬
sleeve bearing	滑动轴承,套筒轴承
groove /gru:v/ n.	凹槽,槽沟
bore /bɔ:/ n.	孔径
annular /'ænjulə/ adj.	环形的,环状的
antifriction bearing	滚动轴承,减摩轴承
roller /'roulə/ n.	滚柱,辊
raceway /'reiswei/ n.	滚道
ball bearing	滚珠轴承
roller bearing	滚柱轴承
needle bearing	滚针轴承
lubricate /'lju:brikeit/ vt.	加润滑剂,使润滑
stress-reversal /'stresri'və:səl/ n.	应力反向
self-aligning /ˌselfə'lainiŋ/ adj.	自动对准的
n.	自动定心,自动调心
accommodate /ə'kɔmədeit/ vt.	使适应,调节
misalignment /ˌmisə'lainmənt/ n.	未对准;位移;角度误差;失调
contaminant /kən'tæminənt/ n.	污染物,杂质

Passage IV Gears

Gears are direct-contact bodies, operating in pairs, that transmit motion and force from one rotating shaft to another, or from a shaft to a slide (rack), by means of successively engaging projections called teeth. There are four main types of gears: spur, helical, worm, and bevel.

Spur and <u>Helical Gears</u>

A gear having tooth elements that are straight and parallel to its axis is known as a <u>spur gear</u>. A spur pair can be used to connect parallel shafts only. Parallel shafts, however, can also be connected by gears of another type, and a spur gear can be mated with a gear of a different type.

To prevent jamming as a result of thermal expansion, to aid lubrication, and to compensate for unavoidable inaccuracies in manufacture, all power-transmitting gears must have backlash. This means that on the pitch circles of a mating pair, the space width on the pinion must be slightly greater than the tooth thickness on the gear, and vice versa. On instrument gears, backlash can be eliminated by using a gear split down its middle, one half being rotatable relative to the other. A spring forces the split gear teeth to occupy the full width of the pinion space.

If an involute spur pinion were made of rubber and twisted uniformly so that the ends rotated about the axis relative to one another, the elements of the teeth, initially straight and parallel to the axis, would become helices. The pinion then in effect would become a helical gear.

Helical gears have certain advantages; for example, when connecting parallel shafts they have a higher load-carrying capacity than spur gears with the same tooth numbers and cut with the same cutter. Because of the overlapping action of the teeth, they are smoother in action and can operate at higher pitch-line velocities than spur gears. The pitch-line velocity is the velocity of the pitch circle. Since the teeth are inclined to the axis of rotation, helical gears create an axial thrust. If used singly, this thrust must be absorbed in the shaft bearings. The thrust problem can be overcome by cutting two sets of opposed helical teeth on the same blank. Depending on the method of manufacture, the gear may be of the continuous-tooth herringbone variety or a double-helical gear with a space between the two halves to permit the cutting tool to run out. Double-helical gears are well suited for the efficient transmission of power at high speeds.

Helical gears can also be used to connect nonparallel, non-intersecting shafts at any angle to one another. Ninety degrees is the commonest angle at which such gears are used. When the shafts are parallel, the contact between the teeth on mating gears is 'line contact' regardless of whether the teeth are straight or helical. When the shafts are inclined, the contact becomes 'point contact'. For this reason, crossed-axis helical gears do not have as much load-carrying capacity as parallel-shaft helicals. They are relatively insensitive to misalign-ment, however, and are frequently employed in instruments and positioning mechanisms where friction is the only force opposing their motion.

Worm and Bevel Gears

In order to achieve line contact and improve the load-carrying capacity of the crossed-axis helical gears, the gear can be made to curve partially around the pinion, in somewhat the same way that a nut envelops a screw. The result would be a cylindrical worm and gear. Worms are also made in the shape of an hourglass, instead of cylindrical, so that they partially envelop the gear. This results in a further increase in load-carrying capacity.

Worm gears provide the simplest means of obtaining large ratios in a single pair. They are usually less efficient than parallel-shaft gears, however, because of an additional sliding movement along the teeth. Because of their similarity, the efficiency of a worm and gear depends on the same factors as the efficiency of a screw. Single-thread worms of large diameter have small lead angles and low efficiencies. Multiple-thread worms have larger lead angles and higher efficiencies. For lead angles of about 15 degrees and a coefficient of friction less than 0.15, the efficiency ranges from about 55 percent to 95 percent, and the gear can drive the worm. Such units make compact speed increasers; they have been used for driving superchargers on aircraft engines. In self-locking worms, the gear cannot drive the worm, and the efficiency is less than 50 percent.

For transmitting rotary motion and torque around corners, bevel gears are commonly used. The connected shafts, whose axes would intersect if extended, are usually but not necessarily at right angles to one another. The pitch surfaces of bevel gears are rolling, <u>truncated cones</u>, and the teeth, which must be tapered in both thickness and height, are either straight or curved. Although curved-tooth bevel gears are called <u>spiral</u> bevel gears, the curve of the teeth is usually a circular arc. The curvature of the teeth results in overlapping tooth action and a smoother transmission of power than with straight teeth. For high speeds and torques, spiral bevel gears are superior to straight bevel gears in much the same way that helical gears are superior to spur gears for connecting parallel shafts.

When adapted for shafts that do not intersect, spiral bevel gears are called <u>hypoid gears</u>. The pitch surfaces of these gears are not rolling cones, and the ratio of their mean diameters is not equal to the speed ratio. Consequently, the pinion may have few teeth and be made as large as necessary to carry the load. This permits higher speed ratios than with intersecting axes, just as crossed-axis helicals and worm gears can provide higher ratios than parallel helicals. The absence of the proportional rolling-pitch surface requirement is a benefit.

The profiles of the teeth on bevel gears are not involutes; they are of such a shape that the tools for cutting the teeth are easier to make and maintain than involute cutting tools. Since bevel gears come in pairs, as long as they are <u>conjugate</u> to one another they need not be conjugate to other gears with different tooth members.

Words and Expressions

helical gear	斜齿轮，螺旋齿轮
spur gear	正齿轮
backlash /'bæklæʃ/ n.	间隙，齿间隙
pinion /'pinjən/ n.	小齿轮
herringbone /'heriŋboun/ n.	人字形；交叉缝式
crossed-axis /'krɔst'æksis/ adj.	轴交叉的
worm gear	蜗轮，蜗杆与蜗轮
coefficient of friction	摩擦系数
truncated cone	截头圆锥体，截体
spiral /'spaiərəl/ adj.	螺旋形的
n.	螺旋形，螺旋，螺线
hypoid gear	偏轴伞齿轮
conjugate /'kɔndʒugeit/ adj.	成对的，共轭的

Exercises

I. **Choose the best answer for each of the following questions.**

1. The most common bearing application is the _____.
   a. support of a rotating shaft
   b. reduction of friction

c. support of a pulley   d. acceleration of a shaft
2. In the design of a bearing the _____ is one of the prime consideration.
   a. speed   b. lubrication
   c. reduction of friction   d. dimension
3. Friction will bring about the following effect except the _____.
   a. loss of power   b. generation of heat
   c. increasing of wear   d. acceleration of speed
4. The amount of sidling friction in journal bearings depends on the following except _____.
   a. materials   b. surface finishes
   c. sliding speeds   d. the type of the shaft
5. The motion retarding effect antifriction bearing is called _____.
   a. rolling resistance   b. sliding friction
   c. rolling friction   d. sliding resistance
6. When selecting the lubricant and motion materials, one must take into account the following factors except _____.
   a. bearing pressures   b. temperature
   c. rubbing velocity   d. loss of power
7. Which of the following is NOT the basic type of antifriction bearing _____ bearings.
   a. ball   b. roller
   c. needle   d. journal
8. Which of the following is limited to radial load applications only?
   a. Needle bearings.   b. Ball bearings.
   c. Sleeve bearings.   d. Journal bearings.
9. The life of an antifriction bearing is measured by _____.
   a. the hours before it breaks down
   b. the number of shaft revolutions that occur prior to fatigue failure
   c. how much lubricant it uses
   d. the minutes it is in function
10. The primary purpose of keys is to _____.
    a. enhance the function of the shaft   b. Prevent relative rotary movement
    c. accelerate the speed   d. lengthen the life of bearings

II. Translate the following passage into Chinese.

Gears are vital factors in machinery. One of first mechanism invented using gears was the clock. In fact, a clock is little more than a train of gears. Considerable study and research have been made on gears in recent years because of their wide use under exacting conditions. They have to transmit heavier loads and run consider gearing the prime element in nearly all classes of machinery.

III. Translate the following passage into English.

轴承有各种类型，如滑动轴承、滚珠轴承、滚柱轴承等等。我们根据不同的需要，使用不同的轴承。尽管滚珠轴承和滚柱轴承的基本设计责任在轴承制造厂家，机器设计人员必须对轴承所要完成的任务做出正确的评价，不仅要考虑轴承的选择，而且还要考虑轴承的正确安装条件。

Unit 8 Mechanical Design

Passage I Introduction to Mechanical Design

The Design Process

A machine is a combination of mechanisms and other components which transforms, transmits, or utilizes energy, force, or motion for a useful purpose. Examples are engines, turbines, vehicles, hoists, printing presses, washing machines, and movie cameras. Many of the principles and methods of design that apply to machines also apply to manufactured articles that are not true machines, from hub caps and filing cabinets to instruments and nuclear pressure vessels. The term 'mechanical design' is used in a broader sense than 'machine design' to include their design. For some apparatus, the thermal and fluid aspects that determine the requirements of heat, flow path, and volume are separately considered. However, the motion and structural aspects and the provisions for retention and enclosure are considerations in mechanical design. Applications occur in the field of mechanical engineering, and in other engineering fields as well, all of which require mechanical devices, such as switches, cams, valves, vessels, and mixers.

Designing starts with a need, real or imagined. Existing apparatus may need improvements in durability, efficiency, weight, speed, or cost. New apparatus may be needed to perform a function previously done by men, such as computation, assembly, or servicing. With the objective wholly or partly defined, the next step in design is the conception of mechanisms and their arrangements that will perform the needed functions. For this, freehand sketching is of great value, not only as record of one's thoughts and as an aid in discussion with others, but particularly for communication with one's own mind, as a stimulant for creative ideas. Also, a broad knowledge of components is desirable, because a new machine usually consists of a new arrangement or substitution of well-known types of components, perhaps with changes in size and material. Either during or following this conceptual process, one will make quick or rough calculations or analyses to determine general size and feasibility. When some idea as to the amount of space that is needed or available has been obtained, to-scale layout drawings may be started.

When the general shape and a few dimensions of the several components become apparent, analysis can begin in earnest. The analysis will have as its objective satisfactory or superior performance, plus safety and durability with minimum weight, and a competitive cost. Optimum proportions and dimensions will be sought for each critically loaded section, together with a balance between the strengths of the several components. Materials and their treatment will be chosen. These important objectives can be attained only by analysis based upon the principles of mechanics, such as those of statics for reaction forces and for the optimum utilization of friction; of dynamics for inertia, acceleration, and energy; of elasticity and strength of materials for stress and deflection; of physical behavior of materials; and of fluid mechanics for lubrication and hydrodynamic drives. The analyses may be made by the same engineer who conceived the arrangement of mechanisms, or, in a large company, they may be made by a separate analysis division or research group. As a result of the analyses, new arrangements and new dimensions may be required. Design is a reiterative and cooperative process, whether done formally or informally, and the analyst can contribute to phases other than his own.

Finally, a design based upon function and reliability will be completed, and a prototype may be built. If its tests are satisfactory, and if the device is to be produced in quantity, the initial design will undergo certain modifications that enable it to be manufactured in quantity at a lower cost. During subsequent years of manufacture and service, the design is likely to undergo changes as new ideas are conceived or as further analyses based upon tests and experience indicate alterations. Sales appeal, customer satisfaction, and manufacturing cost are all related to design, and ability in design is intimately involved in the success of an engineering venture.

Some Rules for Design

In this section it is suggested that, applied with a creative attitude, analyses can lead to important improvements and to the conception and perfection of alternate, perhaps more functional, economical, and durable products. The creative phase need not be an initial and separate one. Although he may not be responsible for the whole design, an analyst can contribute more than the numerically correct answer to a problem that he is asked to solve——more than the values of stress, dimensions, or limitations of operation. He can take the broader view that the specifications or the arrangements may be improved. Since he will become familiar with the device and its conditions of operation before or during his analysis, he is in a good position to conceive of alternatives. It is better that he suggest a change in shape that will eliminate a moment or a stress concentration than to allow construction of a mechanism with heavy sections and excessive dynamic loads. It is better that he scrap his fine analysis, rather than that he later see the mechanism scrapped.

To stimulate creative thought, the following rules are suggested for the designer and analyst. The first six rules are particularly applicable for the analyst, although he may become involved with all ten rules:

1. Apply ingenuity to utilize desired physical properties and to control undesired ones.
2. Recognize functional loads and their significance.
3. Anticipate unintentional loads.
4. Devise more favorable loading conditions.
5. Provide for favorable stress distribution and stiffness with minimum weight.
6. Use basic equations to proportion and optimize dimensions.
7. Choose materials for a combination of properties.
8. Select carefully between stock and integral components.
9. Modify a functional design to fit the manufacturing process and reduce cost.
10. Provide for accurate location and noninterference of parts in assembly.

Words and Expressions

hoist /hɔist/ *n.*	起重机，卷扬机
mixer /ˈmiksə/ *n.*	混合器，搅拌机
sketch /sketʃ/ *vi.*	绘略图；素描
stimulant /ˈstimjulənt/ *n.*	兴奋剂
conceptual /kənˈseptjuəl/ *adj.*	概念上的
layout drawing	布置图，轮廓图
reiterative /riːˈitərətiv/ *adj.*	反复的
prototype /ˈprəutətaip/ *n.*	样机，原型
scrap /skræp/ *vt.*	扔弃
n.	废料，废金属
ingenuity /ˌindʒiˈnjuː(ː)iti/ *n.*	机灵，独创性
stiffness /ˈstifnis/ *n.*	刚度，刚性
stock /stɔk/ *n.*	原料，备料
noninterference /ˈnɔnˌintəˈfiərəns/ *n.*	不互相干扰

Exercises

Ⅰ. **Decide whether the following statements are true or false (T/F).**

( ) 1. Engines, cameras and cams are all machines.
( ) 2. Mechanical design includes not only machine design but also design for the mechanical part of some apparatus.
( ) 3. People start a design because they need something new in their life.
( ) 4. Generally the designer will have a freehand sketch to show the conception of mechanism and their arrangements that will fulfill the need function.
( ) 5. The designer should have a broad knowledge of component.
( ) 6. Rough calculations about the size of the designed machine should be made after the conceptual process.
( ) 7. The designers not only base their analysis on the principles of mechanics but also they'll consider other factors such as weight, cost and safety.
( ) 8. If a design proves functional and reliable, it can be put into production.
( ) 9. Designing is a personal creative process.
( ) 10. A change in shape that will eliminate the possibility of a scrapped mechanism is never too late.

Ⅱ. **Answer the following questions.**

1. How is a machine defined?
2. Why is freehand sketching of great value?
3. When can people start analysis?
4. What does analysis cover?
5. What are the six rules which are specially applicable for the analyst?

Passage Ⅱ Machine Design

The complete design of a machine is a complex process. The designer must have a good background in such fields as statics, kinematics, dynamics, and strength of materials, and in addition, be familiar with the fabricating materials and processes. The designer must be able to assemble all the relevant facts, and make calculations, sketches, and drawings to convey manufacturing information to the shop.

One of the first steps in the design of any product is to select the material from which each part is to be made. Numerous materials are available to today's designers. The function of the product, its appearance, the cost of the material, and the cost of fabrication are important in making a selection. A careful evaluation of the properties of a material must be made prior to any calculations.

Careful calculations are necessary to ensure the validity of a design. Calculations never appear on drawings, but are filed away for several reasons. In case of any part failures, it is desirable to know what was done in originally designing the defective components. Also, an experience file can result from having calculations from past projects. When a similar design is needed, past records are of great help.

The checking of calculations (and drawing dimensions) is of utmost importance. The misplacement of one decimal point can ruin an otherwise acceptable project. For example, if one were to design a bracket to support 100 lb when it should have been figured for 1000 lb, failure would surely be forthcoming. All aspects of design work should be checked and rechecked.

The computer is a tool helpful to mechanical designers to lighten tedious calculations, and provide extended analysis of available data. Interactive systems, based on computer capabilities, have made possible the concepts of computer aided design (CAD) and computer-aided manufacturing (CAM). Through such systems, it is possible for one to transmit conceptual ideas to punched tapes for numerical machine control without having formal working drawings.

Laboratory tests, models, and prototypes help considerably in machine design. Laboratories furnish much of the information needed to establish basic concepts; however, they can also be used to gain some idea of how a product will perform in the field.

Finally, a successful designer does all he can to keep up to date. New materials and production methods appear daily. Drafting and design personnel may lose their usefulness by not being versed in modern methods and materials. A good designer reads technical periodicals constantly to keep abreast of new developments.

Words and Expressions

decimal point	小数点
lighten /ˈlaitn/ v.	减轻，(使)轻松，使发亮
computer-aided manufacturing	计算机辅助制造
punch /pʌntʃ/ n.	冲头，冲压机
vt.	穿孔

Passage Ⅲ Engineering Tolerancing

Introduction

A solid is defined by its surface boundaries. Designers typically specify a component's nominal dimensions such that it fulfils its requirements. In reality, components cannot be made repeatedly to nominal dimensions, due to surface irregularities and the intrinsic surface roughness. Some variability in dimensions must be allowed to ensure manufacture is possible. However, the variability permitted must not be so great that the performance of the assembled parts is impaired. The allowed variability on the individual component dimensions is called the tolerance.

The term tolerance applies not only to the acceptable range of component dimensions produced by manufacturing techniques, but also to the output of machines or processes. For example, the power produced by a given type of internal combustion engine varies from one engine to another. In practice, the variability is usually found to be modeled by a frequency distribution curve, for example the normal distribution (also called the Gaussian distribution). One of the tasks of the designer is to specify a dimension on a component and the allowable variability on this value that will give acceptable performance.

Component Tolerances

Control of dimensions is necessary in order to ensure assembly and interchangeability of components. Tolerances are specified on critical dimensions that affect clearances and interference fits. One method of specifying tolerances is to state the nominal dimension followed by the permissible variation, so a dimension could be stated as 40.000 ± 0.003 mm. This means that the dimension should be machined so that it is between 39.997 mm and 40.003 mm. Where the variation can vary either side of the nominal dimension, the tolerance is called a bilateral tolerance. For a unilateral tolerance, one tolerance is zero, e. g. $40.000^{+0.006}_{0.000}$.

Most organizations have general tolerances that apply to dimensions when an explicit dimension is not specified on a drawing. For machined dimensions a general tolerance may be ± 0.5 mm. So a dimension specified as 15.0 mm may range between 14.5 mm and 15.5 mm. Other general tolerances can be applied to features such as angles, drilled and punched holes, castings, forgings, weld beads and fillets.

When specifying a tolerance for a component, reference can be made to previous drawings or general engineering practice. Tolerances are typically specified in bands as defined in British or ISO standards. Table 8-1 gives a guide for the general applications of tolerances. For a given tolerance, e. g. H7/s6, a set of numerical values is available from a corresponding chart for the size of component under consideration. The section following gives specific examples of this for a shaft or cylindrical spigot fitting into a hole.

Standard Fits for Holes and Shafts

A standard engineering task is to determine tolerances for a cylindrical component, e. g. a shaft, fitting or rotating inside a corresponding cylindrical component or hole. The tightness of fit will depend on the application. For example, a gear located on to a shaft would require a 'tight' interference fit, where the diameter of the shaft is actually slightly greater than the inside diameter of the gear hub in order to be able to transmit the desired torque. Alternatively, the diameter of a journal bearing must be greater than the diameter of the shaft to allow rotation. Given that it is not economically possible to manufacture components to exact dimensions, some variability in sizes of both the shaft and hole dimension must be specified. However, the range of variability should not be so large that the operation of the assembly is impaired. Rather than having an infinite variety of tolerance dimensions that could be specified, national and international standards have been produced defining bands of tolerances, examples of which are listed in Table 8-1, e. g. H11/c11. To turn this information into actual dimensions corresponding tables exist, defining the tolerance levels for the size of dimension under consideration. In order to use this information the following list and Fig. 8-1 give definitions used in conventional tolerancing. Usually the holebased system is used, as this result in a reduction in the variety of drill, reamer, broach and gauge tooling required within a company.

Size: a number expressing in a particular unit the numerical value of a dimension.
Actual size: the size of a part as obtained by measurement.
Limits of size: the maximum and minimum sizes permitted for a feature.
Maximum limit of size: the greater of the two limits of size.
Minimum limit of size: the smaller of the two limits of size.
Basic size: the size by reference to which the limits of size are fixed.
Deviation: the algebraic difference between a size and the corresponding basic size.
Actual deviation: the algebraic difference between the actual size and the corresponding basic size.
Upper deviation: the algebraic difference the maximum limit of size and the corresponding basic size.
Lower deviation: the algebraic difference between the minimum limit of size and the corresponding basic size.
Tolerance: the difference between the maximum limit of size and the minimum limit of size.

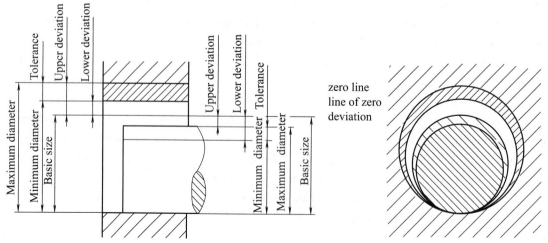

Fig. 8-1　Definition of terms used in conventional torerancing

Shaft: the term used by convention to designate all external features of a part.
Hole: the term used by convention to designate all internal features of a part.

Table 8-1 Example of tolerance bands and typical applications

Class	Description	Characteristic	ISO code	Asembly	Application
Clearance	Loose running fit	For wide commercial tolerances	H11/c11	Noticeable clearance	IC engine exhaust value in guide
	Free running fit	Good for large temperature variations, high running speeds or heavy journal pressures	H9/d9	Noticeable clearance	Multiple bearing shafts, hydraulic piston in cylinder, removable levers, bearing for rollers
	Close running fit	For running on accurate machines and accurate location at moderate speeds and journal pressure	H8/f7	Clearance	Machine tool main bearings, crankshaft and connecting rod bearings, shaft sleeves, clutch sleeves, guide blocks
	Sliding fit	When parts are not intended to run freely, but must move and turn and locate accurately	H7/g6	Push fit without ticeable clearance	Push-on gear wheels and clutches, connecting rod bearings, indicator pistons
	Location clearance fit	Provides snug fit for location of stationary parts, but can be freely assembled	H7/h6	Hand pressure with lubrication	Gears, tailstock sleeves, adjust rings, loose bushes for piston bolts and pipelines
Transition	Location transition fit	For accurate location (compromise between clearance and interference fit)	H7/k6	Easily tapped with hammer	Pulleys, clutches, gears, flywheels, fixed handwheels and permanent levers
	Location transition fit	For more accurate location	H7/n6	Needs pressure	Motor shaft armatures, toothed collars on wheels
Interference	Location interference fit	For parts requiring rigidity and alignment with accuracy of location	H7/p7	Needs pressure	Split journal bearings
	Medium drive fit	For ordinary steel parts or shrink fits on light sections	H7/s6	Needs pressure or temperature difference	Clutch hubs, bearings, bushes in blocks, wheels, connecting rods. Bronze collars on grey cast iron hubs

Words and Expressions

tolerance /ˈtɔlərəns/ n.	公差；
vt.	给（机器部件等）规定公差
nominal /ˈnɔminl/ adj.	公称的，标称的，额定的
intrinsic /inˈtrinsik/ adj.	固有的，本质的
normal distribution	正态分布
weld bead	焊缝
fillet /ˈfilit/ n.	圆角，倒角
spigot /ˈspigət/ n.	插销，塞子；阀门
interference fit	干涉配合，过盈配合，
broach /brəutʃ/ n.	拉刀
v.	拉削
gauge /geidʒ/ n.	（电线等的）直径；（金属板的）厚度；量具
deviation /ˌdiːviˈeiʃən/ n.	偏差，偏移

Passage Ⅳ Conceptual Design

Conceptual design is the generation of solutions to meet the specified requirements. Conceptual design can represent the sum of all subsystems and component parts which go on to make up the whole system. Ion and Smith describe conceptual design as an iterative process comprising a series of generative and evaluative stages which converge to the preferred solution. At each stage of iteration the concepts are defined in greater detail, allowing more thorough evaluation.

It is important to generate as many concepts and ideas as possible or economically expedient. There is a temptation to accept the first promising concept and proceed towards detailed design and the final product. This should be resisted as such results can invariably be bettered. It is worth noting that sooner or later your design will have to compete against those from other manufacturers, so the generation of developed concepts is prudent.

According to McGrath, concepts are often most effectively generated by working individually and then coming together with other members of the design team at a later stage to evaluate the collective concepts. The strengths and weaknesses of the concept should be identified and one of the concepts selected and further developed, or the strengths of several of the concepts combined, or the process repeated, to generate further new concepts. Several techniques are in common use to aid idea and concept generation. These include boundary shifting, brainstorming and synectics, analogies, function trees, morphological analysis and software tools. Boundary shifting involves challenging the constraints defined in the product design specification (PDS) to identify whether they are necessary. For example, the **PDS** may define that steel should be used for a component. Boundary shifting would challenge this specification to see whether it is appropriate and, if not, other materials could be considered. Brainstorming involves a multidisciplinary group meeting together to propose and generate ideas to solve the stated problem. The emphasis within brainstorming is on quantity rather than quality of ideas and criticism of another person's idea is strictly forbidden. Synectics is a sophisticated form of brainstorming aimed at stimulating the thinking process. Conceptual design by analogy involves looking for solutions to equivalent problems. For example, analogies with solutions found in the natural world may provide insight to the problem in hand. The function tree method involves decomposing the function of a product into different subfunctions. Using the function tree method, conceptual design takes place at the subsystem or component level. For example, it may not be possible to produce new concepts for the power plant of an automobile, but it may be possible to generate new concepts for the subsystems or for individual components. Ulrich and Eppinger propose the scheme illustrated in Fig. 8-2 for concept generation.

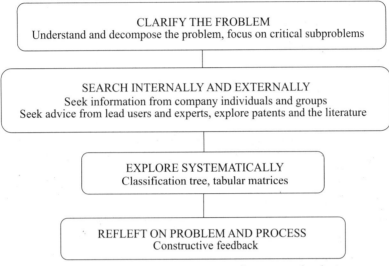

Fig. 8-2 Scheme to aid generation of conceptual solutions

Having generated ideas and concepts, the next step is to evaluate them and select the best concept. One method of evaluation is the use of tabular matrices. These consist of a series of criteria against which the concepts must be marked. The importance of the criteria can be weighed if appropriate and the most suitable concept is identified as the one with the highest overall mark. This method provides a structured technique of evaluation and makes it difficult for individuals within a design team to push their own ideas for irrational reasons.

Having generated the conceptual solutions the next step is to express these so that they are communicable to all involved in the total design process. In practice this may take the form of a drawn scheme or 3D model, either physical or computer generated. By the time the general scheme has been completed and calculations undertaken to determine the solution's compatibility to the PDS, the basis will have been established for the detailed design phase to commence.

Words and Expressions

iterative /'itərətiv/ *adj.*	重复的，反复的
expedient /iks'pi:djənt/ *adj.*	有利的
n.	权宜之计
prudent /'pru:dənt/ *adj.*	谨慎的，精明的，节俭的
brainstorming /'brein,stɔ:miŋ/ *n.*	头脑风暴法

synectics /si'nektiks/ n.　　　　　　　协力创新法；协同学
product design specification　　　　　产品设计说明书
tabular /'tæbjulə/ adj　　　　　　　　制成表的，表格式的

Exercises

Ⅰ. **Choose the appropriate words to complete the sentences and change the form if necessary.**

1. iterative　　　iteration　　　iterate
   a. The teacher _____ the explanation in order that every student understood.
   b. Ion and Smith thought conceptual design is an _____ process.
   c. The speaker's _____ of the demand makes the audience sleepy.
2. evaluation　　　evaluate　　　evaluative
   a. The school has only been open for six months, so it's hard to _____ its success.
   b. The _____ should be based on impartiality.
   c. Conceptual design comprises _____ stages.
3. specific　　　specification　　　specify
   a. The contract _____ red tiles, not slates, for the roof.
   b. The technical _____ of a new car is clearly given.
   c. What are your _____ aims?
4. generative　　　generation　　　generate
   a. The accident _____ a lot of public interest in the nuclear power issue.
   b. This chapter deals with the _____ of electricity.
   c. _____ grammar was once popular.
5. communicate　　　communication　　　communicable
   a. This book is full of complex ideas not easily _____ to non-experts.
   b. This poem _____ the author's despair.
   c. Being deaf and dumb makes _____ very difficult.

Ⅱ. **Select the best choices to complete the sentences.**

1. The allowed variability on the individual component dimensions is called _____.
   a. endurance　　b. tolerance　　c. bearing　　d. standing
2. The car's _____ on mountain roads was impressive.
   a. performance　　b. perfume　　c. perfect　　d. perforce
3. Don't boil the sauces as this can _____ the flavor.
   a. impact　　b. impair　　c. impart　　d. impeach
4. The job is of little _____ interest.
   a. inner　　b. internal　　c. intrinsic　　d. intro
5. It is under _____ agreement that the bank will give 10000 million dollars loan.
   a. bilateral　　b. lateral　　c. part　　d. side
6. There is not much _____ for tall vehicles passing under this bridge.
   a. room　　b. space　　c. crack　　d. clearance
7. We received no notification _____ to today's date.
   a. before　　b. prior　　c. previous　　d. advance
8. You should read the newspapers to keep _____ of current affair.

    a. up   b. on   c. abreast   d. out
9. _____ is a method of solving problems in which all the members of a group suggest ideas which are then discussed.
    a. Brainstorming   b. Deduction   c. Semiarn   d. Induction
10. Your first evaluation will be six months after you _____ employment.
    a. commence   b. commemorate   c. commend   d. comment

Ⅲ. Translate the following passage into Chinese.

As stated previously, the purpose of machine design is to produce a product which will serve a need for man. Inventions, discoveries and scientific knowledge by themselves do not necessarily benefit be derived. It should be recognized, therefore, that a human need must be identified before a particular product is designed.

Ⅳ. Translate the following passage into English.

机械设计是一门通过设计新产品或者改进老产品来满足人类需求的应用技术科学。进行各种机械设计的人员通常被称为设计人员或者设计工程师。机械设计是一项创造性的工作，设计工程师不仅在工作上要有创新性，还必须在机械制图、运动学、动力学、工程材料、材料力学和（机械）制造工艺等方面具有深厚的基础知识。

Unit9 Hot Working and Forming Processes

Passage I Casting

Casting is the introduction of molten metal into a cavity or mold where, upon solidification, it becomes an object whose shape is determined by mold configuration. Casting offers several advantages over other method of medal forming: it is adaptable to intricate shapes, to extremely large pieces, and to mass production; it can provide parts with uniform physical and mechanical properties through out and, depending on the particular material being cast, the design of the part, and the quantity being produced, its economic advantages can surpass other processes.

Categories

Two broad categories of metal-casting processes exist: ingot casting (which includes continuous casting) and casting to shape. Ingot castings are produced by pouring molten metal into a permanent or reusable mold. Following solidification these ingots (or bars, slabs, or billets, as the case may be) are then further processed mechanically into many new shapes. Casting to shape involves pouring molten metal into molds in which the cavity provides the final useful shape, followed only by machining or welding for the specific application.

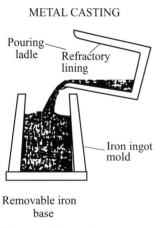

Fig. 9-1 Static ingot casting

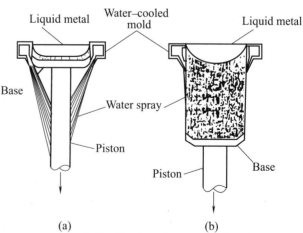

Fig. 9-2 Semicontinuous casting

(a) Molten aluminum solidifies in a water-cooled mold with a movable base.

(b) The piston is moved down so more molten metal can be poured into the reservoir.

Ingot casting Ingot castings make up the majority of all metal castings and are separated into three categories: static cast ingots, semi-continuous or direct-chill cast ingots, and continuous cast ingot.

Static cast ingots Static ingot casting simply involves pouring molten metal into a permanent mold (Fig. 9-1). After solidification, the ingot is withdrawn from the mold and the mold can be reused. This method is used to produce millions of tons steel annually.

Semi-continuous cast ingots A Semi-continuous casting process is employed in the aluminum industry to produce most of the cast alloys from which rod, sheet, strip, and plate configurations are made. In this process molten aluminum is transferred to a water-cooled permanent mold (Fig. 9-2 (a)) which has a movable base mounted on a long piston. After solidification has progressed from the mold surface so that a solid 'skin' is formed, the piston is moved down, and more metal continues to fill the reservoir (Fig. 9-2 (b)). Finally the piston will have moved its entire length, and the process is stopped. Conventional practice in the aluminum industry utilizes suitably lubricated metal molds. However, technological advances have allowed major aluminum alloy producers to replace the metal mold (at least in part) by an electromagnetic field so that molten metal touches the metal mold only briefly, thereby making a product with a much smoother finish than that produced conventionally.

Continuous cast ingots Continuous casting provides a major source of cast material in the steel and copper industry and is growing rapidly in the aluminum industry. In this process molten metal delivered to a permanent mold, and the casting begins much in the same way as in Semicontinuous casting. However, instead of the process ceasing after a certain length of time, the solidified ingot is continually sheared or cut into lengths and removed during casting. Thus the process is continuous, the solidified bar or strip being removed as rapidly as it is being cast. This method has many economic advantages over the more conventional casting techniques; as a result, all modern steel mills produce continuous cast products.

Casting to shape Casting to shape is generally classified according to the molding process, molding material or method of feeding the mold. There are four basic types of these casting processes: sand, permanent-mold, die, and centrifugal.

Sand casting This is the traditional method which still produces the large volume of cast-to-shape pieces. It utilizes a mixture of sand grains, water, clay, and other materials to make high-quality molds for use with molten metal. This 'green sand' mixture is compacted around a pattern (wood, plaster, or metal), usually by machine, to 20%-80% of its bulk density. The basic components of a sand mold and of other molds as well are shown in Fig. 9-3. The two halves of the mold (the cope and drag) are closed over cores necessary to form internal cavities, and the whole assembly is weighted or clamped to prevent floating of the cope when the metal is poured.

Other casting processes which utilize sand as a basic component are the shell, carbon dioxide, investment casting, ceramic molding and plaster molding processes. In addition, there are a large number of chemically bonded sands which are becoming increasingly important.

Permanent-mold casting Many high-quality castings are obtained by pouring molten metal into a mold made of cast iron, steel, or bronze. Semipermanent mold materials such as aluminum, silicon carbide, and graphite may also be used. The mold cavity and the gating system are machined to the desired dimensions after the mold is cast; the smooth surface from machining

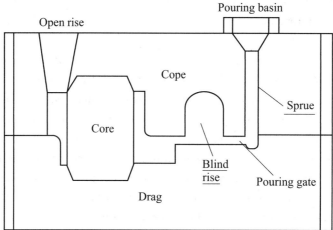

Fig. 9-3　Section through a sand mold showing the gating system and the risers

thus gives a good surface finish and dimensional accuracy to the casting. To increase mold life and to make ejection of the casting easier, the surface of the mold cavity is usually coated with carbon soot or a refractory slurry; these also serve as heat barriers and control the rate of cooling of the casting. The process is used for cast iron and nonferrous alloys with advantages over sand casting such as smoother surface finish, closer tolerances, and higher production rates.

Die casting　A further development of the permanent molding process is die casting. Molten metal is forced into a die cavity under pressures of 100-100000psi. Two basic types of die-casting machines are hot-chamber and cold-chamber. In the hot-chamber machine, a portion of the molten metal is force into the cavity at pressures up to about 2000pis. The process is used for casting low-melting-point alloys such as lead, zinc, and tin.

In the cold-chamber process the molten mental is ladled into the injection cylinder and force into the cavity under pressures which are about 10 times those in the hot-chamber process. High-melting-point alloys such as aluminum-, magnesium-, and copper-base alloys are used in this process. Die casting has the advantages of high production rates, high quality and strength, surface finish on the order of 40-100microinch rms (root mean square), and close tolerances, with thin sections.

Rheocasting　Rheocasting is the casting of a mixture of solid and liquid. In this process the alloy to be cast is melted and then allowed to cool until it is about 50% solid and 50% liquid. Vigorous stirring promotes liquidlike properties of this mixture so that it can be injected in a die-casting operation. A major advantage of this type of casting process is expected to be much reduced die erosion due to the lower casting temperatures.

Centrifugal casting　Inertial forces of rotation distribute molten metal into the mold cavities during centrifugal casting, of which there are three categories: true centrifugal casting, semicentrifugal casting, and centrifuging. The first two processes produce hollow cylindrical shapes and parts with rotational symmetry respectively. In the third process, the mold cavities are spun at a certain radius from the axis of rotation; the centrifugal force thus increases the pressure in the mold cavity.

The rotational speed in centrifugal casting is chosen to give between 40 and 60g acceleration. Dies may be made of forged steel or cast iron. Colloidal graphite is used on the dies to facilitate removal of the casting.

Successful operation of any metal-casting process requires careful consideration of mold design and metallurgical factors.

Words and Expressions

solidification /sə,lidifi'keiʃən/ n.	凝固，固化体（作用）
ingot casting	铸锭，模铸锭
slab /slæb/ n.	板坯，扁坯
semi-continuous /,semikən'tinjuəs/ adj.	半连续的，断断续续的
water-cooled /'wɔːtəkuːld/ adj.	水冷的
piston /'pistən/ n.	活塞，柱塞
reservoir /'rezəvwɑː/ n.	油箱
centrifugal /sen'trifjugəl/ adj.	离心的
bulk density	松装密度，散装密度
cope /kəup/ n.	上箱
drag /dræg/ n.	下箱
pouring basin	烧口杯，外浇杯
sprue /spruː/ n.	浇入口
blind riser	暗冒口
pouring gate	浇口，注口，直浇口
investment casting	熔模铸造法，蜡模铸造法
ceramic molding	陶瓷造型
plaster molding	石膏造型
carbon soot	炭黑
slurry /'slɜːri/ n.	泥浆，浆
root mean square	均方根
rheocasting /'riːəkʌstiŋ/ n.	流变铸造
colloidal /kə'lɔidl/ adj.	胶态的，胶体的

Exercises

I. Choose the best method of metal casting for following casting product according to the passage.

( ) 1. Millions of tons of steel.
( ) 2. Most of the cast alloys in aluminum industry.
( ) 3. Cast material in the steel and copper industry.
( ) 4. The largest volume of cast-to-shape pieces.
( ) 5. High-quality castings.
( ) 6. Low-melting-point alloys such as lead and zinc.
( ) 7. High-melting-point alloys as aluminum, magnesium and copper-base alloys.
( ) 8. Hollow cylindrical shapes and parts:

a. static ingot casting.
b. semi-continuous ingot casting.
c. continuous casting.

d. sand casting.
　　e. permanent-mold casting.
　　f. hot-chamber die casting.
　　g. cold-chamber die casting.
　　h. centrifugal casting.

Ⅱ. Translate the following passage into English.

　　砂型铸造（sand casting）生产的第一步是设计并制作一个合适的模型。铸造模型一般由硬木做成，考虑到在金属液凝固及随后的冷却过程中所产生的收缩，模型的尺寸必须大于最终铸件尺寸。收缩的程度因铸件金属或合金种类的不同而不同。除一些形状极其简单的铸件外，几乎所有铸件的模型都分成两部分或更多的部分，以便于制模。

Passage Ⅱ　Welding

Since the heat of the electric are may be concentrated and effectively controlled for fusion, several welding processes use this method for joining metal. The electric arc consists of a high-current discharge through a thermally ionized gaseous column referred to as a plasma. This gas is composed of similar numbers of electrons and ions, the ions flow out of a negative terminal (cathode) and move toward the positive terminal (anode). In addition to the plasma, there are other maternals such as molhen metals, slags, vapors, and neutral and excited gaseous atoms that are mixed together.

Arc Welding-Consumable Electrodes

Manual arc welding is widely used in the construction and fabrication of metal sheets, plates, and roll-formed products. The equipment includes a source of direct or alternating electric current, a ground, an electrode holder, and proper safety equipment. The latter consists of a helmet with dark eye potection, long sleeves, and a leather apron. The ultraviolet light from the welding arc can cause the equivalent of sunburn or snow bindness.

　　A conventional electrode forms a molten pool in the joint area. A gaseous shield and slag protect the weld deposit from oxidation and rapid loss of heat (Fig. 9-4 (a)). Unskilled operators find the drag-type electrode, with large amounts of iron powder in the electrode coating, much easier to use (Fig. 9-4 (b)). The iron powder increases the rate of deposition, but reduces the penetration and permits the core to burn away so that the coating can drag along the surface and the arc length stays constant, Thereby a good deposit can be made by an operator with relatively little skill.

　　In shielded-metal-arc welding the arc is started by momentarily striking the electrode against the base metal and quickly withdrawing to form an arc. The arc must not be too long, as this gives an opportunity for contamination by the atmosphere, and it is more difficult to control its application to the joint. The current and voltage must be under close control; they are governed by the quality of equipment and its inherent regulating characteristics.

　　When the arc forms between the base metal and the electrode, the immediate surface is melted, and, with the use of an electrode that cannot conduct the heat away rapidly, some of the metal is vaporized. These droplets and the vaporized metal flow along the stream of the arc path to the base metal where they condense, build up, and solidify (Motion-picture studies of this action have been made and are

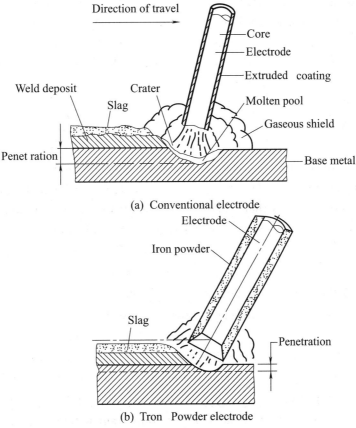

Fig. 9-4 Shielded metal-arc welding with conventional and iron-powder electrodes

available from leading welding equipment suppliers). Therefore, the arc process is primarily a localized casting process that is influenced by the action of the electrode, current, flux, and operator. In the liquid and gaseous state, it is essential that no harmful chemical action (such as oxidation and forming of nitrides) occur, that gas occlusions escape, that flux inclusions be avoided, and that the material cool without tearing or cracking.

The molten metal is protected from contamination by four general methods.

(1) The electrode is coated with a flux that melts and forms a gaseous envelope around the arc and a liquid covering over the molten metal.

(2) An inert gas envelope is blown around the electrode as it melts. The inert gas is argon, helium, or mixtures of argon and helium. This method has proved especially satisfactory in the welding of aluminum, magnesium, and copper alloys.

(3) The end of the electrode is submerged in a granular flux. This surrounds the arc and protects it and the molten metal.

(4) Carbon dioxide is used as a shielding gas to weld low-carbon and allay ferritic steels. Carbon dioxide is less expensive than inert gases and gives deeper penetration into the base metal. When carbon dioxide is used with filler metals of proper chemistry, it produces welds of high quality and soundness. A mixture of carbon dioxide and argon increases the stability of the arc over either a pure carbon dioxide or pure argon gas. Pure carbon dioxide causes

splatter in and about the weld. Pure argon prevents oxidation of the metal with resulting surface tension and uneven surfaces. With a combination of carbon dioxide and argon, slight oxidation takes place and the result is a smooth weld surface. Argon plus 25 percent carbon dioxide is used for welding steel. Especially for stainless steel, argon plus 1 to 5 percent oxygen may be used. Shielding gases are used at rates of 10 to 35ft^3/h.

Passage Ⅲ Forming

Forming can be defined as a process in which the desired size and shape are obtained through the plastic deformations of a material. The stresses induced during the process are greater than the yield strength, but less than the fracture strength, of the material. The type of loading may be tensile, compressive, bending, or shearing, or a combination of these. This is a very economical process as the desired shape, size, and finish can be obtained without any significant loss of material. Moreover, a part of the input energy is fruitfully utilized in improving the strength of the product through strain hardening.

The forming processes can be grouped under two broad categories, namely, cold forming, and hot forming. If the working temperature is higher than the recrystallization temperature of the material, then the process is called hot forming. Otherwise the process is termed as cold forming. The flow stress behavior of a material is entirely different above and below its recrystallization temperature. During hot working, a large amount of plastic deformation can be imparted without significant strain hardening. This is important because a large amount of strain hardening renders the material brittle. The frictional characteristics of the two forming processes are also entirely different. For example, the coefficient of friction in cold forming is generally of the order of 0.1, whereas that in hot forming can be as high as 0.6. Further, hot forming lowers down the material strength so that a machine with a reasonable capacity can be used even for a product having large dimensions.

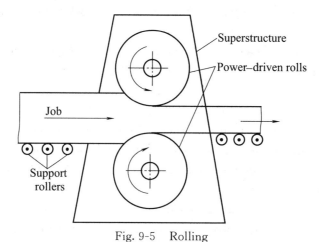

Fig. 9-5 Rolling

The typical forming processes are rolling, forging, drawing, deep drawing, bending, and extrusion. For a better understanding of the mechanics of various forming operations, we shall briefly discuss each of these processes.

Rolling

In this process, the job is drawn by means of friction through a regulated opening between two power-driven rolls (Fig. 9-5). The shape and size of the product are decided by the gap between the rolls and their contours. This is a very useful process for the production of sheet metal and various common sections, e. g., rail, channel, angle, and round.

Forging

In forging, the material is squeezed between two or more dies to alter its shape and size. Depending on the situation, the dies may be open (Fig. 9-6 (a)) or closed (Fig. 9-6 (b)).

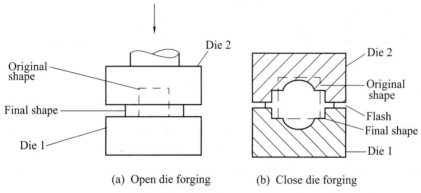

(a) Open die forging   (b) Close die forging

Fig. 9-6 Forging operation

Rawing

In this process, the cross-section of a wire or that of a bar or tube is reduced by pulling the workpiece through the conical orifice of a die. Fig. 9-7 represents the operation schematically. When high reduction is required, it may be necessary to perform the operation in several passes.

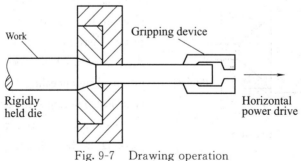

Fig. 9-7 Drawing operation

Deep Drawing

In deep drawing, a cup-shaped product is obtained from a flat sheet metal with the help of a punch and a die. Fig. 9-8 shows the operation schematically. The sheet metal is held over the die by means of a blank holder to avoid defects in the product.

Bending

As the name implies, this is a process of bending a metal sheet plastically to obtain the desired shape. This is achieved by a set of suitably designed punch and die. A typical process is shown schematically in Fig. 9-9.

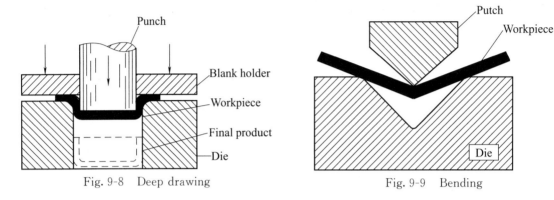

Fig. 9-8 Deep drawing   Fig. 9-9 Bending

Extrusion

This is a process basically similar to the closed die forging. But in this operation, the workpiece is compressed in a closed space, forcing the material to flow out through a suitable opening, called a die (Fig. 9-10). In this process, only the shapes with constant cross-sections (die outlet cross-section) can be produced.

Advantages and Disadvantages of Hot and Cold Forming

Now that we have covered the various types of metal working operations, it would only be appropriate that we provide an overall evaluation of the hot and cold working processes. Such a discussion will help in choosing the proper working conditions for a given situation.

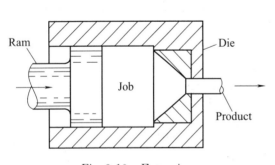

Fig. 9-10 Extrusion

During hot working, a proper control of the grain size is possible since active grain growth takes place in the range of the working temperature. As a result, there is no strain hardening, and therefore there is no need of expensive and time-consuming intermediate annealing. Of course, strain hardening is advisable during some operations (viz., drawing) to achieve an improved strength; in such cases, hot working is less advantageous. Apart from this, strain hardening may be essential for a successful completion of some processes (e. g., in deep drawing, strain hardening prevents the rupture of the material around the bottom circumference where the stress is maximum). Large products and high strength material can be worked upon under hot conditions since the elevated temperature lowers down the strength and, consequently, the work load. Moreover, for most materials, the ductility increases with temperature and, as a result, brittle materials can also be worked upon by the hot working operation. It should, however, be remembered that there are certain materials (viz., steels containing sulphur) which become more brittle at elevated temperatures. When a very accurate dimensional control is required, hot working is not advised because of shrinkage and loss of surface metal due to scaling. Moreover, surface finish is poor due to oxide formation and scaling.

The major advantages of cold working are that it is economical, quicker, and easier to handle because here no extra arrangements for heating and handling are necessary. Further, the mechanical properties normally get improved during the process due to strain hardening. What is more, the control of grain flow directions adds to the strength characteristics of the product. However, apart from other limitations of cold working (viz., difficulty with high strength and brittle materials and large product sizes), the inability of the process to prevent the significant reduction brought about in corrosion resistance is an undesirable feature.

Words and Expressions

fracture /ˈfræktʃə/ n.	断裂
strain hardening	应变硬化，加工硬化，冷作硬化
cold forming	冷成形，冷态成形，冷作成形
hot forming	热成形
recrystallization /riːˌkrɪstəlaɪˈzeɪʃən/ n.	再结晶
hot working	热加工，热处理
deep drawing	拉伸
gap /gæp/ n.	缺口，裂口，间隙，缝隙，差距
channel /ˈtʃænl/ n.	槽钢
superstructure /ˈsjuːpəˌstrʌktʃə/ n.	上部结构
conical /ˈkɔnikəl/ adj.	圆锥的，圆锥形的
orifice /ˈɔrifis/ n.	孔，节流孔
shrinkage /ˈʃriŋkidʒ/ n.	收缩
inability /ˌinəˈbiliti/ n.	无能，无力

Exercises

Ⅰ. Match the following terms in Column (Ⅰ) with the descriptions in Column (Ⅱ).

(Ⅰ)   (Ⅱ)

( ) 1. drawing   a. The shape and size of the product are decided by the gap between the rolls and their contours.

( ) 2. forging   b. The material is squeezed between two or more dies to alter its shape and size.

( ) 3. rolling   c. The cross-section of a wire or that of a bar or tube is reduced by pulling the workpiece through the conical orifice of a die.

( ) 4. extrusion   d. A cup-shaped product is obtained from a flat sheet metal with the help of a die.

( ) 5. bending   e. A desired shape can be obtained by bending a metal sheet plastically.

( ) 6. deep drawing   f. Only the shapes with constant cross-sections can be produced.

( ) 7. cold forming   g. The desired size and shape are obtained through the plastic deformation of a material.

( ) 8. forming   h. The working temperature is lower than the recrystallization temperature of a material.

( ) 9. die   i. The working temperature is higher than the recrystallization temperature of a material.

( ) 10. hot forming   j. It is a suitable opening through which the material is formed to flow out.

II. Translate the following passage into Chinese.

Rolling is the process of shaping metal in a machine called rolling mill. Ingots of metal are rolled by forcing them between two rollers rotating in opposite directions, thus pressing the metal into the required shape. There are two kinds of rolling: hot rolling and cold rolling, before cold rolling, the scale covering the surface of the hot-rolled object should be removed. Cold rolling produces a higher surface finishing sheet and gives it a very exact size. The process has innumerable advantages. Many shapes may be manufactured in quantities at a rapid rate and at a relatively low cost.

Passage IV   Forging

Forging is one of the oldest <u>metalworking</u> processes known to man. As early as 2000 B. C. , forging was used to produce weapons, <u>implements</u>, and jewelry. The process was performed by hand using simple hammers.

Hot forging is defined as the controlled, plastic deformation or working of metals into predetermined shapes by means of pressure or impact blows, or a combination of both. In hot forging, this plastic deformation is performed above the recrystallization temperature to prevent strain hardening of the metal.

During the deformation process, the crystalline structure of the base metal is refined and any nonmetallic or alloy <u>segregation</u> is properly oriented. In bar stock, the grain flow is only in one direction. When the contour of the part is changed, the grain flow lines are cut, rendering the metal more susceptible to fatigue and stress corrosion. Hot forging develops the grain flow so that it follows the outline of the part being formed. The directional alignment of the grains or fibers helps increase strength, ductility, and resistance to impact and fatigue in the metal.

Deformation is affected by the stress inherent in the metal, the microstructural characteristics of the starting material, the temperature at which the deformation occurs, the rate at which the deformation occurs, and the frictional restraint between the material being forged and the die surface.

Forging Processes

Metal flow during the forging process normally falls into two categories: <u>upsetting</u> and <u>extrusion</u>. Upsetting occurs when the metal is compressed parallel to the longitudinal axis of the workpiece. This action enables the metal to flow freely in one direction as in <u>open-die forging</u>, or it can be restrained as in <u>impression-die forging</u>. Extrusion occurs when the metal is compressed parallel to the longitudinal axis of the workpiece and allowed to flow through an orifice in the die cavity.

Open-Die Forging

Open-die forging, also referred to as smith forging, blacksmith forging, hand forging, and flat-die forging, is generally performed without special tooling. The forms obtained and the dimensions maintained are usually dependent upon the skill of the operator and the type of equipment used. However, with the addition of computer control to the equipment, more complex forgings can be produced and better dimensional control is maintained. This equipment may range from the simple anvil and hammer of the blacksmith to giant, computer-controlled, hydraulic presses capable of delivering up to 75000 tons of force and producing single forgings weighing several thousand pounds. Most open-die forgings are simple geometric shapes such as discs, rings, or shafts. Open-die forging is also used in the steelmaking industry to cog ingots or to draw down billets from one size to a smaller one.

The open-die forging process is employed when only a few parts are needed and when the part is too large to be produced in closed dies. Quantities of less than 100 parts are generally good candidates to be produced in open dies because designing and manufacturing closed dies for such a small quantity is often too costly. However, large quantities are produced with open dies. The open-die process is also used to obtain the mechanical properties in a workpiece that are not obtainable by machining. Generally, most forgings begin with the open-die process before the final forging operation.

Impression-Die Forging

In impression-die forging, the workpiece is placed between two dies containing the impression of the forging shape to be produced. The dies are brought together and the workpiece is plastically deformed until the sides come in contact with the walls of the die. As the deformation continues, a small amount of material begins to flow outside the die impression, forming flash. The thin flash cools rapidly, creating a pressure increase inside the workpiece. The increased pressure assists the flow of material into the unfilled portion of the impression. The majority of the forgings produced are done using impression-die forging.

Closed-die forging or flashless forging, which is a special form of impression-die forging, does not depend on the flash to achieve complete die filling. Generally, the material is deformed in a cavity that does not allow excess material to flow outside the impression. Therefore, die design and workpiece volumes are more critical than in impression-die forging so that complete die filling is achieved without generating excess pressures due to overfilling.

Currently, closed-die forging is moving more and more toward near-net-shaped and net-shaped forging. Near-net-shaped parts are those parts that require minor metal removal before assembly. Net-shaped parts have finished functional surfaces that do not require additional metal removal. Gears, airfoils, and high-temperature jet engine disc forgings are being produced using this process.

Some of the more widely used forging processes are ring rolling, orbital forging, isothermal forging, incremental forging, roll forging, wedge rolling, and electric upsetting.

Words and Expressions

metalworking /ˈmetlwɜːkiŋ/ *n.*	金属加工；
adj.	金属制造的
implement /ˈimplimənt/ *n.*	工具，器具
segregation /ˌsegriˈgeiʃən/ *n.*	偏析，分离
upsetting /ʌpˈsetiŋ/ *n.*	镦锻，镦粗
open-die /ˈəupəndai/ *n.*	开式模具
open-die forging	开式模锻造；开式锻模
impression-die forging	压印模锻造
flat-die forging	无模锻造，自由锻造
flash /flæʃ/ *n.*	飞边
flashless /ˈflæʃlis/ *adj.*	无飞边的
overfill /ˌəuvəˈfil/ *vt.*	使满溢，过度填充
near-net-shaped /ˌniənetˈʃeipt/ *adj.*	近净形的
net-shaped /ˈnetʃeipt/ *adj.*	净形的
airfoil /ˈɛəfɔil/ *n.*	机翼，螺旋桨
ring rolling	环锻
orbital forging	轨形锻造
isothermal forging	等温锻造
incremental forging	步进锻造
roll forging	滚锻，轧锻
wedge rolling	楔形滚轧，楔形轧制

Exercises

Ⅰ. **Translate the following passage into Chinese and pay attention the verbs in the sentences.**

1. The basic metal working processes are not likely to change fundamentally.
2. Modern industry needs considerable quantities of this metal, either in the form of iron or in the form of steel.
3. It is necessary to design a mandrel for holding previously threaded workpiece.
4. The analysis of electrical systems requires that the basic definitions be clearly understood.
5. The drilling machine is the second oldest machine tool, having invented shortly after the lathe.
6. It is generally formed by forging and twisting grooves in a flat strip of steel or by milling a cylindrical piece of steel, high-speed steel being commonly used.

Ⅱ. **Translate the following passage into English.**

Forging means the shaping of metal by a series of hammer blows, or by slow application of pressure. The simplest example is a blacksmith's forging of a hot piece of metal by hammering the work-piece on an anvil. Heavy smith's forging is fundamentally similar, differing only in the scale of the operation. The work-piece may be an ingot of 100 tons and the deforming force provided by a massive forging hammer, but the whole process is controlled by the master smith, who decides each time where, and with what force, the blow should take place.

Part2 Equipment and Technology of Machine Manufacture

Unit10 Basic Machining Operations —Turning, Boring and Milling

Passage I Basic Machining Operations

Machine tools have evolved from the early foot-powered lathes of the Egyptians and John Wilkinson's boring mill. They are designed to provide rigid support for both the workpiece and the cutting tool and can precisely control their relative positions and the velocity of the tool with respect to the workpiece. Basically, in metal cutting, a sharpened wedge-shaped tool removes a rather narrow strip of metal from the surface of a ductile workpiece in the form of a severely deformed chip. The chip is a waste product that is considerably shorter than the workpiece from which it came but with a corresponding increase in thickness of the uncut chip. The geometrical shape of the machine surface depends on the shape of the tool and its path during the machining operation.

Most machining operations produce parts of differing geometry. If a rough cylindrical workpiece revolves about a central axis and the tool penetrates beneath its surface and travels parallel to the center of rotation, a surface of revolution is produced (Fig. 10-1 (a)), and the operation is called turning. If a hollow tube is machined on the inside in a similar manner, the operation is called boring (Fig. 10-1 (b)). Producing an external conical surface of uniformly varying diameter is called taper turning (Fig. 10-1 (c)). If the tool point travels in a path of varying radius, a contoured surface like that of a bowling pin can be produced (Fig. 10-1 (d)); or, if the piece is short enough (approximately 1 in.) and the support is sufficiently rigid, a contoured surface could be produced by feeding a shaped tool normal to the axis of rotation (Fig. 10-1 (e)). Short tapered or cylindrical surfaces could also be contour formed.

Flat or plane surfaces are frequently required. They can be generated by radial turning or facing, in which the tool point moves normal to the axis of rotation (Fig. 10-2 (a)). In other cases, it is more convenient to hold the workpiece steady and reciprocate the tool across it in a series of straight-line cuts with a crosswise feed increment before each cutting stroke (Fig. 10-2 (b)). This operation is called planning and is carried out on a shaper. For larger pieces it is easier to keep the tool stationary and draw the workpiece under it as in planning. The tool is fed at each reciprocation. Contoured surfaces can be produced by using shaped tools (Fig. 10-2 (c)).

Multiple-edged tools can also be used. Drilling uses a twin-edged fluted tool for holes with depths up to 5 to 10 times the drill diameter. Whether the drill turns or the workpiece rotates,

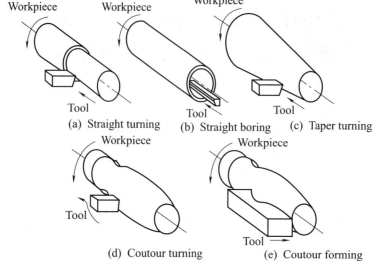

Fig. 10-1 Diagrams showing how surfaces of revolution are generated and formed

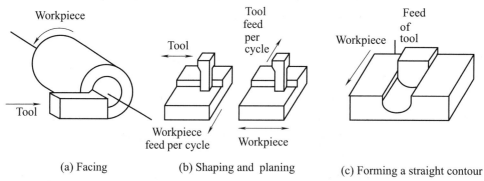

Fig. 10-2 Diagram showing how plane surfaces are generated and formed

relative motion between the cutting edge and the workpiece is the important factor. In milling operations a rotary cutter with a number of cutting edges engages the workpiece, which moves slowly with respect to the cutter. Plane or contoured surfaces may be produced, depending on the geometry of the cutter and the type of feed. Horizontal or vertical axes of rotation may be used, and the feed of the workpiece may be in any of the three coordinate directions.

Basic Machine Tools

Machine tools are used to produce a part of a specified geometrical shape and precise size by removing metal from a ductile material in the form of chips. The latter are a waste product and vary from long continuous ribbons of a ductile material such as steel, which are undesirable from a disposal point of view, to easily handled well-broken chips resulting from cast iron. Machine tools perform five basic metal-removal processes: turning, planning, drilling, milling, and grinding (Table 10-1). All other metal-removal processes are modifications of these five basic processes. For example, boring is internal turning; reaming, tapping, and counterboring modify drilled holes and are related to drilling; hobbing and gear cutting are fundamentally milling operations; hack sawing and broaching are a form of planning and honing; lapping, superfinishing, polishing, and buffing are variants of grinding or abrasive removal operations. Therefore, there are only four types of basic machine tools, which use cutting tools of specific controllable geometry: 1. lathes, 2. planers, 3. drilling machines, and 4. milling machines. The grinding process forms chips, but the geometry of the abrasive grain is uncontrollable.

Table 10-1 Comparison of basic machining operations for ductile materials

Operation	Shape produced	Machine tool	Cutting tool	Relative motion		Surface roughness μin.	Min. prod. tolerance in.
				Tool	Work		
Turning (external)	Surface of revolution (cylindrical)	Lathe, boring machine	Single point			32-500	±0.001
Boring (internal)	Cylindrical (enlarges holes)	Boring machine	Single point			16-250	±0.0001 ±0.001
Shaping and planning	Flat surfaces or Slots	Shaper, planer	Single point			32-500	±0.001
Drilling	Cylindrical (originates holes 0.010 to 4in. dia.)	Drill press	Drill: twin edges		Fixed.	125-250	±0.002
Milling End, form face, slab	Flat and contoured surfaces and slots	Milling machine	Multiple points (cutter teeth)			32-500	±0.001
Grinding Cylindrical Surface Plunge	Cylindrical and flat	Grinding machine	Multiple points (grind wheel)			8-125	±0.0001

The amount and rate of material removed by the various machining processes may be large, as in heavy turning operations, or extremely small, as in lapping or superfinishing operations where only the high spots of a surface are removed.

A machine tool performs three major functions: 1. it rigidly supports the workpiece or its holder and the cutting tool; 2. it provides relative motion between the workpiece and the cutting tool; 3. it provides a range of feeds and speeds usually ranging from 4 to 32 choices in each case.

Speed and Feeds in Machining

Speeds, feeds, and depth of cut are the three major variables for economical machining. Other variables are the work and tool materials, coolant and geometry of the cutting tool. The rate of metal removal and power required for machining depend upon these variables.

The depth of cut, feed, and cutting speed are machine settings that must be established in any metal-cutting operation. They all affect the forces, the power, and the rate of metal removal. They can be defined by comparing them to the needle and record of a phonograph. The cutting speed (V) is represented by the velocity of the record surface relative to the needle in the tone arm at any instant. Feed is represented by the advance of the needle radically inward per revolution, or is the difference in position between two adjacent grooves. The depth of cut is the penetration of the needle into the record or the depth of the grooves.

Words and Expressions

boring mill	镗床
wedge-shaped /'wedʒ'ʃeipt/ *adj.*	楔形的
boring /'bɔːriŋ/ *n.*	镗孔,镗削
taper /'teipə/ *n.*	锥形,锥度
v.	逐渐变细,逐渐减少
taper turning	锥体车削
bowling pin	保龄球棒
feed /fiːd/ *vt.*	供给,进给,走刀
shaped /ʃeipt/ *adj.*	成形的,仿形的
radial /'reidjəl/ *adj.*	径向的,(沿)半径的
facing /'feisiŋ/ *n.*	端面车削,刮削
planing /'pleiniŋ/ *n.*	刨削,刨工
shaper /'ʃeipə/ *n.*	牛头刨床
drill /dril/ *n.*	钻头
shaping /'ʃeipiŋ/ *n.*	牛头刨削
grinding machine	磨床
reaming /'riːmiŋ/ *n.*	铰孔,扩孔,清除毛边,铰削作业
tapping /'tæpiŋ/ *n.*	攻螺纹
counterboring /ˌkauntə'bɔːriŋ/ *n.*	镗孔,锪孔
hobbing /'hɔbiŋ/ *n.*	滚铣,滚齿
hack sawing	弓锯
broaching /'brəutʃiŋ/ *n.*	拉削
honing /'həuniŋ/ *n.*	搪磨,珩磨
lapping /'læpiŋ/ *n.*	研磨,抛光
superfinishing /ˌsjuːpə'finiʃiŋ/ *n.*	超精加工
buffing /'bʌfiŋ/ *n.*	擦光,磨光
variant /'vɛəriənt/ *n.*	变量
planer /'pleinə/ *n.*	龙门刨床
drilling machine	钻床,钻机
milling machine	铣削机,铣床
coolant /'kuːlənt/ *n.*	冷却剂,冷却液
phonograph /'fəunəgrɑːf/ *n.*	留声机,电唱机
tone arm	唱臂,拾音器臂

Passage II   Turning on Lathe centers

The basic operations performed on an engine lathe are illustrated in Fig. 10-3. Those operations performed on external surfaces with a single point cutting tool are called turning. Except for drilling, reaming, and tapping, the operations on internal surfaces are also performed by a single point cutting tool.

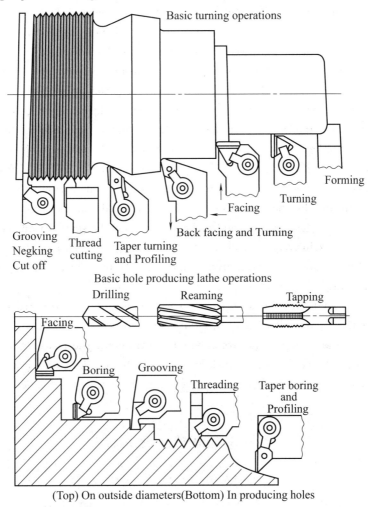

(Top) On outside diameters (Bottom) In producing holes

Fig. 10-3   The basic turning operations performed on a lathe

All machining operations, including turning and boring, can be classified as roughing, finishing, or semi-finishing. The objective of a roughing operation is to remove the bulk of the material as rapidly and as efficiently as possible, while leaving a small amount of material on the work-piece for the finishing operation. Finishing operations are performed to obtain the final size, shape, and surface finish on the workpiece. Sometimes a semi-finishing operation will precede the finishing operation to leave a small predetermined and uniform amount of stock on the work-piece to be removed by the finishing operation.

Generally, longer workpieces are turned while supported on one or two lathe centers. Cone shaped holes, called center holes, which fit the lathe centers are drilled in the ends of the workpiece-usually along the axis of the cylindrical part. The end of the workpiece adjacent to the tailstock is always supported by a tailstock center, while the end near the headstock may be supported by a headstock center or held in a chuck. The headstock end of the workpiece may be held in a four-jaw chuck, or in a collet type chuck. This method holds the workpiece firmly and transfers the power to the workpiece smoothly; the additional support to the workpiece provided by the chuck lessens the tendency for chatter to occur when cutting. Precise results can be obtained with this method if care is taken to hold the workpiece accurately in the chuck.

Very precise results can be obtained by supporting the workpiece between two centers. A lathe dog is clamped to the workpiece; together they are driven by a driver plate mounted on the spindle nose. One end of the workpiece is machined; then the workpiece can be turned around in the lathe to machine the other end. The center holes in the workpiece serve as precise locating surfaces as well as bearing surfaces to carry the weight of the workpiece and to resist the cutting forces. After the workpiece has been removed from the lathe for any reason, the center holes will accurately align the workpiece back in the lathe or in another lathe, or in a cylindrical grinding machine. The workpiece must never be held at the headstock end by both a chuck and a lathe center. While at first thought this seems like a quick method of aligning the workpiece in the chuck, this must not be done because it is not possible to press evenly with the jaws against the workpiece while it is also supported by the center. The alignment provided by the center will not be maintained and the pressure of the jaws may damage the center hole, the lathe center, and perhaps even the lathe spindle. Compensating or floating jaw chucks used almost exclusively on high production work provide an exception to the statements made above. These chucks are really work drivers and cannot be used for the same purpose as ordinary three or four-jaw chucks.

While very large diameter workpieces are sometimes mounted on two centers, they are preferably held at the headstock end by faceplate jaws to obtain the smooth power transmission; moreover, large lathe dogs that are adequate to transmit the power not generally available, although they can be made as a special. Faceplate jaws are like chuck jaws except that they are mounted on a faceplate, which has less overhang from the spindle bearings then a large chuck would have.

Words and Expressions

engine lathe	普通车床
roughing /'rʌfiŋ/ n.	粗加工
tailstock /'teil'stɔk/ n.	[机]尾架，尾座，顶针座
headstock /'hed'stɔk/ n.	机头座，车[刨]床头座，床头座，床头箱，主轴箱
chuck /tʃʌk/ n.	卡盘
collet /'kɔlit/ n.	夹头，有缝夹套
chatter /'tʃætə/ n.	振动，颤动
dog /'dɔg/ n.	销，卡箍
cylindrical grinding	外圆磨削
cylindrical grinding machine	外圆磨床
faceplate /'feis‚pleit/ n.	面板，花盘
overhang /'əuvə'hæŋ/ n.	伸出物，伸出量

Passage Ⅲ Boring

The objective of boring a hole in a lathe is:
1. To enlarge the hole.
2. To machine the hole to the desired diameter.
3. To accurately locate the position of the hole.
4. To obtain a smooth surface finish in the hole.

The motion of the boring tool is parallel to the axis of the lathe when the carriage is moved in the longitudinal direction and the workpiece revolves about the axis of the lathe. When these two motions are combined to bore a hole, it will be concentric with the axis of rotation of the lathe. The position of the hole can be accurately located by holding the workpiece in the lathe so that the axis about which the hole is to be machined coincides with the axis of rotation of the lathe. When the boring operation is done in the same setup of the work that is used to turn and face it, practically perfect concentricity and perpendicularity can be achieved.

The boring tool is held in a boring bar which is fed through the hole by the carriage. A typical boring tool is shown in Fig. 10-4. Variations of this design are used, depending on the job to be done. The lead angle used, if any, should always be small. Also, the nose radius of the boring tool must not be too large. The cutting speed used for boring can be equal to the speed for turning. However, when the spindle speed of the lathe is calculated, the finished, or largest, bore diameter should be used. The feed rate for boring is usually somewhat less than for turning to compensate for the lack of rigidity of the boring bar.

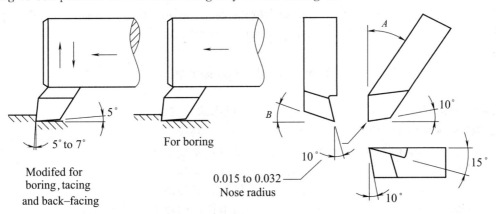

Angle "A" – To suit boring bar
Angle "B" – To suit hole in work
The design is typical, but variations are used to suit different conditions
Fig. 10-4 Design of a typical high-speed steel boring tool

The boring operation is generally performed in two steps; namely, rough boring and finish boring. The objective of the rough-boring operation is to remove the excess metal rapidly and efficiently, and the objective of the finish-boring operation is to obtain the desired size, surface finish, and location of the hole. The size of the hole is obtained by using the trial-cut procedure. The diameter of the hole can be measured with inside calipers and outside micrometer calipers. Basic Measuring Instruments, or inside micrometer calipers can be used to measure the diameter directly. Cored holes and drilled holes are sometimes eccentric with respect to the rotation of the lathe. When the boring tool enters the work, the boring bar will take a deeper cut on one side of the hole than on the other, and will deflect more when taking this deeper cut, with the result that the bored hole will not be concentric with the rotation of the work. This effect is corrected by taking several cuts through the hole using a shallow depth of cut. Each succeeding shallow cut causes the resulting hole to be more concentric than it was with the previous cut. Before the final, finish cut is taken; the hole should be concentric with the rotation of the work in order to make certain that the finished hole will be accurately located.

Shoulders, grooves, contours, tapers, and threads are also bored inside of holes. Internal grooves are cut using a tool that is similar to an external grooving tool. The procedure for boring internal shoulders is very similar to the procedure for turning shoulders. Large shoulders are faced with the boring tool positioned with the nose leading, and using the <u>cross slide</u> to feed the tool. Internal contours can be machined using a tracing <u>attachment</u> on a lathe. The tracing attachment is mounted on the cross slide and the <u>stylus</u> follows the outline of the master profile plate. This causes the cutting tool to move in a path corresponding to the profile of the master profile plate. Thus, the profile on the master profile plate is reproduced inside the bore. The master profile plate is accurately mounted on a special slide which can be precisely adjusted in two directions, in order to align the cutting tool in the correct relationship to the work. This lathe has a <u>cam-lock</u> type of spindle nose which permits it to take a cut when rotating in either direction. Normal turning cuts are taken with the spindle rotating counterclockwise. The boring cut is taken with the spindle revolving in a clockwise direction, or 'backwards'. This permits the boring cut to be taken on the 'back side' of the bore which is easier to see form the operator's position in front of the lathe. This should not be done on lathes having a threaded spindle nose because the cutting force will tend to <u>unscrew</u> the chuck.

Words and Expressions

carriage /ˈkærɪdʒ/ n.		（机床的）拖板
concentricity /ˌkɒnsenˈtrɪsɪti/ n.		同心，同心度
perpendicularity /ˌpəːpənˌdɪkjuˈlærɪti/ n.		垂直，垂直度
boring bar		镗杆，钻杆
trial-cut /ˈtraɪəlˈkʌt/ n.		试切，试切割
inside caliper		内卡钳，内径卡
cross slide		横向滑板，横向架，横拖板
attachment /əˈtætʃmənt/ n.		附件，附加装置
stylus /ˈstaɪləs/ n.		唱针，铁笔
cam-lock /ˈkæmˈlɒk/ n.		偏心夹
unscrew /ˌʌnˈskruː/ vt.		拧松螺丝，拆卸

Passage Ⅳ　Milling

Milling is a machining process for removing material by relative motion between a workpiece and a rotating cutter having multiple cutting edges. In some applications, the workpiece is held stationary while the rotating cutter is moved past it at a given feed rate (traversed). In other applications, both the workpiece and cutter are moved in relation to each other and in relation to the milling machine. More frequently, however, the workpiece is advanced at a relatively low rate of movement or feed to a milling cutter rotating at comparatively high speed, with the cuter axis remaining in a fixed position. A characteristic feature of the milling process is that each milling cutter tooth takes its share of the stock in the form of small individual chips. Milling operations are performed on many different machines.

Since both the workpiece and cutter can be moved relative to one another, independently or in combination, a wide variety of operations can be performed by milling. Applications include the production of flat or contoured surfaces, slots, grooves, recesses, threads, and other configurations.

Milling is one of the most universal, yet complicated machining methods. The process has more variations in the kinds of machines used, workpiece movements, and types of tooling than any other basic machining method. Important advantages of removing material by means of milling include high stock removal rates, the capability of producing relatively smooth surface finishes, and the wide variety of cutting tools that are available. Cutting edges of the tools can be shaped to form any complex surface.

The major milling methods are peripheral and face milling; in addition, a number of related methods exist that are variations of these two methods, depending upon the type of workpiece or cutter.

Peripheral Milling

In peripheral milling, sometimes called slab milling, the milled surface generated by teeth or inserts located on the periphery of the cutter body is generally in a plane parallel to the cutter axis. Milling operations with form-relieved and formed profile cutters are included in this class. The cross section of the milled surface corresponds to the outline or contour of the milling cutter or combination of cutters used.

Peripheral milling operations are usually performed on milling machines with the spindle positioned horizontally; however, they can also be performed with end mills on vertical-spindle machines. The milling cutters are mounted on an arbor which is generally supported at the outer end for increased rigidity, particularly when, because of the conditions of the setup, the cutter or cutters are located at some distance from the nose of the spindle. Peripheral milling should generally not be done if the part can be face milled.

Face Milling

Face milling is done on both horizontal and vertical milling machines. The milled surface resulting from the combined action of cutting edges located on the periphery and face of the cutter is generally at right angles to the cutter axis. The milled surface is flat, with no relation to the contour of the teeth, except when milling is done to a shoulder. Generally, face milling should be applied wherever and whenever possible.

Chip thickness in conventional (up) face milling varies from a minimum at the entrance and exit of the cutter tooth to a maximum along the horizontal diameter. The milled surface is characterized by tooth and revolution marks, as in the case of peripheral milling cutters. The prominence of these marks is controlled by the accuracy of grinding the face cutting edge of the teeth, or by the accuracy of the body/insert combination in indexable cutters and of mounting the cutter so that it runs true on the machine spindle. It is also controlled by the rigidity of the machine and workpiece itself. When the length of the face cutting edge is less than the feed per revolution (or the amount the work has moved in one revolution of the cutter), a series of roughly circular grooves or <u>ridges</u> results on the milled surface. Similar marking is produced by the trailing teeth when they drag on the milled surface of the work. This is known as heel drag.

In face milling, it is important to select a cutter with a diameter suited to the proposed width of cut if best results are to be obtained. Cuts equal in width to the full cutter diameter should be avoided, if possible, since the thin chip section at entry of the teeth results in accelerated tooth wear from abrasion plus a tendency for the chip to weld or stick to the tooth or insert and be carried around and recut. This is detrimental to surface finish. A good ratio of cutter diameter to the width of the workpiece or proposed path of cut is 5 : 3.

Words and Expressions

milling cutter	铣刀
recess /ri'ses/ n.	退刀槽
face milling	铣面
slab milling	平面铣刀
insert /'insə:t/ n.	嵌入，插入，嵌入物
arbor /'ɑ:bə/ n.	柄轴，心轴
ridge /ridʒ/ n.	脊，螺脊

Exercises

Ⅰ. **Choose the best answer for each of the following sentences.**

1. The operations performed on external surface with a single point cutting tool are called _____ .
    a. drilling   b. reaming   c. tapping   d. turning
2. _____ can not be classified as routing, finishing or semi-finishing.
    a. Boring   b. Turning   c. Drilling   d. Screwdriving
3. The objective of _____ operation is to remove the bulk of the material.
    a. finishing   b. roughing   c. cutting   d. machining
4. The end of the workpiece _____ to the tailstock is always supported by a tailstock center.
    a. close   b. related   c. adjacent   d. adequate
5. Faceplate jaws are _____ on a faceplate.
    a. climbed   b. mounted   c. put   d. aligned
6. The motion of the boring tool is _____ to the axis of the lathe.
    a. opposite   b. suitable   c. parallel   d. contrary
7. The axis about which the hole is be machined _____ with axis of rotation of the lathe.
    a. combines   b. coincides   c. connects   d. contracts
8. The boring bar will _____ more when taking the deeper cut on one side of the hole.
    a. adjust   b. deflect   c. degrade   d. rotate

9. The hole should be _____ with the rotation of the work.
   a. identical   b. connected   c. concentric   d. consistent
10. Peripheral milling operation can be performed with end mills on both vertical spindle and _____ spindle machines.
    a. upward   b. horizontal   c. inclinable   d. clockwise
11. Sometimes the finishing operation will be _____ by a semi-finishing operation.
    a. proceeded   b. followed   c. preceded   d. predetermined
12. Can you _____ the position of the hole as quickly as you can?
    a. overhang   b. locate   c. maintain   d. enlarge
13. The _____ of the tower against the sky is very magnificent. Which of the following can not be used to complete the sentence?
    a. profile   b. contour   c. configuration   d. silhouette
14. The mountain is _____ the blue sky.
    a. relieved against   b. released from   c. related to   d. rescued by
15. The small feed rate for boring can _____ the lack of rigidity of the boring bar.
    a. compensate for   b. compensate by
    c. compensate with   d. compensate to

II. Translate the following expressions into Chinese.
   1. center hole   2. lathe dog   3. spindle nose
   4. cylindrical grinding machine   5. faceplate jaw   6. chuck jaw
   7. peripheral milling   8. face milling   9. rough boring
   10. finish boring

III. Match the following words in column (I) with the statements in column (II).
   (I)   (II)
   ( ) 1. spindle   a. part of a machine that holds something
   ( ) 2. caliper   b. a hard quick repeated sound made by machines
   ( ) 3. chuck   c. a part of a machine shaped like a stick
   ( ) 4. chatter   d. a tool used for measuring thickness
   ( ) 5. profile   e. an edge or shape of something seen against a background
   ( ) 6. cutter   f. a tool used for cutting
   ( ) 7. chip   g. a small piece of metal
   ( ) 8. contour   h. the shape of the outer edge of something
   ( ) 9. groove   i. a thin line cut into a surface
   ( ) 10. abrasion   j. an area on the surface that has been damaged by rubbing

IV. Translate the following sentence into Chinese and pay attention to the adjectives and adverbs.
   1. The metal may be fluid, plastic, elastic, ductile or malleable.
   2. Electrical discharge machining has proved especially valuable in the machining of super-tough, electrically conductive materials.
   3. In machining, grinding processes are most often used as finish machining processes.
   4. Boring operations are performed to enlarge, finish and accurately locate holes.
   5. The engine lathe has been replaced in today's production shops by a wide variety of automatic lathes.
   6. The design engineer must be careful in using tolerances of an experimental part.

Unit11 Broaching、Sawing、Drilling and Reaming

Passage Ⅰ Broaching

Broaching is a process for internal or external machining of flat, round, or contoured surfaces. Machines of different types are used to push or pull a multitooth cutting tool or the workpiece in relation to each other to remove material. Each tooth on the cutting tool (broach) is generally higher than the preceding tooth (see Fig. 11-1). As a result, the depth of the cut increases the operation progresses.

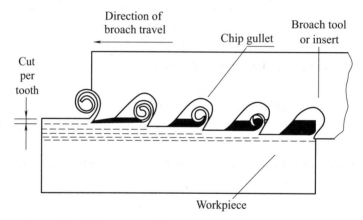

Fig. 11-1 Broach tool on which each successive tooth is generally

Generally, broaching machines differ from other machine tools in that they provide only cutting speed and force—the feed is built into the broach. Infeed, however, is provided by the workholding fixture for some applications. Another exception is helical broaching in which the machine provides rotary motion.

Broaching also differs from other machining processes in that roughing, semifinishing, and finishing teeth are often positioned along the axis of a single tool. This permits completing an operation in a single pass. Several types of broaches are sometimes used in combination to cut different surfaces on the workpiece simultaneously.

Broaching applications are of two major types: external (surface) broaching and internal broaching. Both types are used for machining configurations ranging from flat surfaces to complex contours on or in workpieces varying from small precision components to very large part made from many different materials. For some applications both external and internal broaching are combined in one operation, while broaching is general not considered to be a heavy stock is removal operation, there are applications of surface broaching in which 12.7mm or more of stock is removed in a single pass.

Workpieces with internal surfaces to be broached require a starting hole for insertion of the tool. Surfaces to be broached must be parallel to the direction of tool or work travel, but uniformly rotating sections such as helical gear teeth can be broached by rotating the tool or work as each moves in relation to the other. No obstructions such as protuberances on or in the workpieces can block the passage of the broach, but blind holes may be broached by limiting the travel of a series of short push-type broaches. A recess, however, larger in diameter than the hole to be broached must be provided at the bottom of the blind hole for chip space.

Surface broaching applications are practically unlimited. Any external form can be produced as long as the surfaces are in a straight line and unobstructed. Such forms include slots and keyways, flat and contoured surfaces, rack and gear teeth, and serrations.

An infinite number of forms can also be produced by internal broaching. In addition to machining round, square, rectangular, and other shaped holes, the process is uses to cut contoured surfaces, keyways, splines, serrations, and gear teeth. This method is also used to rifle the bores of gun barrels. Starting holes for internal broaching are generally produced by casting, forging, punching, drilling, or boring.

Broaching Machines

Broaching is done on a variety of types of equipment, including portable units, hand-held pulling units, and machines ranging from small manually operated or powered arbor presses to large horizontal surface broaching machines. Conventional presses, however, are multifunction machines and are seldom used for production broaching. Major requirements for any broaching machine include accurate relative motion between the tool and workpiece and rigid construction to withstand the high forces encountered. Most machines are of simple design and are very reliable.

Classification of Broaching Machines

Broaching machines can be classified by operational characteristics and/or the type of operation performed when the machines are properly tooled. With respect to the direction of cutting stroke, broaching machines are classified as vertical, with the axis of the cutting stroke perpendicular to the floor; horizontal, with the cutting stroke parallel to the floor; and special, encompasses all other variation or combinations. They can be further classified as surface, internal, and universal or combination broaching machines.

Types of power used to drive the broaching machines are also used to describe them. Machines are powered hydraulically or mechanically, with hydraulic drives in greatest use for vertical and smaller horizontal machines. Some machines, however, such as continuous (chain) types and large, horizontal surface broaching types, are almost exclusively powered electromechanically. With the energy savings possible with electromechanical drives, this type of power is now being used on other broaching machines.

Further classification of broaching machines is based on operational characteristics such as single or dual-ram, pulldown or pullup, pushdown or pushup, rotary, continuous, pot-type, and blind spline. A schematic representation of broaching machine classification according to type of drive, direction of cutting stroke, and operational characteristics is presented in Fig. 11-2.

Broaching machines are available with single-, dual-, or variable-speed drives. For some applications, dual-speed controls are desirable to drive the broach at one speed during part of

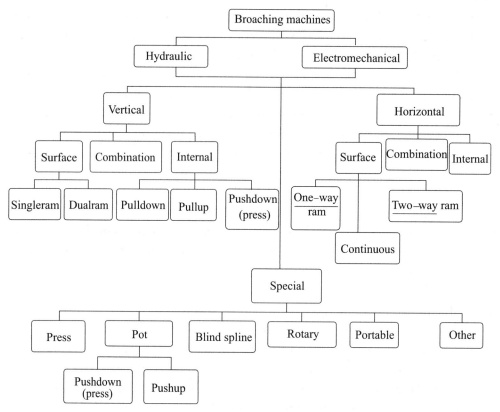

Fig. 11-2 Classification of broaching machines according to type of drive, direction of cutting stroke, and operational characteristics

the stroke and at a second speed during another portion of the stroke.

Machine control systems can range from simple to sophisticate. Advanced control systems available on some machines can accommodate any required sequence of ram motions, loading, clamping, workpiece movement, unclamping, and unloading. Programmable controllers are used on some machines. While numerical control (NC) and computer numerical control (CNC) do not ordinarily lend themselves to the simple requirements of broaching, they have been used for some special applications.

Many different accessories and attachments are available for use with broaching machines. These include reciprocating shuttle, tilting, and dial tables with infeed, crossfeed, or rotary motions for vertical surface broaching machines. Automatic loading/unloading, clamping/unclamping, and broach retrieval systems are often desirable, depending on the application, and chip conveyors are frequently used for high-production applications involving large-volume metal removal. Many different material handing devices are available to automate the broaching process. Broaching machines have been incorporated into transfer lines that also perform other operations such as drilling, boring, and milling.

Broaching Machines Selection

Important factor in selecting a broaching machine for a specific application include the type of cutting tool needed for the operation and the production requirements. Basic machine features to be considered are the configuration, capacity in terms of tons of ram force, ram stroke and speed, and dimensional capacity for tooling and workpiece. Machine size and capacity are functions of the tool and workpiece sizes, broaching power requirements, and available production space.

Vertical broaching machines offer the advantages of reduced floor-space requirements; having the tools move in a vertical plane, thus avoiding possible sag; generally better cutting fluid dispersement and chip-removal facilities; and easier workpiece loading, clamping, and unloading. Disadvantages of some vertical types of machines, compared to horizontal types, include the need for high ceilings or deep floor pits for long stroke machines and, generally, more difficult access for toolchanging. Some small, vertical, table-top machines, however, are relatively inexpensive, and feature fast changeover from one setup to the next.

Horizontal broaching machines usually have the advantage of being able to handle larger and heavier work piece and longer broaches for greater stock removal. They often provide increased versatility in that they can be set up quickly to broach different parts. With the exception of continuous-type machines; special machines; and large, fast, horizontal broaching machines, however, most broaching machines in service and being built today are vertical.

Words and Expressions

multitooth /ˈmʌltituːθ/ n.	多齿
adj.	多齿的
gullet /ˈgʌlit/ n.	锯齿间空隙
broaching machine	拉床
infeed /inˈfiːd/ n.	横进给，横向进磨，横切
protuberance /prəˈtjuːbərəns/ n.	凸起，隆起
unobstructed /ˌʌnəbˈstrʌktid/ adj.	无阻碍的，没有阻挡的，自由的
serration /seˈreiʃən/ n.	锯齿，细齿
rifle /ˈraifl/ n.	在（枪膛）内制来复线
drive /draiv/ vt.	驱动，传动
n.	驱动，传动
electromechanical /iˈlektrəumiˈkænikəl/ adj.	机电式的
pulldown /ˈpulˈdaun/ n.	下拉
pullup /ˈpulˈʌp/ n.	拉起，吸起
pushdown /ˈpuʃˈdaun/ n.	下推
pushup /ˈpuʃˈʌp/ n.	上推
one-way /ˈwʌnˈwei/ adj.	单向的
two-way /ˈtuːˈwei/ adj.	双向的，两路的
clamping /ˈklæmpiŋ/ n.	固定，卡紧
unclamp /ˈʌnˈklæmp/ vt.	松开…的夹钳
accessory /ækˈsesəri/ n.	附件，零件
adj.	附属的，补充的
crossfeed /ˈkrɔsfiːd/ n.	横向送进，横进给
chip conveyor	切屑输送机
sag /sæg/ n.	下垂，垂度

dispersement /dis'pə:smənt/ n.　　　　　分散
toolchanging /'tu:ltʃeindʒiŋ/ n.　　　　刀具更换
table-top /'teibl'tɔp/ adj.　　　　　　　台式的

Exercises

Choose the best answer for each of the following according to the information of the text.

1. A starting hole is needed in workpiece with internal surface to be broached for _____ .
   a. machining configuration　　　　　b. cutting different surfaces
   c. inserting the tool　　　　　　　　d. blocking the passage of the broach
2. The word '_____' cannot be used to describe the broaching machines.
   a. vertical　　　b. special　　　c. universal　　　d. parallel
3. The difference between broaching machines and other machine tools is that broaching machines _____ .
   a. are only for internal machining　　　b. are only for external machining
   c. only provide cutting speed and force　d. are used for cutting metals
4. Each tooth on the cutting tool is generally higher than the preceding tooth, which results in _____ .
   a. decrease of the depth of the cut　　b. rotary motion
   c. increase of the depth of the cut　　d. relative motion
5. The word '_____' cannot be used to describe the advantage of broaching.
   a. high-productivity　　b. economy　　c. versatility　　d. complexity
6. Major requirements for any broaching machine exclude _____ .
   a. accurate relative motion　　　　　b. rigid construction
   c. simple design　　　　　　　　　　d. both a and b
7. When a broaching machine is to be selected, the following factors should be considered except _____ .
   a. type of cutting tool　　　　　　　b. production requirements
   c. basic machine features　　　　　　d. control system
8. Which of the following about machine control system is NOT true?
   a. Machine control system can be either simple or complex?
   b. Dual-speed controls sometimes are necessary to drives the broach.
   c. Advanced control systems on some machines can only provide required sequence of loading.
   d. Some machines are supplied with programmed controllers.
9. The advantages of vertical broaching machine don't include _____ .
   a. reducing floor-space requirements
   b. avoiding possible sag
   c. need for high ceilings
   d. easier workpiece loading, clamping, and unloading
10. Most widely-used broaching machines are _____ .
    a. continuous-type machines　　　　b. special machines
    c. large and fast horizontal machines　d. vertical machines

Passage II Sawing

Sawing is the parting of material by using metal disks, blades, or abrasive disks as the cutting tools. Sawing a piece from stock for further machining is called cutoff sawing, while shaping or forming a piece is referred to as contour sawing.

Machine sawing of metal is performed by five types of saws or processes: hacksawing, band sawing, cold sawing, friction sawing, and abrasive sawing.

Hacksaws are used principally as cutoff tools. The toothed blade, held in tension, is reciprocated across the workpiece. A vise holds the stock in position. The blade is fed into the work by gravity or springs. Sometimes a mechanical or hydraulic feed is used. Automatic machines, handling bar-length stock, are used for continuous production.

Band saws cut rapidly and are suited for either cutoff or contour sawing. The plane in which the blade operates classifies the machine as being either vertical or horizontal. Band saws are basically a flexible endless band of steel running over pulleys or wheels. The band has teeth on one side and is operated under tension. Guides keep it running true. The frame of the horizontal type is pivoted to allow positioning of the workpiece in the vise. Horizontal machines are used for either straight or angular cuts. A table that supports the workpiece and the wide throat between the upright portions of the blade makes the vertical band saw ideal for contour work. Band saws operating at high speed are frequently used as friction saws.

Cold sawing is principally a cutoff operation. The blade is a circular disk with cutting teeth on its periphery. Blades range in size from a few inches to several feet in diameter. The cutting teeth may be cut into the periphery of the disk or they may be inserts of a harder material. The blade moves into the stock with a positive feed. Stock is positioned manually in some cold-sawing machines, while other models are equipped for automatic cycle sawing.

Friction sawing is a rapid process used to cut steel as well as certain plastics. This process is not satisfactory for cast iron and nonferrous metals. Cutting is done as the high-speed blade wipes the metal from the kerf after softening it with frictional heat. Circular alloy-steel blades perform cutoff work, while frictional band saws do both cutoff and contour sawing. Circular blades are frequently cooled by water or air. Circular blades are advanced into the work, while thick work-pieces require power-table feed when friction-cut on a band saw.

Abrasive sawing is a cutoff process using thin rubber or bakelite bonded abrasive disks. In addition to steel, other materials such as nonferrous metals, ceramics, glass, certain plastics, and hard rubber are cut by this method. Cutting is done by the abrasive action of the grit in the disk.

Abrasive disks are operated either wet or dry. For heavy cutting a cooling agent is generally used. The workpiece is firmly held while the wheel traverses through it. Machines are made in manually operated and automatic models.

Words and Expressions

abrasive disk   砂轮，磨盘
contour sawing   仿形锯法

hacksawing /'hæk'sɔːiŋ/ n.　　弓锯法
band sawing　　　　　　　　　带锯法
hacksaw /'hæksɔː/ n.　　　　　弓锯
band saw　　　　　　　　　　 带锯
kerf /kəːf/ n.　　　　　　　　切口，截口，锯痕
friction-cut /'frikʃən'kʌt/ v.　摩擦切割
bakelite /'beikəlait/ n.　　　　酚醛塑料，胶木
grit /grit/ n.　　　　　　　　　磨料粒，小砂粒

Passage Ⅲ　Drilling

Holes are one of the most common features in products manufactured today. Therefore, drilling and other related processes and tools are extremely important. Holes as small as 0.005in may be drilled using special techniques. On the other hand, holes larger than 2 to $2\frac{1}{2}$ in. in diameter are seldom drilled, because other processes and techniques are less expensive.

The twist drill (shown in Fig. 11-3) is the most common type of drill. The shank of the drill is held by the machine tool, which in turn imparts a rotary motion; this shank may be straight or tapered. The body of the drill is typically made up of two spiral grooves known as flutes, which are defined by a helix angle that is generally about 30° but can vary depending on

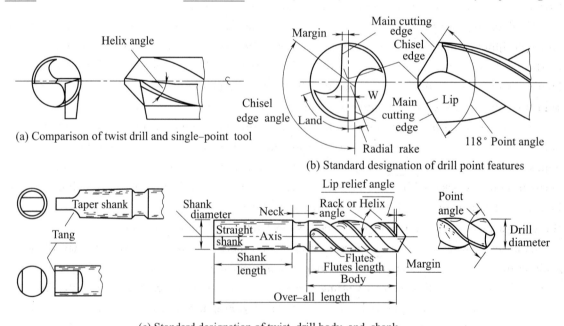

(a) Comparison of twist drill and single-point tool

(b) Standard designation of drill point features

(c) Standard designation of twist-drill body and shank

Fig. 11-3　Geometry of the twist drill

the material properties of the workpiece. The point of the drill (see Fig. 11-3) generally from a 118° angle and includes a 10° clearance angle and chisel edge. The chisel edge is flat with a web thickness of approximately 0.015 x drill diameter. This edge can cause problems in hole location owing to its ability to 'walk' on a surface before engaging the workpiece. In the case of brittle materials, drill point angles of less than 118°are used, while ductile materials use larger points angles and smaller clearance angles.

Complex hole configurations may often be called for; these include multiple diameters, chamfers, countersinks, and combinations of these, as illustrated in Fig. 11-4. In each of these cases it is possible to make special combination drills that can produce the configurations shown in a single operation. Although expensive, they can be economically justified for sufficient volume.

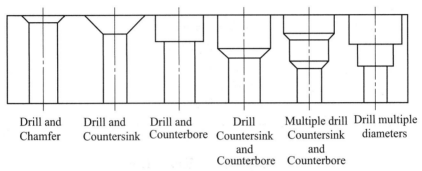

Fig. 11-4　Internal surfaces produced by special-purpose drills

The flat chisel edge, which can 'walk' on the surface of the workpiece, and the long, slender shaft and body of the twist drill, which can deflect, make it difficult to machine holes to tight tolerances. A combination center drill and countersink can be used to accurately start a hole, owing to its small web thickness and its tendency to deflect only very small amounts (because of a relatively large diameter-to-length ratio). Truing of the hole to make it straight is accomplished by boring. Reaming the hole provides a better finish as well as more accurate sizing.

The feed rate of a drill is normally proportional to its diameter, because it depends on the volume of chips the flutes can handle. However the feed is independent of the cutting speed, which is a function of the tool-work combination. A rule of thumb would give a feed rate as approximately $d/65$, so that a $\frac{3}{4}$—in.-diameter drill would have a feed rate of about 0.012in./rev. Although the hole wall tends to support the drill when the hole depth exceeds three times the drill diameter, there is a tendency for buckling to occur and the feed rate should be reduced.

Most drills are made form high-speed steel because of its relatively low cost and ease of manufacture. Some types of carbide drill are now available commercially. The demands of numerically controlled machine tools have led to the development of drills that will produce more precise holes and that will originate a hole in line with the centerline of the drill-press spindle. Drills that have heavier webs, less stickout, double margins, and are ground with a spiral point help meet these new demands.

Words and Expressions

twist drill　　　　　　　　　　［机］麻花钻，螺旋钻
flute /fluːt/ n.　　　　　　　　沟槽
helix /ˈhiːliks/ n.　　　　　　　螺旋线

helix angle	螺旋角
clearance angle	后角，间隙角
chisel edge	横刃，凿锋
web /web/ n.	腹部，缩颈
point angle	顶角
tang /tæŋ/ n.	柄舌
lip relief angle	钻缘后角
margin /'mɑ:dʒin/ n.	钻缘
countersink /'kauntə,siŋk/ vt.	钻孔装埋，打埋头孔
n.	埋头孔，锥形扩孔
counterbore /'kauntə,bɔ:/ n.	镗孔，沉孔
rule of thumb	经验法则
drill-press /'dril,pres/ n.	钻床，压钻机
stickout /'stikaut/ n.	悬臂

Passage IV Reaming

Reaming is a machining process for enlarging, smoothing and/or accurately sizing existing holes by means of multiedge fluted cutting tools (reamers). As the reamers and/or workpiece is rotated and advanced relative to each other, chips are produced to remove relatively small amounts of material from the hole wall. Reaming may be performed on the same type of machines used for drilling.

Accuracy of the hole and quality of finish produced by reaming depends primarily upon the condition of the starting hole, rigidity of the machine and fixture, correct speeds and feeds, a suitable and properly applied cutting fluid, and precise resharpening of dull tools.

Since stock removal is small and must be uniform in reaming, the starting holes (drilled or otherwise produced) must have relatively good roundness, straightness, and finish. Reamers tend to follow the existing centerline of the hole being reamed, and in limited instances it may be necessary to bore the holes prior to reaming to maintain required tolerances. With the proper conditions and operating parameters, reaming can produce close tolerances and smooth finishes.

Reamers

A reamer is a rotary cutting tool, generally of cylindrical or conical shape, intended for enlarging and finishing holes to accurate dimensions. It is usually equipped with two or more peripheral channels or flutes, either parallel to its axis or in a right-or left-hand helix as required. Those with helical flutes provide smooth shear cutting, are less subject to chatter, and produce a better finish. The flutes form cutting teeth and provide channels for removing the chips.

Kinds of Reamers

Reamers are made in many different forms, including solid and inserted-blade types, adjustable and nonadjustable; they are available for either manual operation (hand reamers) or for machine use (chucking reamers). Materials from which cutting elements of most production reamers are made include high-speed steel and cemented carbides.

Carbide reamers These tools are being used increasingly because of their longer life, improved accuracy, and resistance.

Bore reamers These tools combine boring and reaming in a single operation to minimize problems with respect to hole size, straightness, and finish. Single-point bore reamers, for use in applications for which guide bushings can be used, have a single-point cutting edge on the end of the tool, followed by a reaming section. Multipoint bore reamers are available for applications for which bushings cannot be used.

Coolant-fed reamers These tools, having means (usually internal passages) for directing coolant to the cutting edges, offer advantages for some applications, particularly when reaming blind holes. In such applications, reduced friction and temperatures at the reamer/workpiece interface decrease wear and lengthen tool life. In some cases, feeds and speeds can be increased and improved accuracies and smoother finishes obtained. The initial cost of coolant-fed reamers is higher, but increased productivity and improved quality often make them economically desirable.

Reamer Holders/Drivers

Reamers are commonly held and driven by three-jaw chucks, straight sleeves and setscrews, and, for taper shanks, sleeves or sockets. Reamers with adapters for quick-chance chucks are used for production applications.

When reamers must guide themselves into previously made holes, they require floating holders to maintain alignment. There are several types of floating holders. Some permit angular float, others permit a parallel (axial) float, and still others permit both angular and parallel float.

Floating holders have some limitations. If the reamer axis is vertical, floating reamer drives often do a good job of correcting for small amounts of misalignment. When the workpieces rotate, however, as is the case on screw machines, lathes, and some other machine tools, floating holders are sometimes inadequate. This is because relatively large amounts of misalignment are often found on these machines and because the weight of the reamer and holder tend to push the tool into an off-center position.

Some full floating holders, which compensate for both angular and parallel misalignment, are equipped with springs or other components to counterbalance the mass of the holder. A floating holder cannot generally operate both vertically and horizontally and still correct for both angular and parallel misalignment. Application details (vertical or horizontal operation and rotating or stationary tool) should be specified when a floating holder is ordered.

Workholding for Reaming

Jig design and the use of bushings for reaming are essentially the same as for drilling. Major functions of the jigs and bushings are accurate locating, supporting, and securing of the workpieces, and precise guiding of the tools. A difference for reaming is that closer tolerances are generally required on both the jigs and bushings.

Operating Parameters for Reaming

Factors that must be established for efficient and economical reaming include the proper cutting speed, feed rate, and cutting fluid to be used. Other important considerations are resharpening the reamers and troubleshooting the operations.

Words and Expressions

resharpen /ˌriːˈʃɑːpən/ v.	尖刃修磨
hand reamer	手铰刀，手用铰刀
chucking reamer	机用铰刀
floating holder	浮动刀夹
off-center /ˈɔ(ː)fˈsentə/ adj.	偏离中心的
adv.	偏离中心地
jig /dʒɪg/ n.	夹具，钻模
troubleshoot /ˈtrʌblˌʃuːt/ v.	故障检修
n.	排除故障

Exercises

Ⅰ. Choose the best answer for each of the following sentences.

1. When I said some people are stupid, I wasn't _____ you.
    a. referring to   b. relating to   c. responding to   d. refraining from
2. Engine in which pistons move backwards and forwards inside cylinders is called _____ engine.
    a. automatic   b. abrasive   c. reciprocating   d. hydraulic
3. The frontier of the country _____ from the northern hills to the southern coast.
    a. covers   b. ranges   c. moves   d. includes
4. The highway _____ a wild and mountainous region.
    a. travels   b. traverses   c. transverses   d. transfers
5. On the stage, a _____ graceful ballet dancer is performing attractively and the audiences are cheering up.
    a. thin   b. slim   c. slender   d. bony
6. The price of this kind of machining tools increases are _____ to the increases in the costs of production.
    a. proportional   b. prepositional   c. provisional   d. principal
7. The style of architecture in this region _____ the ancient Greeks.
    a. originated by   b. originated from   c. originated after   d. originated in
8. The _____ of the drill is held by the machine tool, which in turn imparts a rotary motion.
    a. body   b. shank   c. point   d. edge
9. The truing of the hole to make it straight can be done by _____.
    a. drilling   b. reaming   c. boring   d. grinding
10. The _____ of the metal caused it to crack.

a. hardness   b. rigidity   c. firmness   d. stiffness

II. Translate the following expressions into Chinese.

1. cutoff sawing   2. contour sawing   3. hack sawing   4. band sawing
5. cold sawing   6. friction sawing   7. abrasive sawing   8. carbide sawing
9. bore reamer   10. coolant-fed reamer

III. Translate the following passage into English.

金属切削加工在制造业中得到了广泛的应用。其特点是工件在加工前具有足够大的尺寸，可以将工件最终的几何形状尺寸包容在里面。不需要的材料以切屑、颗粒等形式被去除掉。切削是获得所需的工作尺寸公差和表面质量的必要手段。

Unit 12　Lathes and Other Machines

Passage I　Lathes, Boring Machines and Planing Machine

Lathes

Lathes are designed to rotate the workpiece and feed the cutting tool in the direction necessary to generate the required <u>machined surface</u>.

The most common form of lathe is the <u>turret</u> lathe shown <u>diagrammatically</u> in Fig. 12-1 (a); it consists of a horizontal <u>bed</u> supporting the headstock, the carriage and the turret. The workpiece is gripped in a chuck or collet or is mounted on a faceplate mounted on the end of the <u>main spindle</u> of the machine.

The rotation of the workpiece is provided by an electric motor driving the main spindle through a series of gears.

Cutting tools are mounted on the cross slide and on the turret. The tool on the cross slide can be driven or fed parallel to or normal to the axis of rotation of the workpiece. The turret can be indexed to bring the various tools into position and can be driven or fed along the bed of the lathe.

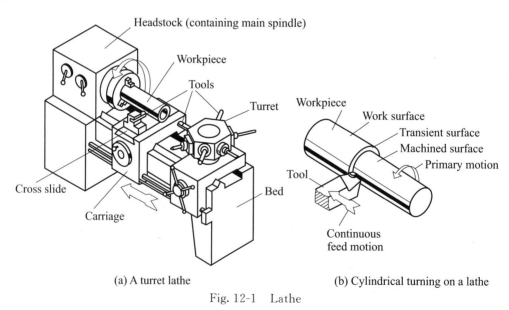

(a) A turret lathe　　　　　　　　　(b) Cylindrical turning on a lathe

Fig. 12-1　Lathe

Modern turret lathes are provided with computer control of all of the workpiece and tool motions. These are known as computer numerical control (CNC) lathes and the tool or the cross slide can be fed in any direction in the horizontal plane to generate a required contour on the workpiece.

Fig. 12-1 (b) shows a cylindrical surface being generated by rotation of the workpiece and the movement of the carriage along the lathe bed; this operation is known as cylindrical turning.

The feed-motion setting on the lathe is the distance moved by the tool during each revolution of the workpiece. The feed f for all machine tools is defined as the displacement of the tool relative to the workpiece, in the direction of feed motion, per stroke or per revolution of the workpiece or tool. Thus, to turn a cylindrical surface of length l_w, the number of revolutions of the workpiece is l_w/f, and the machining time t_m, is given by

$$t_m = l_w/(fn_w)$$

where n_w is the rotational speed of the workpiece.

It should be emphasized at this point that t_m is the time for one pass of the tool (one cut) along the workpiece. This single pass does not necessarily mean, however, that the machining operation is completed. If the first cut is designed to remove a large amount of material at high feed (roughing cut), the forces generated during the operation will probably have caused significant deflections in the machine structure. The resulting loss of accuracy may necessitate a further machining operation at low feed (finish cut) to bring the workpiece diameter within the limits specified and to provide a smooth machined surface. For these reasons, the workpiece is often machined oversize during the roughing cut, leaving a small amount of material that will subsequently be removed during the finishing cut.

Vertical-Boring Machine

A horizontal-spindle lathe is not suitable for turning heavy, large diameter workpieces. The axis of the machine spindle would have to be so elevated that the machine operator could not easily reach the tool- and work-holding devices. In addition, it would be difficult to mount the workpiece on a vertical faceplate or support it between centers; for this reason a machine that operates on the same principle as a lathe, but has a vertical axis, is used and is known as a vertical-boring machine (Fig. 12-2). Like the lathe, this machine rotates the workpiece and applies continuous, linear feed motion to the tool.

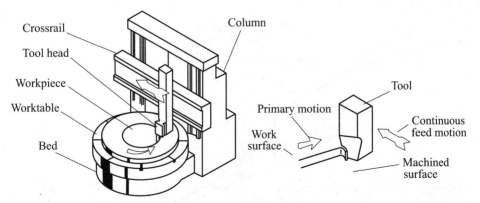

Fig. 12-2   Faxing on a vertical-boring machine

Single-point tools are employed and the operations carried out are generally limited to turning, facing, and boring.

The horizontal work-holding surface, which facilitates the positioning of large workpieces consists of a rotary table having radial T slots for clamping purposes.

Horizontal-Boring Machine

Another machine described here that uses single-point tools and has a rotary primary motion is a horizontal-boring machine (Fig. 12-3). This machine is needed mostly for heavy noncylindrical workpieces in which an internal cylindrical surface is to be machined. In general, the words horizontal or vertical used when describing a machine tool refer to the orientation of the machine spindle that provides primary motion (main spindle). Thus, in the horizontal borer, the main spindle is horizontal.

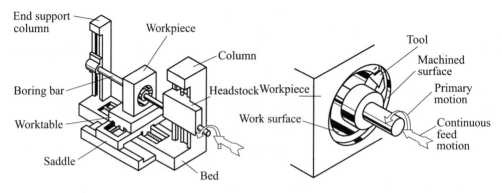

Fig. 12-3 Boring on a horizontal-boring machine

The principal feature of the machine is that the workpiece remains stationary during machining, and all the generating motions are applied to the tool. The most common machining process is boring and is shown in the figure. Boring is achieved by rotating the tool, which is mounted on a boring bar connected to the spindle, and then feeding the spindle, boring bar, and tool along the axis of rotation. The machine-tool motions which can be used to move the workpiece are for positioning of the workpiece and are not generally employed white machining is taking place. A facing operation can be carried out by using a special toolholder (Fig. 12-4) that feeds the tool radially as it rotates.

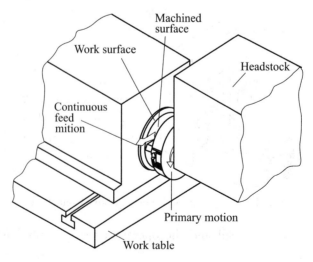

Fig. 12-4 Facing on a horizontal-boring machine

Again, the equations developed earlier for the machining time, and the metal-removal rate in boring and facing will apply.

Planing Machine

The planer is suitable for generating flat surfaces on very large parts. With this machine (Fig. 12-5) a linear primary motion is applied to the workpiece and the tool is fed at right angles to this motion. The primary motion is normally accomplished by a rack-and-pinion drive using a variable speed motor and the feed motion is intermittent. The work is held on the machine table using the T slots provided. The machining time t_m and metal-removal rate Z_w can be estimated as follows:

$$t_m = b_w/(fn_r)$$

where b_w is the width of the surface to be machined, n_r is the frequency of cutting strokes and f is the feed. The metal-removal rate Z_w during cutting is given by

$$Z_w = fa_p v$$

where v is the cutting speed, and a_p is the depth of cut (the depth of the layer of material to be removed).

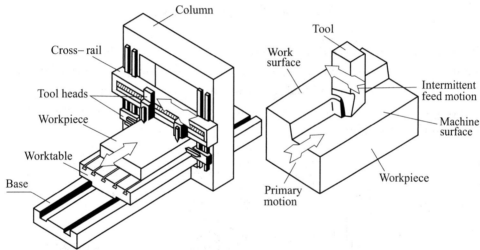

Fig. 12-5 Production of a flat surface on a planer

Words and Expressions

machined surface	加工面
turret /'tʌrit/ n.	转刀架，转塔
diagrammatically /ˌdaiəgrə'mætikəli/ adv.	用图解法
bed /bed/ n.	床身
main spindle	主轴
transient surface	过渡面
roughing cut	粗切削
necessitate /ni'sesiteit/ vt.	使需要，使成为必需
elevate /'eliveit/ vt.	升高，增加
facilitate /fə'siliteit/ vt.	提供

orientation /ˌɔːriənˈteɪʃən/ n.　　方向，方位，定位，倾斜性
rack-and-pinion /ˈrækˈəndˈpinjən/ n.　　齿条与齿轮
intermittent /ˌintə(ː)ˈmitənt/ adj.　　间歇的，断断续续的
base /beis/ n.　　基座，底座

Exercises

Answer the following questions in detail according to the information of the text.

1. Why is the work-piece often machined oversize during the roughing cut?
2. How is the feed for all machine tools defined?
3. Why is a vertical-boring machine used to operate on the same principle as a lathe to replace a horizontal-spindle lathe?
4. What is the limit of single-point tools?
5. What do the words 'horizontal' and 'vertical' refer to when they are used to describe machine tools?

Passage Ⅱ　Drill press

A drill press (Fig. 12-6) can perform only those operations where the tool is rotated and fed along its axis of rotation. The workpiece always remains stationary during the machining process. On small drill presses, the tool is fed by the manual operation of a <u>lever</u> (known as <u>sensitive drilling</u>). Both the <u>worktable</u> and the <u>head</u> can be raised and lowered to accommodate workpieces of different heights.

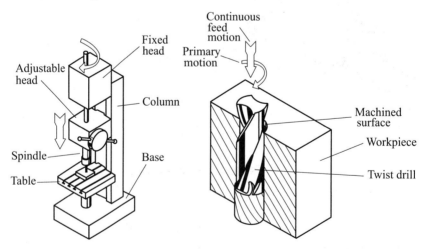

Fig. 12-6　Drilling on a drill press

The most common operation performed on this machine is drilling with a twist drill to generate an internal cylindrical surface. This tool has two cutting edges, each of which removes its share of the work material.

The machining time t_m is given by

$$t_m = l_w / (f n_t)$$

where l_w is the length of the hole produced, f is the feed (per revolution) and n_t is the rotational speed of the tool.

The metal-removal rate Z_w may be obtained by dividing the volume of material removed during one revolution of the drill by the time for one revolution. Thus

$$Z_w = (\pi/4) f d_m^2 n_t$$

where d_m is the diameter of the machined hole. If an existing hole of diameter d_w is being enlarged, then

$$Z_w = (\pi/4) f (d_m^2 - d_w^2) n_t$$

Because the chips removed by the cutting edges take a helical form and travel up the drill flutes, twist drills are usually considered suitable for machining holes having a length no more than five times their diameter. Special drills requiring special drilling machines are available for drilling deeper holes.

The workpiece is often held in a vise bolted to the machine worktable. The drilling of a concentric hole in a cylindrical workpiece, however, is often carried out on a turret lathe with the drill mounted on the turret.

Large twist drills are usually provided with a taper shank. This shank is designed to be inserted in a corresponding taper hole in the end of the machine spindle.

Small twist drills have a parallel shank and are held in a three-jaw chuck of the familiar type used in hand drills. These chucks are provided with a taper shank for location in the drill-press spindle or in the tailstock of a lathe.

Several other machining operations can be performed on a drill press, and some of the more common ones are illustrated in Fig. 12-7. The <u>center-drilling</u> operation produces a shallow, conical hole with clearance at the bottom. This center hole can provide a guide for a subsequent drilling operation to prevent the drill point from 'wandering' as the hole is started. The reaming operation is intended for finishing a previously drilled hole. The reamer is similar to a drill, but has several cutting edges and straight flutes. It is intended to remove a small amount of work material only, but it considerably improves the accuracy and surface finish of a hole. The <u>spot-facing</u> operation is designed to provide a flat surface around the end of a hole and perpendicular to its axis; this flat surface can provide a suitable seating for a washer and nut for example.

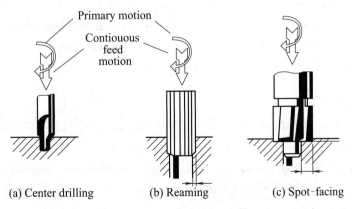

(a) Center drilling   (b) Reaming   (c) Spot-facing

Fig. 12-7 Some drill-press operations

Words and Expressions

lever /ˈliːvə/ n.	手柄
sensitive drilling	手压钻削
worktable /ˈwəːkˈteibl/ n.	工作台
head /hed/ n.	（动力）头，颈部
center drilling	打中心孔
spot-facing /ˌspɔtˈfeisiŋ/ n.	锪孔，锪端面

Passage Ⅲ Grinding Wheels and Grinding Machines

Grinding Wheels

A grinding wheel is made up of many small grit particles held together by a bonding material. It may properly be called a cutting tool with many cutting teeth, since each projection from the face of the wheel cuts a tiny chip resembling the larger chips made by the cutting tools described earlier. The two kinds of grit most commonly used are silicon carbide and aluminum oxide, both in a crystalline form. The crystals are crushed; the resultant particles of grit, sorted as to size, are bonded by some material, such as vitrified clay, glass, rubber, shellac, or phenolic resin. The cutting surface of the wheel may be the periphery, the side, or both the periphery and the side.

As the cutting edges of the small grit particles become dull, the cutting forces increase and pull these dull particles from the bonding material. This exposes new sharp grit particles and is the natural wear of the wheel. If the contour of the cutting face of a grinding wheel includes too sharp an angle, the particles of grit at this point are not sufficiently supported and cause rapid wear of the wheel by prematurely pulling out of the bonding material.

There are many cutting edges to share the dulling effect of intermittent cuts, so that the minimum thickness of chip that can be removed by grinding may be less than the thickness of the cutting edge of the grit. Since this edge is extremely thin, it is practicable to machine certain surfaces to a greater degree of accuracy by the use of a grinding wheel than by the use of any other cutting tool. The wheel pressure required to remove minute chips is light and causes comparatively little deflection of the work or the wheel.

Grinding Machines

The more common types of grinding machines are the universal, cylindrical, internal, vertical-surface, horizontal-surface, and centerless grinders.

Universal and cylindrical grinders Work may be mounted between the centers and chucked in the spindle of a universal grinding machine. For cylindrical grinding, the table, on which the spindle and tailstock are mounted, is parallel to the axis of the grinding wheel. For other grinding operations it is possible to swivel the spindle head, feed the grinding wheel horizontally toward the table, and give the grinding wheel a short reciprocating motion parallel to the table motion. The cylindrical grinder is a production machine confined to grinding straight and taper cylindrical work.

Internal grinder The internal grinder is used to finish internal surfaces, such as engine cylinders, ball-bearing races, and similar work that requires excellent accuracy and high finish. The work is revolved against the grinding wheel in an opposite direction and at a much slower speed than the wheel. The wheel must be smaller in diameter than the surface to be ground, and when this surface is of small diameter, the revolutions per minute of the wheel must be extremely high in order to produce the necessary surface speed on the periphery of the wheel. A small wheel wears very rapidly, so that the work should be designed with very little stock to be removed by grinding. Adequate wheel clearance should be allowed at the ends of the cut.

Surface grinders A surface grinder is a general-purpose machine tool used to finish machine a plane surface. There are two types, the horizontal and the vertical. In the horizontal type the axis of the grinding wheel is horizontal, and grinding is done on its periphery. In the vertical type, the axis of the grinding wheel is vertical, and grinding is done on its bottom face. Both types of grinders may have either a reciprocating table or a revolving table. Magnetic material may be held to these tables by magnetic chucks. Nonmagnetic material is clamped or bolted to the tables. Surface grinders with rotary tables are particularly adapted to grinding a number of like small pieces simultaneously.

Centerless grinder The centerless grinder is a repetitive machine tool used to produce a fine, accurate finish on cylindrical, conical, and spherical surfaces, such as piston pins, roller and ball bearings, taper pins, and small shafts. It is by far the most economical method of producing such surfaces if the quantities are such as to justify the setup. The principal elements of this machine are the grinding wheel, regulating wheel, and the work rest. These three elements, properly located with respect to each other, serve to support and guide the work while it is being ground, no other support or guide being necessary. The regulating wheel controls the rotational speed of the work and the rate of feed.

The through-feed method is used to grind cylindrical parts that have no interfering shoulders. The work is passed between the wheels from one side of the machine, entering with a rough surface and emerging from the other side with an accurately finished surface. The infeed method of grinding is used to grind cylindrical parts that have interfering shoulders and conical or formed surfaces. The work is placed upon the work support, and the latter, together with the regulating wheel, is fed forward, forcing the work against the grinding wheel. The grinding wheel has its periphery shaped to the profile desired in the work.

Words and Expressions

grinding wheel 砂轮
crystalline /ˈkristəlain/ adj. 水晶的，结晶的，水晶般的
vitrified /ˈvitrifaid/ adj. 陶瓷的，玻璃化的

vitrified clay 玻化焦
shellac /ʃəˈlæk/ n. 虫胶
phenolic resin 酚醛树脂
prematurely /ˌpreməˈtjuəli/ adv. 过早地，早熟地
through-feed /ˈθruːˈfiːd/ n.. 贯穿进给，贯穿进刀

Passage Ⅳ Milling Machines

Horizontal-Milling Machine

There are two main types of milling machines: horizontal and vertical. In the horizontal-milling machine shown in Fig. 12-8, the milling cutter is mounted on a horizontal arbor driven by the main spindle.

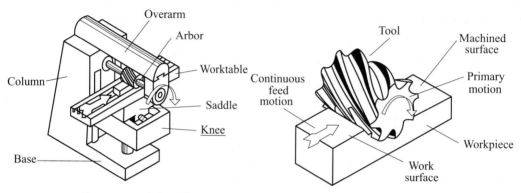

Fig. 12-8 Slab milling on a knee-type horizontal-milling machine

The simplest operation, slab milling, is used to generate a horizontal surface on the workpiece as shown in Fig. 12-8. When estimating the machine time t_m in a milling operation, it should be remembered that the distance traveled by the cutter will be larger than the length of the workpiece. This extended distance is illustrated in Fig. 12-9 in which it can be seen that the cutter travel distance is given by $l_w + \sqrt{a_e(d_t - a_e)}$, where l_w is the length of the workpiece, a_e is the depth of cut, and d_t the diameter of the cutter. Thus, the machining time is given by

$$t_m = [l_w + \sqrt{a_e(d_t - a_e)}]/v_f$$

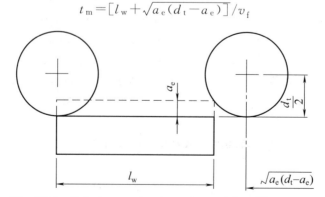

Fig. 12-9 Relative motion between a slab-milling cutter and the workpiece during machining time

where v_f is the feed speed of the workpiece.

The metal-removal rate Z_w will be equal to the product of the feed speed and the cross-sectional area of the metal removed, measured in the direction of feed motion. Thus, if a_p, is equal to the workpiece width,

$$Z_w = a_e a_p v_f$$

There are some other horizontal-milling operations. In form cutting, the special cutter has cutting edges shaped to form the cross section required on the workpiece. These cutters are generally expensive to manufacture, and form milling would only be used when the quantity of production is sufficiently large. In slotting, a standard cutter is used to produce a rectangular slot in a workpiece. Similarly in angular milling, a standard cutter machines a triangular slot. The <u>straddle-milling</u> operation shown in the figure is only one of an infinite variety of operations that can be carried out by mounting more than one cutter on the machine arbor. In this way, combinations of cutters can machine a wide variety of cross-sectional shapes. When cutters are used in combination, the operation is often called <u>gang milling</u>.

Work holding is accomplished either by using a machine vise bolted to the worktable or by direct clamping of the workpiece onto the worktable using the T slots provided.

Vertical-Milling Machine

A wide variety of operations involving the machining of horizontal, vertical, and inclined surfaces can be performed on a vertical-milling machine. As the name of the machine implies, the spindle is vertical. In the knee-type machine illustrated in Fig. 12-10, the workpiece can be fed either:

1. Along the vertical axis by raising or lowering the knee.
2. Along a horizontal axis by moving the <u>saddle</u> along the knee.
3. Along a horizontal axis by moving the table across the saddle.

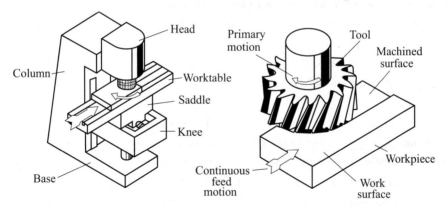

Fig. 12-10 Face milling on a knee-type milling machine

In larger vertical-milling machines, the saddle is mounted directly on the bed, and relative motion between the tool and workpiece along the vertical axis is achieved by motion of the head up or down the <u>column</u>; these machines are called bed-type, vertical-milling machines.

A typical face-milling operation, where a horizontal flat surface is being machined, is shown in Fig. 12-10. The cutter employed is known as a face-milling cutter. In estimating the machining time t_m allowance should again be made for the additional relative motion between the cutting tool and workpiece. The total motion when the path of the tool axis passes over the workpiece is given by (l_w+d_t) and, therefore, the machining is given by

$$t_m=(l_w+d_t)/v_f$$

where l_w is the length of the workpiece, d_t is the diameter of the cutter and v_f is the feed speed of the workpiece.

When the path of the tool axis does not pass over the workpiece,

$$t_m=[l_w+2\sqrt{a_e(d_t-a_e)}\,]/v_f$$

where a_e is the width of the cut in vertical milling.

The metal-removal rate Z_w in both cases is given by equation $Z_w=a_e a_p v_f$.

Work holding is again accomplished by a machine vise or by using the T slots in the machine table.

Words and Expressions

knee /niː/ n.	升降台
straddle /ˈstrædl/ adj.	跨式的
straddle-milling /ˈstrædlˈmiliŋ/ n.	跨铣法
gang milling	组合铣削
saddle /ˈsædl/ n.	滑板，座板
column /ˈkɔləm/ n.	立柱

Exercises

Ⅰ. **Choose the best answer for each of the following sentences.**

1. _____ can only perform these operations where the tool is rotated and fed along its axis of rotation.
   a. A lever   b. A drill press   c. A machining tool   d. A taper shank
2. _____ are usually suitable for machining holes having a length more than five times their diameter.
   a. Sensitive drills   b. Special drills   c. Twist drills   d. Cutting edges
3. In slotting, a _____ is used to produce a rectangular slot in a workpiece.
   a. standard cutter   b. cutting edge   c. special cutter   d. milling machine
4. When the quantity of production is sufficiently large, we had better use _____.
   a. horizontal milling   b. form milling   c. angular milling   d. gang milling
5. In larger vertical-milling machines the _____ is mounted directly on the bed.
   a. head   b. workpiece   c. knee   d. saddle
6. Grinding is generally considered a finishing process used to obtain a fine surface finish and extremely accurate dimensional _____.
   a. shapes   b. figures   c. sizes   d. tolerances
7. Grinding wheels are composed of _____ grains or grit plus a bonding material.
   a. abrasive   b. sensitive   c. sharp   d. minute

8. Usually, the power headstock and tailstock are held on a _____ which in turn is mounted on the main table.
   a. worktable   b. platform   c. surface   d. contour
9. Milling machines may generally be classed as horizontal or vertical depending on the power spindle's axis of _____ .
   a. operation   b. rotation   c. motion   d. combination
10. On machines with a _____ head, the cutter may be tilted to the desired angle.
    a. vertical   b. horizontal   c. universal   d. movable

Ⅱ. **Translate the following expressions into Chinese.**
   1. roughing cut   2. finish cut   3. vertical-boring machine
   4. horizontal- boring machine   5. drill press   6. twist drill
   7. grinding wheel   8. sensitive drilling   9. angular milling
   10. cutting teeth

Part3 Computerized Manufacturing and Mechatronics Technologies

Unit13   Technologies of Numerical Control and Mechatronics

Passage I   Numerical Control of Production Equipments (I)

Numerical control (NC) is a form of programmable automation in which the processing equipment is controlled by means of numbers, letters, and other symbols. The numbers, letters, and symbols are coded in an appropriate format to define a program of instructions for a particular workpart or job. When the job changes, the program of instructions is changed. The capability to change the program is what makes NC suitable for low-and medium-volume production. It is much easier to write new programs than to make major alterations of the processing equipment.

Basic Components of NC

A numerical control system consists of the following three basic components:
Program of instructions
Machine control unit
Processing equipment

The general relationship among the three components is illustrated in Fig. 13-1. The program is fed into the control unit, which directs the pressing equipment accordingly.

The program of instructions is the detailed step-by-step commands that direct the process-

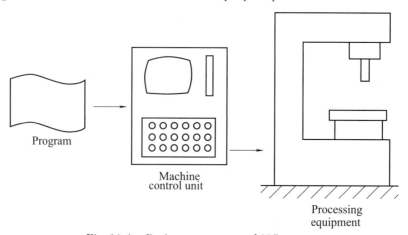

Fig. 13-1   Basic components of NC system

ing equipment. In its most common form, the commands refer to positions of a machine tool spindle with respect to the worktable on which the part is fixtured. More advanced instructions include selection of spindle speeds, cutting tools, and other functions. The program is coded on a suitable medium for submission to the machine control unit. The most common medium in use over the last several decades has been 1-in.-wide punched tape. Because of the widespread use of the punched tape, NC is sometimes called 'tape control'. However, this is a <u>misnomer</u> in modern usage of numerical control. Coming into use more recently have been magnetic tape cassettes and floppy diskettes.

The machine control unit (MCU) consists of the electronics and control hardware that read and interpret the program of instruction and convert it into mechanical actions of the machine tool or other processing equipment.

The processing equipment is the third basic component of an NC system. It is the component that performs useful work. In the most common example of numerical control, one that performs machining operations, the processing equipment consists of the worktable and spindle as well as the motors and controls needed to drive them.

Types of Control Systems

There are two basic types of control systems in numerical control: point-to-point and contouring. In the point-to-point system, also called positioning, each axis of the machine is driven separately by leadscrews, and depending on the type of operation, at different velocities. The machine moves initially at maximum velocity in order to reduce nonproductive time but decelerates as the tool reaches its numerically defined position. Thus in an operation such as drilling or punching, the positioning and cutting take place sequentially. After the hole is drilled or punched, the tool retracts, moves rapidly to another position, and repeats the operation. The path followed from one position to another is important in only one respect: The time required should be minimized for efficiency. Point-to-point systems are used mainly in drilling, punching, and straight milling operations.

In the contouring system, also known as the continuous path system, positioning and cutting operations are both along controlled paths but at different velocities. Because the tool cuts as it travels along a prescribed path, accurate control and synchronization of velocities and movements are important. The contouring system is used on lathes, milling machines, grinders, welding machinery, and machining centers.

Movement along the path, or <u>interpolation</u>, occurs incrementally, by one of several basic methods. In all interpolations, the path controlled is that of the center of rotation of the tool. Compensation for different tools, different diameter tools, or tool wear during machining, can be made in the NC program.

There are a number of interpolation schemes that have been developed to deal with the various problems that are encountered in generating a smooth continuous path with a contouring-type NC system. They include:
 Linear interpolation
 Circular interpolation
 <u>Helical</u> interpolation
 Parabolic interpolation

Cubic interpolation

Each of these interpolation procedures permits the programmer (or operator) to generate machine instructions for linear or curvilinear paths, using a relatively few input parameters. The interpolation module in the MCU performs the calculations and directs the tool along the path.

Linear interpolation is the most basic and is used when a straight-line path is to be generated in continuous-path NC. Two-axis and three-axis linear interpolation routines are sometimes distinguished in practice, but conceptually they are the same. The programmer is required to specify the beginning point and end point of the straight line, and the feed rate that is to be followed along the straight line. The interpolator computes the feed rates for each of the two (or three) axes in order to achieve the specified feed rate.

Linear interpolation for creating a circular path would be quite inappropriate because the programmer would be required to specify the line segments and their respective end points that are to be used to approximate the circle. Circular interpolation schemes have been developed that permit the programming of a path consisting of a circular arc by specifying the following parameters of the arc: the coordinates of its end points, the coordinates of its center, its radius, and the direction of the cutter along the arc. The tool path that is created consists of a series of straight-line segments, but the segments are calculated by the interpolation module rather than the programmer. The cutter is directed to move along each line segment one by one in order to generate the smooth circular path. A limitation of circular interpolation is that the plane in which the circular arc exists must be a plane defined by two axes of the NC system.

Helical interpolation combines the circular interpolation scheme for two axes described above with linear movement of a third axis. This permits the definition of a helical path in three-dimensional space.

Parabolic and cubic interpolation routines are used to provide approximations of free-form curves using higher-order equations. They generally require considerable computational power and are not as common as linear and circular interpolation. Their applications are concentrated in the automobile industry for fabricating dies for car body panels styled with free-form designs that cannot accurately and conveniently be approximated by combining linear and circular interpolations.

Programming for NC

A program for numerical control consists of a sequence of directions that causes an NC machine to carry out a certain operation, machining being the most commonly used process. Programming for NC may be done by an internal programming department, on the shop floor, or purchased from an outside source. Also, programming may be done manually or with computer assistance.

The program contains instructions and commands. Geometric instructions pertain to relative movements between the tool and the workpiece. Processing instructions pertain to spindle speeds, feeds, tools, and so on. Travel instructions pertain to the type of interpolation and slow or rapid movements of the tool or worktable. Switching commands pertain to on/off position for coolant supplies, spindle rotation, direction of spindle rotation, tool changes, workpiece feeding, clamping, and so on.

(1) **Manual Programming** Manual part programming consists of first calculating dimensional relationships of the tool, workpiece, and work table, based on the engineering drawings of the part, and manufacturing operations to be performed and their sequence. A program sheet is then prepared, which consists of the necessary information to carry out the operation, such as cutting tools, spindle speeds, feeds, depth of cut, cutting fluids, power, and tool or workpiece relative positions and movements. Based on this information, the part program is prepared. Usually a paper tape is first prepared for trying out and <u>debugging</u> the program. Depending on how often it is to be used, the tape may be made of more durable <u>Mylar</u>.

(2) **Computer-Aided Programming** Computer-aided part programming involves special symbolic programming languages that determine the coordinate points of corners, edges, and surfaces of the part. Programming language is the means of communicating with the computer and involves the use of symbolic characters. The programmer describes the component to be processed in this language, and the computer converts it to commands for the NC machine. Several languages having various features and applications are commercially available. The first language that used English-like statements was developed in the late 1950s and is called APT (for Auto matically Programmed Tools). This language, in its various expanded forms, is still the most widely used for both point-to-point and continuous-path programming.

Computer-aided part programming has the following significant advantages over manual methods:

Use of relatively easy to use symbolic language.

Reduce programming time. Programming is capable of accommodating a large amount of data concerning machine characteristics and process variables, such as power, speeds, feed, tool shape, compensation for tool shape changes, tool wear, <u>deflections</u>, and coolant use.

Reduced possibility of human error, which can occur in manual programming.

Capability of simple changeover of machining sequence or from machine to machine.

Lower cost because less time is required for programming.

Selection of a particular NC programming language depends on the following factors:

a) Level of expertise of the personnel in the manufacturing facility.

b) Complexity of the part.

c) Type of equipment and computers available.

d) Time and costs involved in programming.

Because numerical control involves the insertion of data concerning workpiece materials and processing parameters, programming must be done by operators or programmers who are knowledgeable about the relevant aspects of the manufacturing processes being used. Before production begins, programs should be verified, either by viewing a simulation of the process on a CRT screen or by making the part from an inexpensive material, such as aluminum, wood, or plastic, rather than the material specified for the finished part.

Words and Expressions

misnomer /mis'nəumə/ *n*.　　　　　　　误称
interpolation /intə:pəu'leiʃn/ *n*.　　　　插补
helical /'helikəl/ *adj*.　　　　　　　　螺旋状的

module /'mɔdju:l/ n.　　　　　　　　组件，模块
debug /di:'bʌg/ v.　　　　　　　　　调试，排出程序中的错误
Mylar /'mailɑ:(r)/ n.　　　　　　　聚酯薄膜
deflection /diflekʃən/ n.　　　　　偏转，偏差，偏斜，挠度

Passage Ⅱ　Numerical Control of Production Equipments (Ⅱ)

The most common application of numerical control is for machine tool control. This was the first application of NC and is today the most important commercially. In this section we discuss the machine tool applications of NC with emphasis on metal machining.

Machine Tool Technology for NC

Each of the five machining processes is carried out on a machine tool designed to perform that process. Turning is performed on a lathe, drilling is done on a drill press, milling on a milling marching, and so on. There are several different types of grinding operations with a corresponding variety of machines to perform them. Numerical control machine tools have been designed for nearly all of the machining processes. The list includes:

　　Drill presses
　　Milling machines, vertical spindle and horizontal spindle
　　Turning machines, both horizontal axis and vertical axis
　　Horizontal and vertical boring mills
　　Profiling and contouring mills
　　Surface grinders and cylindrical grinders

In addition to the machining process, NC machine tools have also been developed for other metalworking professes. These machines include:
　　Punch presses for sheet metal hole punching
　　Presses for sheet metal bending

The introduction of numerical control has had a pronounced influence on the design and operation of machine tools. One of the effects of NC has been that the proportion of time spent by the machine cutting metal under program control is significantly greater than with manually operated machines. This causes certain components, such as the spindle, drive gears, and feed screws, to wear more rapidly. These components must be designed to last longer on NC machines. Second, the addition of the electronic control unit has increased the cost of the machine, therefore requiring higher equipment utilization. Instead of running the machine on only one shift, which was the convention with manually operated machines, NC machines are often operated two or even three shifts to obtain the required payback. Also, the NC machines are designed to reduce the time consumed by the nonprocessing elements in the operation cycle, such as loading and unloading the workpart, and changing tools. Third, the increasing cost to labor has altered the relative roles of the operator and the machine tool. Consider the role of the human operator. Instead of being the highly skilled worker who controlled every aspect of the part production, the tasks of the operator have been reduced to part loading and unloading, tool changing, chip clearing, and the like. In this way, one operator can often run two or three automatic machines. The role and functions of the machine tool have also changed. NC machines are designed to be highly automatic and capable of combining several operations in one setup their formerly required several different machines. These changes are best exemplifies by a new type of machine that did not exit prior to the advent and development of numerical control: the machining center.

The machining center, developed in the late 1950s, is a machine tool capable of performing several different machining operations on a workpart in one setup under program control. The machining center is capable of milling, drilling, reaming, tapping, boring, facing, and similar operations. In addition, the features that typically characterize the NC machining center include the following:

Automatic tool-changing capability. A variety of machining operations means that a variety of tools is required. The tools are contained on the machine in a tool magazine or drum. When a tool needs to be changed, the tool drum rotates to the proper position, and an automatic tool changing mechanism, operating under program control, exchanges the tool in the spindle and the tool in the drum.

Automatic work part positioning. Most machining centers have the capability to rotate the job relative to the spindle, thereby permitting the cutting tool to access four surfaces of the part.

Pallet shuttle. Another feature is that the machining center has two (or more) separate pallets that can be presented to the cutting tool. While machining is being performed with one pallet in position in front of the tool, the other pallet is in a safe location away from the spindle. In this way, the operator can be unloading the finished part from the prior cycle and fixturing the raw workpart for the next cycle while machining is being performed on the current workpiece.

Machining centers are classified as vertical or horizontal. The descriptor refers to the orientation of the machine too spindle. A vertical machining center has its spindle on a vertical axis relative to the worktable, and a horizontal machining center has its spindle on a horizontal axis. This distinction generally results in a difference in the type of work that is performed on the machine. A vertical machining center is typically used for flat work that requires tool access

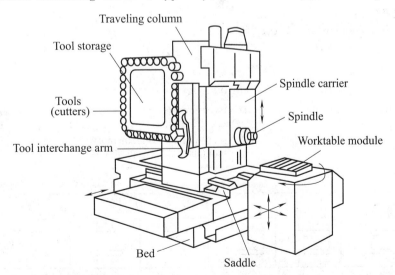

Fig. 13-2 Schematic illustration of a horizontal spindle machining center, equipped with an automatic tool changer. Tool magazines can store 120 cutting tools or more

from the top. A horizontal machining center is used for cube-shaped parts where tool access can best be achieved on the sides of the cube.

An example of an NC horizontal machining center, capable of many of the features described above, is shown in Fig. 13-2.

The success of the machining center has resulted in the development of similar machine tools for other metalworking processes. One example is the turning center, designed as a highly automated and versatile machine tool for performing turning, facing, drilling, threading, and related operations.

DNC and CNC

The development of numerical control was a significant achievement in batch and job shop manufacturing, from both a technological and a commercial viewpoint. There have been two enhancements and extensions of NC technology, including:

Direct numerical control

Computer numerical control

1. Direct Numerical Control

Direct numerical control can be defined as a manufacturing system in which a number of machines are controlled by a computer through direct connection and in real time. The tape reader is omitted in DNC, thus relieving the system of its least reliable component. Instead of using the tape reader, the part program is transmitted to the machine tool directly from the computer memory. In principle, one computer can be used to control more than 100 separate machines (One commercial DNC system during the 1970s boasted a control capability of up to 256 machine tools). The DNC computer is designed to provide instructions to each machine tool on demand. When the machine needs control commands, they are communicated to it immediately.

Fig. 13-3 illustrates the general DNC configuration. The system consists of four components:

Central computer

Bulk memory, which stores the NC part programs

Telecommunication lines

Machines tool

The computer calls the part program instructors from bulk storage and sends them to the individual machines as the need arises. It also receives data back from the machines. This two-

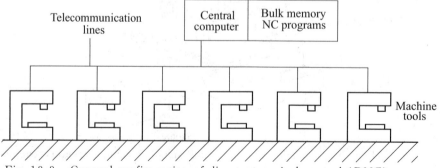

Fig. 13-3 General configuration of direct numerical control (DNC) system

way information flow occurs in real time, which means that each machine's requests for instructions must be satisfied almost instantaneously. Similarly, the computer must always be ready to receive information from the machines and to respond accordingly. The remarkable feature of the DNC system is that the computer is servicing a large number of separate machine tools, all in real time. Depending on the number of machines and the computational requirements that are imposed on the computer, it is sometimes necessary to make use of satellite computers, as shown in Fig. 13-4. These satellites are smaller computers, and they serve to take some of the burden off the larger central computer. Each satellite controls several machines. Groups of part program instructions are received from the central computer and stored in buffers. They are then dispensed to the individual machines as required. Feedback data from the machine are also stored in the satellite's buffer before being collected at the central computer.

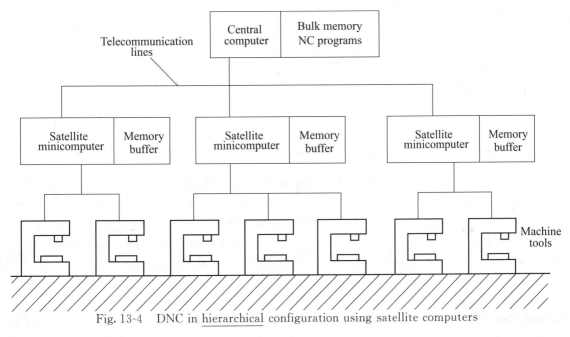

Fig. 13-4 DNC in hierarchical configuration using satellite computers

2. Computer Numerical Control

Since the introduction of DNC, there have been dramatic advances in computer technology. The physical size and cost of a digital computer has been significantly reduced at the same time that its computational capabilities have been substantially increased. In numerical control, the result of these advances has been that the large hard-wired MCUs of conventional NC has been replaced by control units based on the digital computer. Initially, minicomputers were utilized in the early 1970s. As further miniaturization occurred in computers, minicomputers were replaced by today's microcomputers.

Computer numerical control is an NC system using dedicated microcomputer as the machine control unit. Because a digital computer is used in both CNC and DNC, it is appropriate to distinguish between the two types of system. There are three principal differences:

DNC computers distribute instructional data to, and collect data from, a large number of machines. CNC computers control only one machine, or a small number of machines.

DNC computers occupy a location that is typically remote from the machines under their control. CNC computers are located very near their machine tools.

DNC software is developed not only to control individual pieces of production equipment, but also to serve as part of a management information system in the manufacturing sector of the firm. CNC software is developed to augment the capabilities of a particular machine tool.

The general configuration of a computer numerical control system is pictured in Fig. 13-5. As illustrated in the diagram, the controller has a tape reader for initial entry of a part program. In this regard, the outward appearance of a CNC system is similar to that of a conventional NC machine. However, the way in which the program is used in CNC is different. With a conventional NC system, the punched tape is cycled through the tape reader for each workpart in the batch. The MCU reads in a block of instructions on the tape, executing that block heir proceeding to the next block. In CNC, the entire program is entered once and stored in computer memory; the machining cycle for each part is controlled by the program contained in memory rather than from the tape itself.

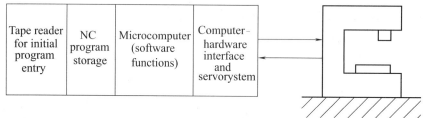

Fig. 13-5　General configuration of a computer numerical control (CNC) system

Control algorithms contained in the computer convert the part program instructions into actions of the machine tool (or other processing equipment). Certain functions are carried out by hard-wired components in the MCU. For example, circular interpolation calculations are often performed by hard-wired circuits rather than by stored program. Also, a hardware interface is required to make the connections with the machine tool servosystems.

3. CNC control features

In previous the important features and functions of the machine control unit in numerical control were described. CNC has made possible additional features beyond what is normally found in a conventional hard-wired MCU. Some of them features include the following:

Storage of more than one part program. With improvements in computer technology, many of the newer CNC controllers have a large enough capacity to store more than a single program. This translates into the capability to store either one very large program or several small and medium-sized programs.

Use of diskettes. There is a growing use of floppy disks for part programs in manufacturing. The capacity of an 8-in. Diskette is the approximate equivalent of 8000 ft of punched tape. Because of this more modern storage technology, many CNC controllers have the optional capability to read in programs stored on disks as well as punched tape.

Program editing at the machine tool site. To deal with the mistakes in part programming, CNC systems permit the program to be edited while it is in computer memory. Hence, the process of testing and correcting the program can be done entirely at the machine site rather than returning to the programming office in the shop to make the tape corrections. In addition to part program corrections, editing can also be done to optimize the cutting conditions of the machining cycle. After correcting and optimizing the program, a tape punch can be connected to the CNC controller in order to obtain a revised version of the tape for future use.

Fixed cycles and programming subroutines. The increased memory capacity and the ability to program the control computer in CNC provides the opportunity to store frequently used machining cycles in memory that can be called by the part program. Instead of writing the instructions for the particular cycle into every program, a code is written into the program to indicate that the cycle should be executed. Some of these cycles require the definition of certain parameters in order to execute. An example is a bolt hole circle, in which the diameter of the bolt circle, the spacing of the bolt holes, and other parameters must be specified. In other cases, the particular machining cycle used by the shop would not require parameter definition.

Interpolation. Some of the interpolation schemes are normally executed only on a CNC system because of the computational requirements. Linear and circular interpolations are often hare-wired into the control unit. Helical, parabolic, and cubic interpolations are usually executed in a stored program algorithm.

Positioning features for setup. Setting up the machine tool for a certain job involves installing and aligning the fixture on the machine tool table. This must be accomplished so that the machine axes are aligned with the workpart. The alignment task can be facilitated using certain features that are made possible by software options in a CNC system. Position set is one of these features. With position set, the operator is not required to position the fixture on the machine table with extreme accuracy. Instead, the machine tool axes are referenced to the location of the fixture by using a target point or set of target points on the work or fixture.

Cutter length compensation. This is similar to the preceding feature but applies to tool length and diameter. In older-style controls, the cutter dimensions had to be set very precisely in order to agree with the tool path defined in the part program. Other methods for ensuring accurate tool path definition have been incorporated into newer CNC controls. One method involves manually entering the actual tool dimensions into the MCU. These actual dimensions may differ from those originally programmed. Compensations are then automatically made in the computed tool path. Another more recent innovation is to use a tool length sensor built into the machine. In this method, the cutter is mounted in the spindle and brought into contact with the sensor to measure its length. This measured value is then used to correct the programmed tool path.

Diagnostics. Many modern CNC machines possess an on-line diagnostics capability, which monitors certain aspects of the machine tool and MCU operation to detect malfunctions or signs of impending malfunctions. When a malfunction is detected, or measurements indicate that a breakdown is about to occur, a message is displayed on the controller's CRT monitor. Depending on the seriousness of the malfunction, the system can be stopped or maintenance can be scheduled for a nonproduction shift. Another use of the diagnostics capability is to help the repair crew determine the reason for a break down of the machine tool. One of the biggest problems when a machine failure occurs is often in diagnosing the reason for the breakdown. By monitoring and analyzing its own operation, the system can determine and communicate the reason for the failure.

Communications interface. With the trend toward interfacing and networking in plants today, most modern CNC controllers are equipped with a standard communications interface to allow the particular machine tool to be linked to other computers and computer-driven devices.

Words and Expressions

pallet /'pælit/ n.		托盘，货盘
DNC=Distributed numerical Control		直接数控
CNC=Computerized numerical Control		计算机数控
batch /bætʃ/ adj.		分批的，间歇式的
hierarchical /ˌhaiəˈrɑːkikəl/ adj.		分层的，体系的，等级的，层次的，分级的
management /ˈmænidʒmənt/ n.		操纵，处理
augment /ɔːgˈment/ v.		增大，扩大
block /blɔk/ n.		滑轮，阻滞
vt.		阻碍，阻塞
servosystem /ˈsəːvəuˌsistəm/ n.		伺服系统
align /əˈlain/ v.		排成一线
facilitated /fəˈsiliteitd/ v.		使容易，促进
incorporate /inˈkɔːpəreit/ vt.		结合，收编，合并
malfunction /mælˈfʌŋkʃən/ n.		故障、工作不正常

Passage Ⅲ Industrial Robot

Introduction

Industrial robots are relatively new electromechanical devices that are beginning to change the appearance of modern industry. Industrial robots are not like the science fiction devices that possess human-like abilities and provide companionship to space travelers. Research to enable robots to 'see', 'hear', 'touch', and 'listen' has been underway for two decades and is beginning to bear fruit. However, the current technology of industrial robots is such that most robots contain only an arm rather than all the anatomy a human possesses. Current control only allows these devices to move from point to point in space, performing relatively simple task. The Robotics Institute of America defines a robot as 'a reprogrammable multifunction manipulator designed to move material, parts, tools, or other specialized devices through variable programmed motions for the performance of a variety of tasks'. A NC machining center would qualify as a robot if one were to interpret different types of machining as different functions. Most manufacturing engineers do not consider a NC machining center a robot, even though these machines have a number of similarities. The power drive and controllers of both NC machines and robots can be quite similar. Robots, like NC machines can be powered by electrical motors, hydraulic systems, or pneumatic systems. Control for either device can be either open-loop or closed-loop. In fact, many of the developments used in robotics have evolved from the NC industry, and many of the manufacturers of robots also manufacture NC machines or NC controllers.

A physical robot is normally composed of a main frame (or arm) with a wrist and some tooling (usually some type of gripper) at the end of the frame. An auxiliary power system may also be included with the robot. A controller with some type of teach pendant, joy-stick, or key-pad is also part of the system. A typical robotic system is shown in Fig. 13-6.

Robots are usually characterized by the design of the mechanical system. A robot whose main frame consists of three linear axes is called a Cartesian robot. The Cartesian robot derives its name from the coordinate system. Travel normally takes place linearly in three-space. Some Cartesian robots are constructed like a gantry to minimize deflection along each of the axes. These robots are referred to as gantry robots. Fig. 13-7 shows examples of Cartesian robots. These robots behave and can be controlled similarly to conventional three-axis NC machines. Gantry robots are generally the most accurate physical structure for robots. Gantry robots are commonly used for assembly where tight tolerance and exact location are required.

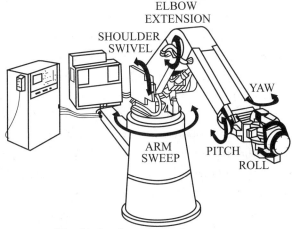
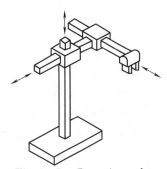

Fig. 13-6 A typical robot system Fig. 13-7 Cartesian robot

A cylindrical robot is composed of two linear axes and one rotary axis. This robot derives its name from the work envelope (the space in which it operates), which is created by moving the axes from limit to limit. Fig. 13-8 shows typical cylindrical robots. Cylindrical robots are used for a variety of applications, but most frequently for material-handling operations.

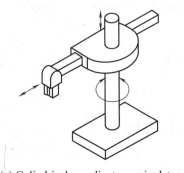
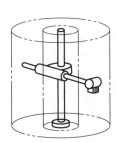

(a) Cylindrical coordinate manipulator (b) Work volume shapeof cylindrical manipulator

Fig. 13-8 Cylindrical robots

Programming a Robot

In order for a device to qualify as a robot, it must be easily reprogrammable. Nonprogrammable mechanisms, regardless of their potential flexibility by reassembly or rewiring, do not qualify as robots. A class of devices that fits this category are fixed or variable-sequence robots. Many of these robots are pneumatically driven. Rather than controlling the robot path, the device is driven to fixed stops or switches via some form of ladder logic. Although the ladder programming qualifies for the deliration of a robot, the switches or stops must normally be physically moved in order to alter the tasks being performed. Drive actuators or motors are turned 'on' or 'off' depending on the desired sequence of tasks and switch states. Robot operations for this type of system are normally limited Io rather simple applications.

Programming of more conventional robots normally takes one of three forms: (1) walk-through or pendant teaching, (2) lead-through teaching, (3) offline programming. Each robot normally comes with one or more of these types of programming systems. Each has advantages and disadvantages depending on the application being considered.

Walk-through or pendant teaching or programming is the most commonly used robot programming procedure. In this type of programming, a pendant that normally contains one or more joy-sticks is used to move the robot throughout its work envelope. At the end of each teach point, the current robot position is saved. As was the case with NC machines, some robots allow the programmer the option of defining the path between points. Again, these robots are called continuous-path systems. Systems that do not allow the user to spiffy the path taken are called point-to-point systems. Many continuous-path robots allow the user to define the path to take between successive points. That is, the user may define a straight-line, circular, or joint-interpolated path. In a straight-line path, the robots move between successive points in a straight-line in Cartesian space. Circular moves, as the name implies take place in circles along one of the major planes. The path that the robot takes using a joint-interpolation scheme is not always easy to determine. In joint interpolation, each of the robot joints are moved at a constant rate so that all the axes start and stop at the same time. For Cartesian rebels, straight-line and joint-interpolation schemes produce the same path. For the other types of robot systems, this is not true.

Pendant programming systems normally have supplemental commands that allow the programmer to perform auxiliary operations such as close the end-effectors, wait, pause, cheek the status of a switch or several switches, return a complete status to a machine, etc. The programmer walks the robot through the necessary steps required to perform a task, saving each intermediate step along with the auxiliary information. The teach pendant used to program the Fanuc M1 robot is shown in Fig. 13-9.

Lead-through programming is one of the simplest programming procedures used to program a robot. As the name implies,

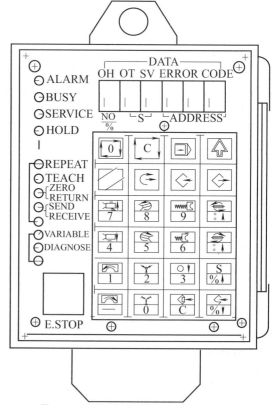

Fig. 13-9 Fanuc M1 teach pendant

the programmer simply physically moves the robot through the required sequence of motions. The robot controller records the position and speed as the programmer leads the robot through tile operation. The power is normally shut down while the programmer is leading the robot through the necessary moves, so that the robot will not generate any 'glitches' that might injure the operator. Although lead-through programming is the easiest programming method to learn, it does introduce some severe limitations to the robot's application. For instance, when the robot is being led through the operation, the operator carries the weight of the robot. The gears, motor and lead screw may introduce a false resolver reading, so that when the weight of the robot, and perhaps a part, must be supported by the system the actual end-effectors position may be significantly different from the position taught to robot. Another problem with this method is that since the position and speed are recorded as the robot is being led through the desired path, a significant amount of data is generated. This data must he stored and later recalled. Storage and retrieval space and time can cause the programmer problems. Perhaps the major problem associated with lead-through programming is that the human who leads the robot through the process is capable of only finite accuracy and may introduce inconsistencies into the process. Human-induced errors and inaccuracies eliminate some of the major advantages of using robots.

Offline programming for robots is a relatively new technology that provides several advantages over both lead-through and teach programming. The principles of offline programming are similar to using an offline language such as APT for NC programming. Several languages have been developed at major universities as well in industry throughout the U. S.. Examples of these languages include VAL created by Unimation, AR-Basic by American Robot Corp., ARMBASIC by Microdot, Inc. and AMI by IBM. To illustrate offline programming, AR-Basic will be used. AR-Basic allows the user to:

(1) Define the position of the robot.

(2) Control the motion of the robot.

(3) Input and output control data.

AR-Basic is an interpretive BASIS system that employs many of the same functions as the familiar BASIC programming language. In AR-Basic, points and tools are defined as a set of primitive data. Points are defined using the convention:

$$X, Y, Z, R, P, Y$$

Where X, Y, and Z are the Cartesian space occupied by the end-effectors, and R, P and Y are the roll, pitch and yaw of the tool. Each of the point definitions can be specified as either absolute or relative points (again defined in a similar manner as for NC machines).

Tool-definition commands are used to define the location of any tooling that might be required for an operation. The tool definition specifies the midpoint of the robot's faceplate, and consists of the same six data used to describe a point.

The robot is set into motion using a set of motion control commands. The motion commands allow the programmer to:

(1) Define the type of path to take (straight-line, circular, or joint-coordinated).

(2) Define the end of tooling speed.

(3) Define the frame of reference.

(4) Define the current tool tip.

AR-Basic also allows the programmer to input and output data to any device to which the robot is interfaced. Analog and digital data can be sent to A/D converters, D/A converters, parallel, or serial I/O ports.

Words and Expressions

manipulator /mə'nipjuleitə/ n.	操作手，机械手
pneumatic /njuː'mætik/ adj.	气动的
pneumatically adv.	气动地
pendant /'pendənt/ n.	控制板，悬挂式操纵台
joy-stick /'dʒɔi,stik/ n.	操纵杆
key-pad=keyboard n.	键盘
Cartesian /kɑː'tizjən/ n.	笛卡儿的，笛卡儿坐标系
gantry /'gæntri/ n.	（起重机）门形框架
envelope=envelop /'enviləup/ n.	包络（线、面），信封
option /'ɔpʃən/ n.	可选品，选择，备选件
joint-interpolated	联合插补
supplemental /ˌsʌpli'mentl/ adj.	辅助的
end-effector	端（立）铣刀
resolver /ri'zɔvə/ n.	解析器，解算装置
retrieval /ri'triːvəl/ n.	（可）取回，（可）恢复
pitch /pitʃ/ n.	节距
yaw /jɔː/ n.	侧滑角
faceplate /'feispleit/ n.	卡盘

Passage IV Adaptive Control of Machine Tools

One of the principal reasons for using numerical control (including DNC and CNC) is that NC reduces the nonproductive time in manufacturing. This is accomplished through a reduction in the following elements, which constitute a significant portion of total production time:
- Work piece handling.
- Setup of the job.
- Lead times between receipt of an order and production.
- Tool changes.
- Operator delays.

Because these nonproductive elements are reduced relative to total production time, a larger proportion of the machine tool's time is spent in actually machining the workpart. Although NC has a significant effect on downtime, it can do relatively little to reduce the in-process time compared to a conventional machine tool. The most promising answer for reducing the in-process time lies in the use of adaptive control (sometimes abbreviated AC). Whereas numerical control guides the sequence of tool positions or the path of the tool during machining, adaptive control determines the proper speeds and/or feeds during machining as a function of variations in such factors as work-material hardness, width or depth of cut, air gaps in the part geometry, and so on. Adaptive control has the capability to re-

spond to and compensate for these variations during the process. Numerical control does not have this capability. Accordingly, adaptive control should be utilized in applications where the following conditions are found:
- The in-process time consumes a significant portion of the total production time.
- There are significant sources of variability in the job for which adaptive control can compensate. In essence, adaptive control adapts speed and/or feed to these variable conditions.

Adaptive Control Defined

For a machining operation, the term adaptive control denotes a control system that measures certain output process variables and uses these to control speed and/or feed. Some of the process variables that have been used in adaptive control machining systems include spindle deflection or force, torque, cutting temperature, vibration amplitude, and horsepower. In other words, nearly all the metal-cutting variables that can be measured have been tried in experimental adaptive control systems. The motivation for developing an adaptive machining system lies in trying to operate the process more efficiently. The typical measures of performance in machining have been metal removal rate and cost per volume of metal removed.

The chronological development of machining adaptive control has been interesting. Starting in the early 1960s, the Bendix Research Laboratories began their attempts to develop an adaptive controller that could be used for metal machining and other processes. This work was sponsored by the U.S. Air Force. At about the same time, Cincinnati Milacron also initiated work on a similar system. What they both found was that it was extremely difficult to develop practical systems that could measure the true performance of the machining process. The reason was the general inability to measure the important process variables accurately in a machine shop environment. They also found that these initial systems were very expensive. Consequently, the adaptive control machines that were finally put into operation were somewhat less sophisticated (and less expensive) than the research adaptive systems developed earlier. The difference between the practical AC systems and the earlier research AC systems prompted the definition of two distinct forms of adaptive control for machining.

Adaptive Control optimization (ACO). These systems are represented by the early Bendix research on adaptive control machining. In this form of adaptive control, an index of performance is specified for the system. This performance index should be a measure of overall process performance, such as production rate or cost per volume of metal removed. The objective of the adaptive controller is to optimize the index of performance by manipulating speed and/or feed in the operation.

Adaptive Control Constraint (ACC). These are represented by the systems that were ultimately employed in production. In this form of adaptive control, constraint limits are imposed on the measured process variables. The objective of the adaptive controller is to manipulate speed and/or feed to maintain the measured variables at or below their constraint limit values.

Current-day adaptive control machining systems generally fall into the second category-adaptive control constraint systems. Basically, most ACO systems attempt to maximize the ratio of work material removal rate to tool wear rate. In other words, the index of performance is

$$IP = \text{a function of } \frac{MRR}{TWR}$$

where
$$MRR = \text{material removal rate}$$
$$TWR = \text{tool wera rate}$$

The trouble with this performance index is that TWR cannot be readily measured on-line with today's measurement technology. Hence, the IP above cannot be monitored during the process. Eventually, sensors will be developed to a level at which the true process performance can be measured on-line. When this occurs, adaptive control optimization systems will become more prominent.

Three Function of Adaptive Control

To evaluate its performance and to response accordingly, the adaptive controller is furnished with the capacity to perform the following three functions: identification, decision, and modification. It may be difficult, in any given adaptive control system, to separate out the components of the system that perform these three functions; nevertheless, all three must be present for adaptation to occur.

(1) Identification function. This involves determining the current performance of the process or system. Normally, the performance quality of the system is defined by some relevant index of performance. The identification function is concerned with determining the current value of this performance measure by making use of the feedback data from the press. Since the environment will change over time, the performance of the system will also change. Accordingly, the identification function is one that must proceed over time more or less continuously. Identification of the system may involve a number of possible measurement activities. It may involve estimation of a suitable mathematical model of the press or computation of the performance index from measurements of process variables. It could include a comparison of the current performance quality with some desired optimal performance.

(2) Decision function. Once the system performance is determined, the next function of adaptive control is to decide how the control mechanism should be adjusted to improve process performance. This decision procedure is carried out by means of a preprogrammed logic provided by the system designer. Depending on the logic, the decision may be to change one or more of the controllable inputs to the process; it may be to alter some of the internal parameters of the controller, or some other decision.

(3) Modification function. The third adaptive function is to implement the decision. While the decision function is a logic function; modification is concerned with a physical or mechanical change in the system. It is a hardware function rather than a software function. The modification involves changing the system parameters or variables so as to drive the process toward a more optimal state.

Operation of an ACC System

Typical applications of adaptive control machining are in profile or contour milling jobs on an NC machine tool. Feed is used as the controlled variable, and cutter force and horsepower are used as the measured variables. It is common to attach an adaptive controller to an NC machine tool. Numerical control machines are a natural starting point for AC for two reasons. First, NC machine tools often possess the required servomotors on the table axes to accept automatic control. Second, the usual kinds of machining jobs for which NC is used possess the sources of variability that make AC feasible. Several large companies have retrofitted their NC machines to include adaptive control. One company, Macotech Corporation in Seattle, Washington, specializes in retrofitting NC machine tools for other manufacturing firms. The adaptive control retrofit package consists of a combination of hardware and software components. The typing hardware components are:

(1) Sensors mounted on the spindle to measure cuter deflection (force).

(2) Sensors to measure spindle motor current. This is used to provide an indication of power consumption.

(3) Control unit and display panel to operate the system.

(4) Interface hardware to cannel the AC system to the existing NC or CNC control unit.

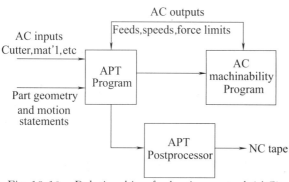

Fig. 13-10 Relationship of adaptive control (AC) software to APT program

The software in the AC package consists of a machinability program, which can be called as an APT MACRO statement. The relationship of the machinability program in the part programming press is shown in Fig. 13-10. The inputs to the program include cutting parameters such as cutter size and geometry, work material hardness, size of cut, and machine tool characteristics. From calculations based on these parameters, the outputs from the program are feed rates, spindle speeds, and cutter force limits for each section of the cut. The objective in these computations is to determine cutting conditions which will maximize metal removal rates. The NC part programmer would ordinarily have to specify feeds and speeds for the machining job. With adaptive control, these conditions are computed by the machinability program based on the input data supplied by the part programmer.

In machining, the AC system operates at the force value calculated for the particular cutter and machine tool spindle. Maximum production rates are obtained by running the machine at the highest feed rate consistent with this force level. Since force is dependent on such factors as depth and width of cut, the end result of the control action is to maximize metal removal rates within the limitations imposed by existing cutting conditions.

Fig. 13-11 shows a schematic diagram illustrating the operation of the AC system during the machining process. When the force increases due to increased workpiece hardness or depth or width of cut, the feed rate is reduced to compensate. When the force decreases, owing to decreases in the foregoing variables or airgaps in the part, feed rate is increased to maximize the rate of metal removal.

Fig. 13-11 shows an air-gap override feature which monitors the cutter force and determines if the cuter is moving through ear or through metal. This is usually sensed by means of a low threshold value of cutter force. If the actual cutter force is below this threshold level, the controlled assumes that the cutter is passing through an air gap. When an air gap is sensed, the feed rate is doubled or tripled to minimize the time wasted traveling across tile air gap. When the cutter reengages metal on the other side of the gap, the feed reverts back to the cutter force mode of control.

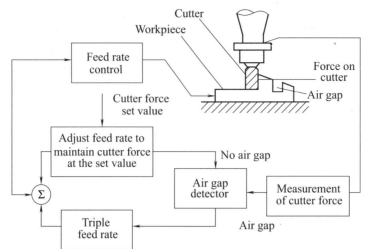

Fig. 13-11　Configuration of typical adaptive control machining system that uses cutter forces as the measured process variable

More than one process variable may be measured in an adaptive control machining system. Originally, attempts were made to employ three measured signals in the Bendix system: temperature, torque, and vibration. Currently, the Macotech system has used both cutter load and horsepower generated at the machine motor. The purpose of the power sensor is to protect the motor from overload when the initial removal rate is constrained by spindle horsepower rather than spindle force.

Benefits of Adaptive Control in Machining

A number of potential benefits accrue to the user of an adaptive control machine tool. The advantage gained will depend on the particular job under consideration. There are obviously many machining situations for which adaptive control cannot be justified.

(1) Increased production rates. Productivity improvement was the motivating force behind the development of adaptive control machining. On-line adjustments to allow for variations in work geometry, material, and tool wear provide the machine too with the capability to achieve the highest metal removal rates that are consistent with existing conditions. This capability translates into more parts per hour. Given the right application, adaptive control will yield significant gains in production rate compared to conventional machining or numerical control.

(2) Increased tool life. In addition to higher production rates, adaptive control will generally provide a more efficient and uniform use of the cutter throughout its tool life. Because adjustments are made in the feed rate to prevent severe loading of the tool, fewer cutters will be broken.

(3) Greater part protection. Instead of setting the cutter force constraint limit on the basis of maximum allowable cutter and spindle deflection, the force limit can be established on the basis of work size tolerance. In this way, the part is protected against an out-to-tolerance condition and possible damage.

(4) Less operator intervention. The advent of adaptive control machining has transferred the control of the process even further out of the hands of the operator and into the hands of management via the part programmer.

(5) Easier part programming. A benefit of adaptive control, which is not so obvious concerns the task of part programming. With ordinary numerical control, the programmer must plan the speed and feed for the worst conditions that the cutter will encounter. He or she may have to try out the program several times before being satisfied with the choice of cutting conditions. In adaptive control part programming, the selection of feed is pretty much left to the controller unit rather than to the part programmer. The constraint limit on force, horsepower, or other variable must be determined according to the particular job and cutter used. However, this can often be calculated from known parameters for the programmer by the system software. In general, the part programmer's task requires a much less conservative approach than for numerical control. Less time is needed to generate the tape for a job, and fewer tryouts are necessary.

Words and Expressions

vibration /vaiˈbreiʃən/ n.	振动，摆动，摇动
vibration amplitude	振幅
AC=Adaptive Control	自适应控制
manipulate /məˈnipjuleit/ vt.	操作
modification /mɔdifiˈkeiʃən/ n.	改进了的形式
contour /ˈkɔntuə/ vt.	曲面仿形
servomotor /ˈsəːvəuˌməutə/ n.	伺服电机
retrofit /ˈretrəˌfit/ v.	改进，改造
machinability /məʃiːnəˈbiliti/ n.	机械加工性，切削性
APT=Automatically Programming Tools	自动编程工具

Unit 14 CAD/CAM/CAPP

Passage I CAD and CAM

Computer-aided design (CAD) and computer-aided manufacturing (CAM) use digital computers, with their high speed and accuracy, as the integrating force throughout the entire process from engineering design to product manufacture. CAD/CAM evolves from and brings together such technologies as numerical control and computer technology. Tied together by the common usage of digital data, and fed by a continuous stream of electronics developments, numerical control and the digital computer have reached the maturity to permit a level of integration that brings us to the threshold of the long-envisioned automatic factory.

The various computerized functions under CAD/CAM fall into three general areas:
1. Design/drafting, or computer-aided engineering.
2. Planning/scheduling, or management information systems.
3. Fabrication, or manufacturing automation.

A conceptualized or idealized CAD/CAM system is shown in Fig. 14-1. This shows how the user interacts with the computer via a graphics terminal, designing and controlling the manufacturing process from start to finish with information stored in a shared data base. With the advent of interactive graphics, the problem of the user entering data and instructions into the computer with stacks of coded punched cards or reels of tape went away. No longer was the

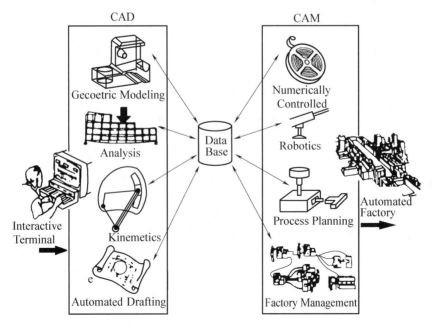

Fig. 14-1 Conceptual CAD/CAM system

user required to be experienced in computer programming and operation to use the machine. With interactive graphics, the user communicates with the computer in display-screen pictures. No knowledge of computers is required to operate these systems, and the communication is in real time, which means that the computer's response to the user's instructions is almost instantaneous. In CAD/CAM, the requirement is for the solution of three-dimensional mechanical design and manufacturing problems. Interacting with the computer via keyboard and lightpen or other pencil-like devices, the designer specifies points and lines on the display screen to quickly construct a display-screen drawing or model. This is in reality the representation of the diagram-stored in the computer data base.

With a stroke of the pen, or by pushing a button, the designer can move, magnify, rotate, flip, copy, or otherwise manipulate the entire design or any part of it. For example, by pushing a button the designer may issue a flip command to produce a mirror image of a display for modeling symmetrical parts, or a translate command may be used to create models for linear parts. A cross, section may be defined and then translated linearly to create a surfaced model. In a similar manner, circular parts can be easily modeled with a rotate command in which a cross section is rotated about a central axis to model parts. These operations take advantage of the computer's capability to repeat detailed operations quickly and flawlessly.

In working with a complex model, the designer can temporarily erase portions of it from the screen to see the area under construction more clearly. The deleted area is recalled later to complete the model. Portions of the model may be enlarged to view and add minute details accurately. The model may be moved and rotated on the screen for viewing at any angle. Mechanisms such as linkages and gears in the assembly may be animated on the screen to ensure proper check for interferences and ease of operation. When the design is complete, the system may then be used to produce detailed engineering drawings.

After part geometry is defined with the completed model, the designer can have the computer calculate physical properties such as weight, volume, surface area, moment of inertia, and center of gravity. The finite-element method may be used to determine the stress, deflections, and other structural characteristics. After such an analysis, the display screen may show color-coded stress plots, the deflected shape of a part subjected to a given load, or an animated mode shape that shows how the structure might vibrate and deform in operation.

The result is that with a CAD/CAM system engineers and designers can view complex forms from various angles at the push of a button instead of having to construct costly, time-consuming models and mock-ups. Changes can be made quickly and inexpensively at the keyboard without requiring drawing changes, or modification of a physical model. In addition, the computer displays can produce realistic simulations of product operation before any hardware is actually produced.

After design completion, the resultant geometric data stored in the computer memory may be used to produce numerical control instructions for making the parts on automated machine tools, or to generate the artwork and drill tapes for automated printed circuit card fabrication. Many CAD/CAM system can now produce NC instructions automatically for a range of different part types. Tool paths may be simulated on the monitor to validate, verify, and modify the program more rapidly.

An engineer at a computer-aided design graphics terminal can design a part, analyze stresses and deflections, study part dynamics, and then produce engineering drawings automatically. From the geometric description provided by computer-aided design, manufacturing engineers may produce numerical control instructions, generate process plans and work instructions, program robots, and provide plant management information with a computer-aided manufacturing system. With an integrated CAD/CAM system, a design is created and the manufacturing process is controlled and executed with a single computer system. These highly sophisticated systems are becoming a way of life at increasing numbers of plants throughout the industrialized world. As CAD/CAM capabilities have increased, costs for these systems have decreased to the point where a company can install a system for a few hundred thousand dollars, which puts them within the budget of many manufacturers.

In summary, CAD/CAM is comprised of distinct functional areas. The experts group CAD functions into four major categories:

1. Geometric modeling.
2. Engineering analysis.
3. Kinematics.
4. Automated drafting.

CAM technology also centers around four major areas or categories:

1. Numerical control.
2. Process planning.
3. <u>Robotics</u>.
4. Factory management.

For CAD/CAM to realize its full potential, the technology of the CAM functions must be advanced to the level of CAD sophistication and CAD/CAM functions must be combined into a truly integrated system. Efforts to do this are under way, and the technology is changing so rapidly that it is difficult to remain abreast of the state of the art without a continuing and sustained effort.

Words and Expressions

numerical control	数字控制
threshold /'θreʃhəuld/ n.	门槛，界限
envision /in'viʒən/ vt.	想象，预见
computer-aided engineering	计算机辅助工程
management information system	管理信息系统
conceptualize /kən'septjuəlaiz/ vt.	构思；使概念化
graphics terminal	图形终端
share /ʃɛə/ n.	份，均分
data base	数据库
advent /'ædvənt/ n.	到来，出现，来临
interactive graphics	交互式图形学
stack /stæk/ n.	堆；堆栈
reel /ri:l/ n.	卷盘，磁带盘
instantaneous /ˌinstən'teinjəs/ adj.	瞬间的

flip /flip/ vi. 交换；翻页
flawlessly /ˈflɔːlisli/ adv. 无缺点的
animate /ˈænimeit/ vt. 动画制作
moment of inertia 转动惯量
finite-element /ˈfainaitˈelimənt/ n. 有限元
mock-up /ˈmɔkʌp/ n. 实体模型
resultant /riˈzʌltənt/ adj. 合成的；作为结果而发生的
artwork /ˈɑːtwəːk/ n. 工艺图；照相原图图纸
robotics /ˈrəubɔtiks/ n. 机器人学

Passage Ⅱ SolidWorks

SolidWorks (stylized as SOLIDWORKS), is a solid modeling computer-aided design (CAD) and computer-aided engineering (CAE) computer program that runs on Microsoft Windows (Fig. 14-2). SolidWorks is published by Dassault Systèmes.

According to the publisher, over 2 million engineers and designers at more than 165,000 companies used SolidWorks as of 2013. Also according to the company, fiscal year 2011-12 revenue for SolidWorks totalled $483 million.

Market

DS Solidworks Corp. has sold over 1.5 million licenses of SolidWorks worldwide. This includes a large proportion of educational licenses. The Sheffield Telegraph comments that Solidworks is the world's most popular CAD software. Its user base ranges from individuals to large corporations, and covers a very wide cross-section of manufacturing market segments. Commercial sales are made through an indirect channel, which includes dealers and partners throughout the world. In the United States, the first reseller of SolidWorks, in 1995, was Computer Aided Technology, Inc, headquartered in Chicago. Directly competitive products to SolidWorks include Solid Edge, and Autodesk Inventor. SolidWorks also partners with third party developers to add functionality in niche market applications like finite element analysis, circuit layout, tolerance checking, etc. SolidWorks has also licensed its 3D modeling capabilities to other CAD software vendors, notably ANVIL.

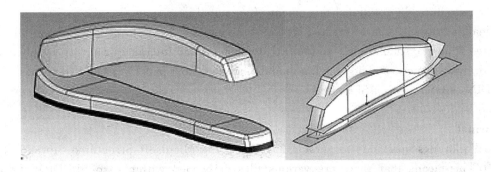

Fig. 14-2 screen shot captured from a SolidWorks top-down design approach

Modeling methodology

SolidWorks is a solid modeler, and utilizes a parametric feature-based approach to create models and assemblies. The software is written on Parasolid-kernel.

Parameters refer to constraints whose values determine the shape or geometry of the model or assembly. Parameters can be either numeric parameters, such as line lengths or circle diameters, or geometric parameters, such as tangent, parallel, concentric, horizontal or vertical, etc. Numeric parameters can be associated with each other through the use of relations, which allows them to capture design intent.

Design intent is how the creator of the part wants it to respond to changes and updates. For example, you would want the hole at the top of a beverage can to stay at the top surface, regardless of the height or size of the can. SolidWorks allows the user to specify that the hole is a feature on the top surface, and will then honor their design intent no matter what height they later assign to the can.

Features refer to the building blocks of the part. They are the shapes and operations that construct the part. Shape-based features typically begin with a 2D or 3D sketch of shapes such as bosses, holes, slots, etc. This shape is then extruded or cut to add or remove material from the part. Operation-based features are not sketch-based, and include features such as fillets, chamfers, shells, applying draft to the faces of a part, etc.

Building a model in SolidWorks usually starts with a 2D sketch (although 3D sketches are available for power users). The sketch consists of geometry such as points, lines, arcs, conics (except the hyperbola), and splines. Dimensions are added to the sketch to define the size and location of the geometry. Relations are used to define attributes such as tangency, parallelism, perpendicularity, and concentricity. The parametric nature of SolidWorks means that the dimensions and relations drive the geometry, not the other way around. The dimensions in the sketch can be controlled independently, or by relationships to other parameters inside or outside of the sketch.

In an assembly, the analog to sketch relations are mates. Just as sketch relations define conditions such as tangency, parallelism, and concentricity with respect to sketch geometry, assembly mates define equivalent relations with respect to the individual parts or components, allowing the easy construction of assemblies. SolidWorks also includes additional advanced mating features such as gear and cam follower mates, which allow modeled gear assemblies to accurately reproduce the rotational movement of an actual gear train.

Finally, drawings can be created either from parts or assemblies. Views are automatically generated from the solid model, and notes, dimensions and tolerances can then be easily added to the drawing as needed. The drawing module includes most paper sizes and standards (ANSI, ISO, DIN, GOST, JIS, BSI and SAC).

File format

SolidWorks files (previous to version 2015) use the Microsoft Structured Storage file format. This means that there are various files embedded within each SLDDRW (drawing files), SLDPRT (part files), SLDASM (assembly files) file, including preview bitmaps and metadata sub-files. Various third-party tools can be used to extract these sub-files, although the subfiles in many cases use proprietary binary file formats.

Words and Expressions

modeling /'mɔdljŋ/ n.　　　　　造型，（图画等的）立体感
licenses /'lajsns/ n.　　　　　许可证，执照；特许
cross-section　　　　　　　　横断面；横截面图
niche /nitʃ/ adj.　　　　　　有商机的
parametric /'pærə'metrik/ n.　（变）数的，参（变）量的
sketch /sketʃ/ n.　　　　　　素描；草图；梗概

Exercises

Ⅰ. **Translate the following passage into Chinese.**

Parameters refer to constraints whose values determine the shape or geometry of the model or assembly. Parameters can be either numeric parameters, such as line lengths or circle diameters, or geometric parameters, such as tangent, parallel, concentric, horizontal or vertical, etc. Numeric parameters can be associated with each other through the use of relations, which allows them to capture design intent.

Ⅱ. **Translate the following passage into English.**

SolidWorks 软件功能强大，组件繁多。SolidWorks 有功能强大、易学易用和技术创新三大特点，这使得 SolidWorks 成为领先的、主流的三维 CAD 解决方案。SolidWorks 能够提供不同的设计方案、减少设计过程中的错误以及提高产品质量。SolidWorks 不仅提供如此强大的功能，而且对每个工程师和设计者来说，操作简单方便、易学易用。

Passage Ⅲ　　Finite Element Method

The introduction

In mathematics, the finite element method (FEM) is a numerical technique for finding approximate solutions to boundary value problems for partial differential equations. It uses subdivision of a whole problem domain into simpler parts, called finite elements, and variational methods from the calculus of variations to solve the problem by minimizing an associated error function. Analogous to the idea that connecting many tiny straight lines can approximate a larger circle, FEM encompasses methods for connecting many simple element equations over many small subdomains, named finite elements, to approximate a more complex equation over a larger domain.

Basic concepts

The subdivision of a whole domain into simpler parts has several advantages:
- Accurate representation of complex geometry
- Inclusion of dissimilar material properties

- Easy representation of the total solution
- Capture of local effects.

A typical work out of the method involves (1) dividing the domain of the problem into a collection of subdomains, with each subdomain represented by a set of element equations to the original problem, followed by (2) systematically recombining all sets of element equations into a global system of equations for the final calculation. The global system of equations has known solution techniques, and can be calculated from the initial values of the original problem to obtain a numerical answer.

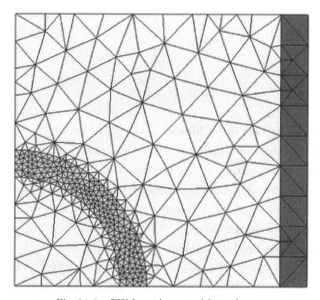

Fig. 14-3 FEM mesh created by software

FEM mesh created by an analyst prior to finding a solution to a magnetic problem using FEM software. Colours indicate that the analyst has set material properties for each zone, in this case a conducting wire coil in orange; a ferromagnetic component (perhaps iron) in light blue; and air in grey. Although the geometry may seem simple, it would be very challenging to calculate the magnetic field for this setup without FEM software, using equations alone.

In the first step above, the element equations are simple equations that locally approximate the original complex equations to be studied, where the original equations are often partial differential equations (PDE). To explain the approximation in this process, FEM is commonly introduced as a special case of Galerkin method. The process, in mathematical language, is to construct an integral of the inner product of the residual and the weight functions and set the integral to zero. In simple terms, it is a procedure that minimizes the error of approximation by fitting trial functions into the PDE. The residual is the error caused by the trial functions, and the weight functions are polynomial approximation functions that project the residual. The process eliminates all the spatial derivatives from the PDE, thus approximating the PDE locally with a set of algebraic equations for steady state problems, a set of ordinary differential equations for transient problems.

These equation sets are the element equations. They are linear if the underlying PDE is linear, and vice versa. Algebraic equation sets that arise in the steady state problems are solved using numerical linear algebra methods, while ordinary differential equation sets that arise in the transient problems are solved by numerical integration using standard techniques such as Euler's method or the Runge-Kutta method.

In step (2) above, a global system of equations is generated from the element equations through a transformation of coordinates from the subdomains' local nodes to the domain's global nodes. This spatial transformation includes appropriate orientation adjustments as applied in relation to the reference coordinate system. The process is often carried out by FEM software using coordinate data generated from the subdomains.

FEM is best understood from its practical application, known as finite element analysis (FEA). FEA as applied in engineering is a computational tool for performing engineering analysis. It includes the use of mesh generation techniques for dividing a complex problem into small elements, as well as the use of software program coded with FEM algorithm (Fig. 14-3). In applying FEA, the complex problem is usually a physical system with the underlying physics such as the Euler-Bernoulli beam equation, the heat equation, or the Navier-Stokes equations expressed in either PDE or integral equations, while the divided small elements of the complex problem represent different areas in the physical system.

FEA is a good choice for analyzing problems over complicated domains (like cars and oil pipelines), when the domain changes (as during a solid state reaction with a moving boundary), when the desired precision varies over the entire domain, or when the solution lacks smoothness. For instance, in a frontal crash simulation it is possible to increase prediction accuracy in "important" areas like the front of the car and reduce it in its rear (thus reducing cost of the simulation). Another example would be in numerical weather prediction, where it is more important to have accurate predictions over developing highly nonlinear phenomena (such as tropical cyclones in the atmosphere, or eddies in the ocean) rather than relatively calm areas.

The structure of finite element methods

Finite element methods are numerical methods for approximating the solutions of mathematical problems that are usually formulated so as to precisely state an idea of some aspect of physical reality.

A finite element method is characterized by a variational formulation, a discretization strategy, one or more solution algorithms and post-processing procedures. Examples of variational formulation are the Galerkin method, the discontinuous Galerkin method, mixed methods, etc.

A discretization strategy is understood to mean a clearly defined set of procedures that cover (a) the creation of finite element meshes, (b) the definition of basis function on reference elements (also called shape functions) and (c) the mapping of reference elements onto the elements of the mesh. Examples of discretization strategies are the h-version, p-version, hp-version, x-FEM, isogeometric analysis, etc. Each discretization strategy has certain advantages and disadvantages. A reasonable criterion in selecting a discretization strategy is to realize nearly optimal performance for the broadest set of mathematical models in a particular model class.

There are various numerical solution algorithms that can be classified into two broad categories; direct and iterative solvers. These algorithms are designed to exploit the sparsity of matrices that depend on the choices of variational formulation and discretization strategy.

Postprocessing procedures are designed for the extraction of the data of interest from a finite element solution. In order to meet the requirements of solution verification, postprocessors need to provide for a posteriori error estimation in terms of the quantities of interest. When the errors of approximation are larger than what is considered acceptable then the discretization has to be changed either by an automated adaptive process or by action of the analyst. There are some very efficient postprocessors that provide for the realization of super <u>convergence</u>.

Applications

A variety of specializations under the umbrella of the mechanical engineering discipline (such as aeronautical, biomechanical, and automotive industries) commonly use integrated FEM in design and development of their products. Several modern FEM packages include specific components such as thermal, electromagnetic, fluid, and structural working environments. In a structural simulation, FEM helps tremendously in producing stiffness and strength visualizations and also in minimizing weight, materials, and costs.

FEM allows detailed visualization of where structures bend or twist, and indicates the distribution of stresses and displacements. FEM software provides a wide range of simulation options for controlling the complexity of both modeling and analysis of a system. Similarly, the desired level of accuracy required and associated computational time requirements can be managed simultaneously to address most engineering applications. FEM allows entire designs to be constructed, refined, and optimized before the design is manufactured.

This powerful design tool has significantly improved both the standard of engineering designs and the methodology of the design process in many industrial applications. The introduction of FEM has substantially decreased the time to take products from concept to the production line. It is primarily through improved initial prototype designs using FEM that testing and development have been accelerated. In summary, benefits of FEM include increased accuracy, enhanced design and better insight into critical design parameters, virtual prototyping, fewer hardware prototypes, a faster and less expensive design cycle, increased productivity, and increased revenue. FEA has also been proposed to use in stochastic modelling for numerically solving probability models.

Words and Expressions

finite element method	有限元方法
numerical /njuːˈmerikl/ *adj.*	数字的，用数字表示的，数值的
partial /ˈpaːʃl/ *n.*	[数学] 偏微商
complex /ˈkɔmpleks/ *adj.*	复杂的；难懂的；复合的
subdivision /sʌbdjˈviʒn/ *n.*	分支；细分，一部
precisely /priˈsaisli/ *adv.*	精确地；恰好地；严谨地，严格地；一丝不苟地
algorithm /ˈælgəriðəm/ *n.*	演算法；运算法则；计算程序
iterative /ˈiterətiv/ *adj.*	重复的，反复的，迭代的
convergence /kənˈvɜːdʒəns/ *n.*	会聚；集收敛；集合
solver /ˈsɔlvə(r)/ *n.*	求解器
postprocessing	后处理
discretization /diskriːtiˈzeiʃən/ *n.*	离散化

Exercises

Ⅰ. **Decide whether the following statements are true or false (T/F).**

(   ) 1. In mathematics, the finite element method (FEM) is a numerical technique for finding approximate solutions to boundary value problems for partial differential equations.

(   ) 2. FEM uses a whole problem domain.

(   ) 3. Accurate representation of complex geometry is one advantage of the subdivision of a whole domain into simpler parts.

(   ) 4. Finite element methods are numerical methods for approximating the solutions of mathematical problems that are usually formulated so as to precisely state an idea of some aspect of physical reality.

(   ) 5. There are various numerical solution algorithms that can be classified into two broad categories: direct and iterative solvers.

(   ) 6. The finite element method cannot improve both the standard of engineering designs and the methodology of the design process in many industrial applications.

Ⅱ. **Answer the following questions.**

1. What is finite element method?
2. What are finite elements? How to generate the finite elements?
3. What are the advantages of the subdivision of a whole domain into simpler parts?
4. What is the work out of the FEM?
5. Why is FEM useful?

Ⅲ. **Translate the following passage into Chinese.**

In mathematics, the finite element method (FEM) is a numerical technique for finding approximate solutions to boundary value problems for partial differential equations. It uses subdivision of a whole problem domain into simpler parts, called finite elements, and variational methods from the calculus of variations to solve the problem by minimizing an associated error function. Analogous to the idea that connecting many tiny straight lines can approximate a larger circle, FEM encompasses methods for connecting many simple element equations over many small subdomains, named finite elements, to approximate a more complex equation over a larger domain.

Ⅳ. **Translate the following passage into English.**

有限元分析是用较简单的问题代替复杂问题后再求解。它将求解域看成是由许多称为有限元的小的互连子域组成,对每一单元假定一个合适的(较简单的)近似解,然后推导求解这个域总的满足条件(如结构的平衡条件),从而得到问题的解。这个解不是准确解,而是近似解,因为实际问题被较简单的问题所代替。由于大多数实际问题难以得到准确解,而有限元不仅计算精度高,而且能适应各种复杂形状,因而成为行之有效的工程分析手段。

Passage Ⅳ   Computer Aided Process Planning (CAPP)

Process planning is concerned with determining the sequence of individual manufacturing operations needed to produce a given part or product. The resulting operation sequence is documented on a form typically referred to as a route sheet. The route sheet is a listing of the production operations and associated machine tools for a workpart or assembly.

Closely related to process planning are the functions of determining appropriate cutting conditions for the machining operations and setting the time standards for the operations. All three functions-planning the process, determining the cutting conditions, and setting the time standards have traditionally been carried out as tasks with a very high manual and clerical content. They are also typically routine tasks in which similar or even identical decisions are repeated over and over. Today, these kinds of decisions are being made with the aid of computers.

Traditional process planning

There are variations in the level of detail found in route sheets among different companies and industries. In the one extreme, process planning is accomplished by releasing the part print to the production shop with the instructions 'make to drawing'. Most firms provide a more detailed list of steps describing each operation and identifying each work center.[2] In any case, it is traditionally the task of the manufacturing engineers or industrial engineers in an organization to write these process plans for new part designs to be produced by the shop. The process planning procedure is very much dependent on the experience and judgment of the planner. It is the manufacturing engineer's responsibility to determine an optimal routing for each new part design. However, individual engineers each have their own opinions about what constitutes the best routing. Accordingly, there are differences among the operation sequences developed by various planners. We can illustrate rather dramatically these differences by means of an example.

In one case, a total of 42 different routings were developed for various sizes of a relatively simple part called an 'expander sleeve'. There were a total of 64 different sizes and styles, each with its own part number. The 42 routings included 20 different machine tools in the shop. The reason for this absence of process standardization was that many different individuals had worked on the parts: 8 or 9 manufacturing engineers, 2 planners, and 25 NC part programmers. Upon analysis, it was determined that only two different routings through four machines were needed to process the 64 part numbers. It is clear that there are potentially great differences in the perceptions among process planners as to what constitutes the 'optimal' method of production.

In addition to this problem of variability among planners, there are often difficulties in the conventional process planning procedure. New machine tools in the factory render old routings less than optimal. Machine breakdowns force shop personnel to use temporary routings, and these become the documented routings even after the machine is repaired. For these reasons and others, a significant proportion of the total numbers of process plans used in manufacturing are not optimal.

Automated process planning

Because of the problems encountered with manual process planning, attempts have been made in recent years to capture the logic, judgment, and experience required for this important function and incorporates them into computer programs. Based on the characteristics of a given part, the program automatically generates the manufacturing operation sequence. A computer-aided process planning (CAPP) system offers the potential for reducing the routine clerical work of manufacturing engineers. At the same time, it provides the opportunity to generate production routings, which are rational, consistent, and perhaps even optimal. Two alternative approaches to computer-aided process planning have been developed. These are:

(1) Retrieval-type CAPP systems (also called <u>variant</u> systems).
(2) Generative CAPP systems.

The two types are described in the following two sections.

Retrieval-Type Process Planning Systems

Retrieval-type CAPP systems use parts classification and coding and group technology as a foundation. In this approach, the parts produced in the plant are grouped into part families, distinguished according to their manufacturing characteristics. For each part family, a standard process plan is established. The standard process plan is stored in computer files and then <u>retrieved</u> for new workparts which belong to that family. Some form of parts classification and coding system is required to organize the computer files and to permit efficient retrieval of the appropriate process plan for a new workpart. For some new parts, editing of the existing process plan may be required. This is done when the manufacturing requirements of the new part are slightly different from the standard. The machine routing may be the same for the new part, but the specific operations required at each machine may be different. The complete process plan must document the operations as well as the sequence of machines through which the part must be routed. Because of the alterations that are made in the retrieved process plan, these CAPP systems are sometimes also called by the name 'variant system'.

Fig. 14-2 will help to explain the procedure used in a retrieval process planning system. The user would initiate the procedure by entering the part code number at a computer terminal. The CAPP program then searches the part family matrix file to determine if a match exists. If the file contains an identical code number, the standard machine routing and operation sequence are retrieved from the respective compeller files for display to the user. The standard process plan is examined by the user to permit any necessary editing of the plan to make it <u>compatible</u> with the new part design. After editing, the process plan formatter prepares the paper document in the proper form.

If an exact match cannot be found between the code numbers in the computer file and the code number for the new part, the user may search the machine routing file and the operation sequence file for similar parts that could be used to develop the plan for the new part. Once the process plan for a new part code number has been entered, it becomes the standard process for future parts of the same classification.

In Fig. 14-4 the machine routing file is distinguished from the operation sequence file to emphasize that the machine routing may apply to a range of different part families and code numbers. It would be easier to find a match in the machine routing file than in the operation sequence file. Some CAPP retrieval systems would use only one such file, which would be a combination of operation sequence file and machine routing file.

The process plan formatter may use other application programs. These could include programs to compute machining conditions, work standards, and standard costs. Standard cost programs can he used to determine total product costs for pricing purposes.

A number of retrieval-type computer-aided process planning systems have been devel-

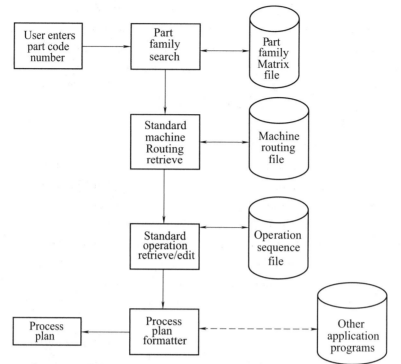

Fig. 14-4 Information flow in a retrieval-type computer-aided process planning systems

oped. These include MIPLAN, one of the MICLASS modules, the CAPP system developed by Computer-Aided Manufacturing-International, COMCAPP V by MDSI, and systems by individual companies. We will use MIPLAN as an example to illustrate these industrial systems.

Example

MIPLAN is a computer-aided process planning package available from the organization for industrial Research, Inc, of Waltham, Massachusetts. It is basically a retrieval-type CAPP system with some additional features. The MIPLAN system consists of several modules, which are used in an interactive, conversational mode.

To operate the system, the user can select any of four different options to create the profess plan for a new part:

(1) The first option is a retrieval approach in which the user inputs a part code number and a standard process plan is retrieved from the compeer file for possible docking. To generate the part code number, the planner may select to use the MICLASS interactive parts classification and coding system.

(2) In the second option, a process plan is retrieved from the computer files by entering an existing part number (rather than a part code number). Again, the existing process plan can be edited by the user, if required.

(3) A process plan can be created from scratch, using standard text material stored in computer files. This option is basically a specialized word-processing system in which the planner selects from a menu of text related to machines and processes. The process plan is assembled from text passages subject to editing for the particular requirements of the new part.

(4) The user can call up an incomplete process plan from the computer file. This may

occur when the user is unable to complete the process plan for a new part at one setting. For example, the planner may be interrupted in the middle of the procedure to solve some emergency problem. When the procedure is resumed, the incomplete plan can be retrieved and finished.

After the process plan has been completed using one to the four MIPLAN options, the user can have a paper document printed out by the computer. A typical MIPLAN output is shown in Fig. 14-5. It is also possible for the user to store the completed process plan (or the partially completed plan as with option 3) in the computer files, or to purge an existing plan from the files. This might be done, for example, when an old machine tool is replaced by a more productive machine, and this necessitates changes in some of the standard process plans.

ORGANIZATION FOR INDUSTRIAL RESEARCH, INC. FACILITY-F1								
PART NUMBER: A63799			S/O#	PRJ#	ORDER QTY	MINIMUM QTY	DUE DATES	PRE#
PART NAME: SHAFT, ARM			A34UB	45D3	1000	935	249	2
PLNG REV:02	DWG REV:0							
PLANNER: ADAMS								
INSPECTIONS				CODE# :1310-1181-2111-0000-0100-0000-00				
	#1	#2	#3	SPECIAL INSTRUCTIONS/HANDLING: 1/2"DIA MS-5000H. R. STEEL(2"LGTHS)				
MFG ENG Q/A		FHB PC AH						
OPEN NO	MACH TOOL	OPERATION DESCRIPTION-ASSY INSTRUCTIONS				SETUP TIMES	PIECE TIMES	OPR
0010	5145	S/UCOLLET ROUGH TURN MACHINE PER TAPE NO. LS982A 0.440 DIA. BY 1.750 LENGTH 0.300 DIA. BY 0.8120 LENGTH 0.275 DIA. BY 0.4375 LENGTH FLNISH 3/64 GROOVES (TYP) AND CHAMERS 0.270 DIA. BY 0.375 LENGTH CHAMFER CUTOFF TO 1.906				2.00	0.173	
0015	1026	#2CENTERS BOTH ENDS				0.25		
0020	9401	CRBURIZE AND HARDER				0.50	0.004	
0030	4063	S/U BETWEEN CENTERS GRING OD HOLD CONCERTRICITY HOLD 0.4200 DIM. HOLD 0.2600 DIM. HOLD 0.2815 DIM. HOLD 0.2600 DIM.				0.25		
0040	9501	BLART TO CLEAN						
0050	9201	CHROME PLATE PER PRINT				0.38	0.001	
0060	9805	FINAL INSPECT						

Fig. 14-5 Route sheet generated by MIPLAN

Computer graphics can be utilized to enhance the MIPLAN output. This possibility is illustrated in Fig. 14-6, which shows a tooling setup for the machining operation described. With this kind of pictorial process planning, drawings of workpart details, tool paths, and other information can be presented visually to facilitate communication to the manufacturing shops.

PART NO:190105	PART NAME: FRONT PLATE	FORMAT:
PLNG REV:1	DWG REV:A	PLANNING:ADAMS
CODE#:8798-3711-1189-3433-1400-0000-0000-00		

0040	5002 MACHINE PER TAPE #1
	SET UP IN FIXTURE#1
	WITH STD ANGLEPLATE
	#A123 PER SKETCH
	ROUGH AND FINISH FACE
	-HOLD0.25+ -0.02DIM
	USE 4" DKA FACE MILL
	C-DRILL(3)HOLES
	DRILL(1) HOLES3/8 DIA
	DRILL(2) TOOLING HOLES
	5/16 DIA
	DRILL(2) TOOLING HOLES
	0.365/0.370 DIA
	AND REAM TO 0.365/0.370 DIA
	SET UP=2.50
	PIECE TIME=0.350

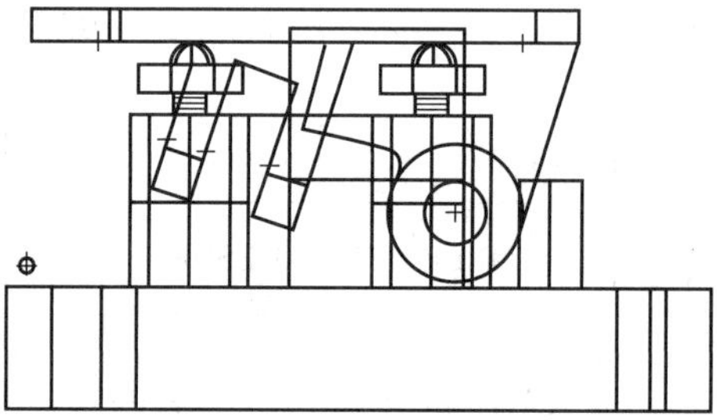

Fig. 14-6 Pictorial process planning

Generative Process Planning Systems

Generative process planning involves the use of the computer to create an individual process plan from scratch, automatically and without human assistance. The computer would employ a set of algorithms to progress through the various technical and logical decisions toward a final plan for manufacturing. Inputs to the system would include a comprehensive description of the workpart. This may involve the use of some form of part code number to summarize the workpart data, but it does not involve the retrieval of existing standard plans. Instead, the generative CAPP system synthesizes the design of the optimum process sequence, based on an analysis of part geometry, material, and other factors which would influence manufacturing decisions.

In the ideal generative process planning package, any part design could be presented to the system for creation of the optimal plan. In practice, current generative-type systems are far from universal in their applicability. They tend to fall short of a truly generative capability, and they are developed for a somewhat limited range of manufacturing processes.

Benefits of CAPP

Whether it is a retrieval system or a generative system, computer-aided process planning offers a number of potential advantages over manually oriented process planning.

(1) **Process rationalization.** Computer-automated preparation of operation routings is more likely to be consistent, logical, and optimal than its manual counterpart. The process plans will be consistent because the same computer software is being used by all planners. We avoid the tendency for <u>drastically</u> different process plans from different planners. The process plans tend to be more logical and optimal because the company has presumably incorporated the experience and judgment of its best manufacturing people into the process planning computer software.

(2) **Increased productivity of process planners.** With computer-aided process planning, there is reduced clerical effort, fewer errors are made, and the planners have immediate access to the process planning data base. These benefits translate into higher productivity of the process planners. One system was reported to increase productivity by 600% in the process planning function.

(3) **Reduced turnaround time.** Working with the CAPP system, the process planner is able to prepare a route sheet for a new part in less time compared to manual preparation. This leads to an overall reduction in manufacturing lead time.

(4) **Improved <u>legibility</u>.** The computer-prepared document is neater and easier to read than manually written route sheets. CAPP systems employ standard text, which facilitates interpretation of the process plan in the factory.

(5) **Incorporation of other application programs.** The process planning system can be designed to operate in conjunction with other software packages to automate many of the time-consuming manufacturing support functions.

Words and Expressions

variation /ˌvɛəriˈeiʃən/ n.　　偏差
expander sleeve　　膨胀套
potential /pəˈtenʃəl/ adj.　　潜在的
perception /pəˈsepʃən/ n.　　理解，理会
temporary /ˈtempərəri/ adj.　　暂时的，临时的
variant /ˈvɛəriənt/ n.　　变种，变式
retrieve /riˈtriːv/ v.　　检索
compatible /kəmˈpætəbl/ adj.　　兼容的，协调的，相容的
drastically /ˈdræstikəli/ adv.　　严重的，猛烈的，急剧的，严格的
legibility /ledʒiˈbiliti/ n.　　易解（读），清晰度

Exercises

Ⅰ. **Translate the following passage into Chinese.**

Most manufacturing engineers would agree that, if 10 different planners were asked to develop a process plan for the same part, they would probably come up with ten different plans. Obviously, all there plans can't reflect the most efficient manufacturing methods and in fact, there is no guarantee that any of them will constitute the optimum method for manufacturing the part.

Ⅱ. Translate the following passage into English.

计算机正在将制造业带入信息时代。计算机长期以来在商业和管理方面得到了广泛的应用，它正在作为一种新的工具进入到工厂中，而且它如同蒸汽机在100多年前使制造业发生改变那样，正在使制造业发生着变革。在将来计算机可能会是一个企业生存的基本条件，许多现今的企业将会被生产能力更高的企业组合所取代。

Unit 15 Advanced Technology of Manufacturing

Passage I Group Technology

Group technology is a manufacturing philosophy that involves identifying and grouping components having similar or related attributes in order to take advantage of their similarities in the design and/or manufacturing phases of the production cycle. Historically, this novel principle first came into being here in the United States in 1920, when Frederick Taylor supported the idea of grouping parts that required special operations. He was followed by the Jones and Larson Machine Company in the early 1920s, which used a crude form of group technology to build machine tools. Their manufacturing approach involved such principles as departmentalization by product rather than by process and minimizing the routing paths. Today, group technology is implemented through the application of well-structured classification and coding systems and supporting software to take advantage of the similarities of component.

Reasons for Adopting Group Technology

Modern manufacturing industries are racing a lot of challenges caused by growing international competition and fast-changing market demands. These challenges, which are exemplified in the following list, have been and can be successfully met by group technology.

(1) There is an industrial trend toward low-volume production (small lot sizes) of a wider variety of products in order to meet the rising demand for specially ordered products in today's affluent societies. In other words, the share of the batch-type production in industry is growing day after day, and it is anticipated that 75 percent of all manufactured parts will be in small lot sizes.

(2) As a result of the first factor, the conventional shop organization (i. e., departmentalization by process) is becoming very inefficient and obsoletes because of the wasteful routing paths of the products batwing the various machine tool departments.

(3) There is a need to integrate the design and manufacturing phases in order to cut short the lead time, thus winning a competitive situation in the international market.

Benefit of Group Technology

Benefits in product design. Concerning design of products, the principal benefit of group technology is that it enables product designers to avoid 'reinventing the wheel', or duplicating engineering efforts. In other words, it eliminates the possibility of designing a product that was previously designed because it <u>facilitates</u> storage and easy retrieval of engineering designs. When an order of a part is released, the part is first coded, and then existing designs that match that code are retrieved from the company's library of designs stored in the memory of a computer, thus saving a large amount of time in design work. If the exact part design is not included in the company's computerized files, a design close enough to the required one can be retrieved and modified in order to satisfy the requirements. A further advantage of group technology is that it promotes standardization of design features, such as corner radii, chamfers, and the like, thus leading to the standardization of production tools and work-holding devices.

Standardization of tooling and setup. Since parts are grouped into families, a flexible design for a work-holding device (jig or fixture) can be made for each family in such a manner that it can accommodate every member of that family, thus reducing the cost of fixturing by reducing the number of fixtures required. Also, it is obvious that a machine setup can be made once for the whole family (because of the similarities between the parts of a family) instead of a machine setup for each of the individual parts.

More efficient material handling. When the plant layout is based on the group technology principles, i.e., dividing the plant into cells, each consisting of a group of different machine tools and wholly devoted to the production of a family of parts, material handling is more efficient because of the minimal routing paths of parts between machine tools achieved in this case. This is in contrast with the 'messy' flow lines in the case of the conventional departmentalization-by-process layout. That comparison is clearly illustrated in Fig. 15-1, which indicates both cases.

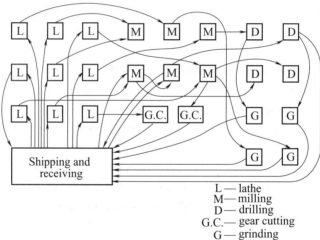

(a) when departmentalization is by process

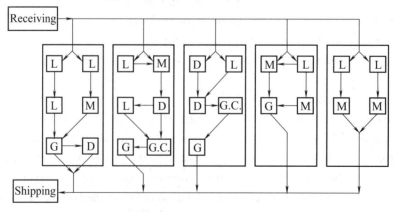

(b) when group technology rules are applied

Fig. 15-1 Flow of parts processed in a plant

Improving economies of batch-type production. Usually, batch-type production involves a wide variety of nonstandard parts, seemingly with nothing in common. Therefore, grouping parts (and processes) in families enables achieving economies that are obtainable only in mass production.

Easter scheduling. Grouping the parts into families facilitates the task of scheduling, since this work will be done for each family instead of for each part.

Reduced work-in-process and lead time. Reduced work-in-process (WIP) and lead time result directly from reduced setup and material-handling time. In other words, parts are not redundantly transferred between machining departments, since material handling is carried out efficiently within each of the individual cells. This is in contrast to the production in a typical plant with a process-type layout, where a piece that requires only a few minutes of machining may spend days on the shop floor. This latter situation involves increased WIP, which adversely affects the inventory turnover and the cash-flow cycle. Also, lead time for a product manufactured in a plant designed according to group technology principles is far shorter than that of a product manufactured in a plant with a process-type layout.

Faster and more rational process planning. Group technology paves the way for automated process planning. This can be achieved through proper parts classification and coding system, where a detailed process plan for each part is stored under its code and thus can be easily retrieved.

Factors Preventing Widespread Application of Group Technology

Problems associated with rearrangement of physical equipment. As we saw, group technology is always associated with the concept of cellular manufacturing. The latter necessitates rearrangement of the existing physical equipment (machine tools) to form the cells. This, in fact, involves costly and cumbersome work, which is sometimes difficult to justify.

The large amount of up-front work needed. In order to implement group technology, it would seem that every single part in the inventory of the industrial corporation must be coded so that part families can be established. This appears to be a big task, which creates a barrier to any tendency toward implementing group technology. However, any manufacturing corporation actually deals with ordered and similar groups of parts because of the area of specialty of that corporation and/or its product line (i.e., range of products). Accordingly, an appropriable approach for solving the problem of up-front work is to do that task gradually, by coding just the blueprints released to the workshop. As a result, the numbers of truly new (uncoded) parts released to the workshop tend to level out after a short period of time.

Natural resistance to anything new. We as human beings try to keep away from the risky unknown. This very reason makes many managers and administrators avoid adapting new concepts and philosophies such as group technology.

Classification and Coding of Parts

In order to implement a classification and coding system based on group technology principles successfully, parts must be classified according to suitable features; then a meaningful code is assigned to reflect those features. The process of retrieving or grouping parts because of similar features therefore becomes a simple one. As a matter of fact, ZIP codes exemplify the basic features of a classification and coding scheme. The ZIP code indicates a geographic location by progressively classifying it into subdivisions, starting with the state and proceeding to county, city, neighborhood, and street. Codes that are numerically close indicate locations that are, in reality, geographically close as well. In fact, it is this latter particular feature that enables the formation of a family of similar parts based on only codes, without the need for physically examining the parts or their drawings.

Although many classification and coding systems have been developed all over the world, none of them as yet has become a universally standard one. This is mainly because of the fact that a system must meet the specific needs of the organization for which it has been developed. It is, therefore, the right approach to develop a group technology classification and cording scheme based on the specific needs of the client or to tailor an existing turnkey system to meet those needs.

As previously mentioned, there are many benefits for group technology; these can fall within two main areas of application, design and manufacturing. Although it is always the ultimate goal to combine the advantages of group technology in both areas, this is usually very difficult to achieve, and the result is either a design-oriented or a manufacturing-oriented system.

Construction of a coding system. A coding system may be based only on numbers or only on alphabets, or it can also be alphanumeric. When using alphabetical codes, each position (or digital location) can have 26 different alternatives, but the alternative values are only limited to 10 per position when numerical codes are used. Consequently, alphabets are employed to widen the scope of a coding scheme and make it more flexible.

There are basically two types of code constructions, namely, monotonies and polycodes. Monocodes which are also referred to as hierarchical, or tree-striate, codes, are based on the approach that each digit amplifies the information given in the preceding digit. It is, therefore, obvious that the meaning of each digit (or what a digit indicates) is dependent upon the digits preceding it. Monocodes tend to be short and are shape-oriented. However, they do not directly indicate the attributes of components because of their hierarchical structure. Consequently, they are usually used for design storage and retrieval and are not successful for manufacturing applications.

On the contrary, the meaning of each digit in a polycode is completely independent of any other digits and provides information that can be directly recognized from its code. For this latter reason the polycode is sometimes referred as the attribute code. The basic idea is illustrated in Fig. 15-2, which indicates the way a polycode, is structured. We can easily see that a polycode is generally manufacturing-oriented, because the easily identifiable attributes help the manufacturing engineer determine the processing requirements of parts. Moreover, a polycode involves a string of features, a structure that makes it particularly suitable for computer analysis. Nevertheless, polycode tend to be long, and a digit location must be reserved whether or not that particular feature applies to a part of a family being coded. It is, therefore, a common industrial practice to use a hybrid construction, combining the advantages of each of the two basic codes while eliminating their disadvantages. In a combination type, the first digit divides the whole group of parts into subgroups, where shorter polycodes are employed. Also, in order to eliminate completely the possibility of error when coding a part, an interactive conversational computer program is employed, where the computer asks questions and automatically

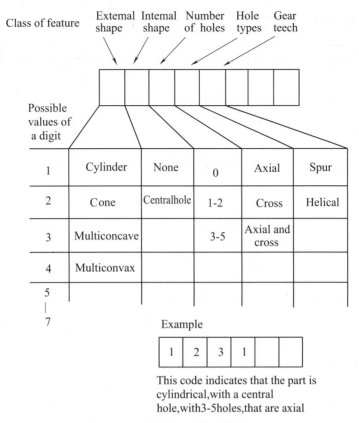

Fig. 15-2 Structure of a polycode

assigns a code for the part based on answers provided by the user at the computer terminal. An example of that automated coding is the MICLASS system (Metal Institute Clarification System), which was developed by the Netherlands Organization for Applied Scientific Research and has gained industrial application in the United States during tube last decade.

Design of Production Cells

It is time to see how a production cell can be designed. But, before doing so, we need to understand a new concept, namely, the composite part. This is a hypothetical part that has all attributes possessed by all of the individual parts of a family. Consequently, the processes required to manufacture the parts of a family would all be employed to produce the composite part representing that family. Any part that is a member of that family can then be obtained by deleting, as appropriate, some of the operations required for producing the composite part. Fig. 15-3 illustrates that concept of the composite part consisting of all processing attributes of all the parts of the family, which are also shown in that figure.

The next step is to design the machining cell to provide all machining capabilities based on the processing attributes of the composite part for the family of parts that is to be manufactured in that machining cell. The number of each kind of machine tool depends upon how frequently that machining operation is needed. In other words, the number of each kind of machine tool in a machining cell is not necessarily the same for all the different kinds of machine tools in the cell. After determining the kinds and numbers of machine tools in the cell,

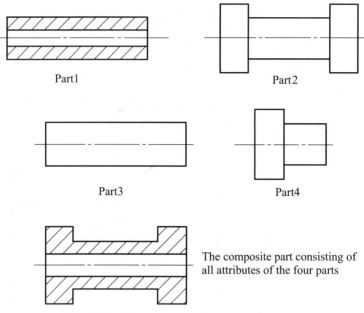

Fig. 15-3　The concept of a composite part

the layout of machines within that cell is planned to achieve efficient flow of workpieces through the cell. Of course, the cells are also arranged to guarantee easy flow of raw stock into the cells and finished products out.

Words and Expressions

facilitate /fə'siliteit/ v.		使容易，促进
promote /prə'məut/ vt.		提倡，鼓励
messy /'mesi/ adj.		凌乱的
redundant /ri'dʌndənt/ adj.		多余地，重复地
process planning		工艺规程设计
cumbersome /'kʌmbəsəm/ adj.		笨重的
barrier /'bæriə/ n.		障碍
orient /'ɔːriənt/ vt.		定…的方向
alphanumeric /ˌælfənjuː'merik/ adj.		字母数字混合编制的
hybrid /'haibrid/ adj.		混合的

Passage II　Cellular Manufacturing

Cellular manufacturing is the concept of organizing plant facilities and process planning for family-of-parts manufacture. The plant's machine tools are divided into cells, each serving a particular part family.

One approach is to have as few cells as possible, each serving a major part division, so that there is a redundancy of principal or core machines in each cell. The core machines are usually multifunction NC machines, with peripheral machines as necessary to offer complete part processing within the cell.

This approach would provide substantial flexibility, simplify the balancing of work loads, and achieve a considerable share of the savings inherent in cellular manufacturing, even without direct numerical control and automatic work handling. Such features could be added in a later phase of the project.

The second approach is to dedicate each (smaller) cell to a narrow part family, using state-of-art machine and control technology. This approach can provide very efficient part production. It lends itself to time-phased project planning. One cell can pay for the next. Maintaining balanced work loads in a smaller cell may be more difficult than doing so in the next larger cell.

Where the part has considerable diverse work content (many operations), and several machines are needed, the flow-line principle may be applicable. Here parts are moved from station to station along a straight line or a circular path. If straight line, work transfer can be provided by conveyor, a shuttle arrangement, or a rail-mounted robot. This arrangement lends itself to prismatic parts. If circular, work transfer is by means of a fixed-base, general-purpose robot that has considerable sweep in the horizontal plane (Fig. 15-4).

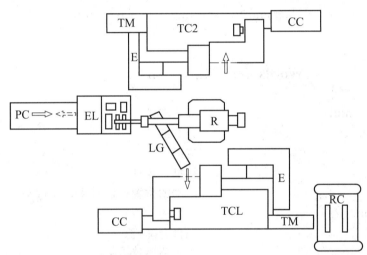

An articulated six-axis, floor-mounted robot (R) with extended horizontal sweep loads and unloads the two CNC turning centers (TC1, TC2). Other system elements include the two-level, two-way parts conveyor (PC) with pallet elevator (EL), laser gage (LG) and individual machine electric and control cabinets (E), chip conveyor(CC), and tool storage matrix (TM) with automatic tool changer. With several such cells networked into a system, entire tool storage matrices can be interchanged, tool transport being provided by automatic guided vehicle (RC).

Fig. 15-4 Typical advanced flexible manufacturing cell for processing parts of rotation

For part of rotation in particular, multiple-function machines are frequently paired with a robot that loads and unloads both machines and presents workpieces to an integrated inspection station. The cell may have two turning centers, or two grinding machines, or both a turning center and a grinding machine.

In some cases, the turning machines are identical and offer the choice of doing one part complete on one machine and another part on the second machine, or on higher-volume parts running the part on either machine to keep both busy doing identical work, or using two setting with the robot not only transferring work but swinging the workpiece end for end between settings.

On longer-cycle parts, the above-mentioned tasks may not utilize all of the robot's time. The robot could also help clear chips, do a deburring operation, or even perform a secondary operation.

On larger, heavier parts or larger machines, or certain machine configurations or groupings of several machines, it may be possible to so configure the cell as to permit use of an overhead gantry-mounted robot. On some smaller, lighter work an integral, machine-mounted robotic arm for part loading/unloading may be feasible.

Carousel, racetrack, or comparable multistation automatic work changers for machine centers permit such machines to run for long periods lightly attended or unattended. This feature, together with automatic tool change, multiple-part program secondary operation. storage, and other features permit certain stand-alone machines to function as flexible minicells.

In robotized cells, the robot's computer usually has sufficient capacity to act as a system coordinator. An inspection station may require its own computer or programmable control for handling and analyzing inspection data and transmitting compensation instructions to machine controllers.

Words and Expressions

family-of-part	/ˈfæmiliəvˈpɑːt/ n.	成族零件
time-phased	/taimˈfeizd/ adj.	分时的
flow-line	/fləuˈlain/ n.	流线
sweep	/swiːp/ n.	扫描,摇杆
end for end		两端的位置颠倒过来,反过来
articulated	/ɑːˈtikjuleitid/ adj.	铰接的
pallet elevator		托盘升降机
laser gage		激光测厚仪
control cabinet		操纵台,控制柜
storage matrix		存储矩阵
automatic tool changer		自动换刀装置
tool changer		换刀器,换刀装置
gantry	/ˈgæntri/ n.	台架
carousel	/ˌkærəˈsel/ n.	圆盘传送带
machine center		加工中心
minicell	/ˈminisel/ n.	微单元
coordinator	/kouˈɔːdineitə/ n.	协调者

Passage Ⅲ Machine Centers

Known in the 1960s as ATCs, or automatic tool changers, machining centers originated out of their capability to perform a variety of machining operations on a workpiece by changing their own cutting tools. Thus began a tool change and additional feature/capability revolution among machine tool builders that continues to escalate by adding improvements and enhancements to the staggering array of machining center choices.

Machining centers, ever in the early years of 'turret drills', began to affect manufacturing operations. Their adoption, in many cases, served as a shop's introduction to numerical control. And their high productivity frequently has forced a rethinking of part setup and processing requirements. Statically, they have become well accepted as a separate class of machine.

Today, machining center usage continues to expand from stand-alone job shop applications to flexible manufacturing cells and systems. However, the increased utilization and higher chip-removal rates of automated applications place considerable wear, tear, stress, and strain on a cell or system's most value-added component.

Machining centers, just like turning centers, are classified as either vertical or horizontal. Vertical machining centers continue to be widely accepted and used, primarily for flat parts and where there-axis machining is required on a single part face such as in mold and die work. Horizontal machining centers are also widely accepted and used, particularly with large, boxy, and heavy parts and because they lend themselves to easy and accessible pallet shuttle transfer when used in a cell or FMS application.

Selection of either a vertical or horizontal machining center mainly depends on the part type, size, weight, application, and, in many cases, personal preference.

Machining center construction has improved to accommodate higher spindle speeds, feeds, and horsepower requirements, along with overall higher utilization rates and increased performance requirements. Machine beds, for the most part, are still the more traditional cast-iron or welded-steel plating. However, computer modeling of the final structures, using such techniques as finite-element analysis, has become more widespread. As a result, castings now routinely feature internal ribs and fabricated steel shapes and braces that have been optimized to yield fewer distortions when the machine is in a loud or cut condition.

Spindle head improvements have advanced to accommodate a fifth axis (and more) of movement, which greatly enhances a machining center's versatility. Key to the new designs are pitch and roll motions right in the spindle head. The additional axes of movement are a necessity, particularly on large machining centers, where the workpiece cannot be easily moved and the tool must tilt and pivot to machine the stationary clamped part. But spindle heads that move in more than three primary axes are also becoming more popular for smaller workpieces. Parts previously machined in several settings on ram-type universal milling machines are moving over to small machining centers to be completed in one part setting.

Some machine tool vendors now offer horizontal-vertical spindles. These are similar in appearance to right-angle spindle attachments that have long been available to change the spindle orientation by 90 degrees. Machines such as these continue to gain acceptance and prominence because they decrease the nonvalue-added setup and piece-handling time and increase the value-added chip-making time. Overall, there is an apparent trend to adding more features, other than just rotation for machining, at the spindle. This means that heads generally are becoming more complicated.

Characteristics demanded of machining center spindles by modern high-performance cutting tool materials include stiffness, running accuracy (runout), axial load-carrying capacity, thermal stability, and axial freedom for thermal expansion. Most importantly though, the demand is for speed. In some cases, spindle speeds have exceeded the 6000~7000 rpm range, depending on the manufacturer and application required.

By today's definition, a machining center must include an automatic tool changer. Tool-storage and tool-change mechanisms vary among the diversified machine tool suppliers, as some are front, side, or top mounted. The advantages of having tools stored away from the working spindle include less contamination from flying chips and better protection for an operator changing tools during machining. The double-ended, 180-degree indexing arm continues to be the most popular approach, although various designs of the tool gripping and clamping mechanisms will vary among builders.

More cutting tools are needed with modern machining centers, which means more tool storage capacity is required. Machining requirements for cells and systems demand that backup tools be available on-line to replace a broken tool or a worn-out tool before it breaks. Tools stored at machining centers fit into individual pockets of a machine tool's magazine or tool matrix. Pocket designs vary, ranging from simple holes cut into a disk-shaped carrousel to individually machined pockets assembled into a chain to interconnected plastic pockets.

Words and Expressions

staggering /ˈstægəriŋ/ adj.	交错的，摇摆的
turret drill	六角机床
statistically /stəˈtistikəli/ adv.	统计上地，统计
tear /tɛə/ n.; v.	扯裂，撕裂
value-added /ˌvæljuːˈædid/ adj.	有附加值的，增值的
boxy /ˈbɔksi/ adj.	箱状的，四四方方的
horsepower /ˈhɔːsˌpauə/ n.	马力，输出功率
overall /ˈəuvərɔːl/ adv.	大体上
welded-steel /ˈweldidˈstiːl/ n.	焊接钢
plating /ˈpleitiŋ/ n.	镀件
computer modeling	计算机模拟
routinely /ruːˈtiːnli/ adv.	例行公事地
fabricated steel	预制钢
distortion /disˈtɔːʃən/ n.	扭曲，变形
primary axis	主坐标轴
nonvalue-added /ˌnɔnˈvæljuːˈædid/ adj.	没有附加值的，不增值的
piece-handing time	工件装卸时间
chip-making /ˈtʃipˈmeikiŋ/ adj.	制造切屑的
running accuracy	旋转精度
runout /ˈrʌnaut/ n.	跳动，径向跳动
load-carrying capacity	负荷能力，承载能力
thermal stability	热稳定性，耐热性
double-ended /ˈdʌblˌendid/ adj.	双端的

worn-out /ˌwɔːnˈaut/ *adj*.	不能再用的，磨破的
fit into	适合
pocket /ˈpɔkit/ *n*.	槽
magazine /ˌmæɡəˈziːn/ *n*.	仓库
carrousel /ˌkæruˈzel/ *n*.	回转车

Passage IV   Flexible Manufacturing Systems

What is FMS?

Definitions of FMS, or Flexible Manufacturing Systems, are plentiful and in many respects are dependent on the ultimate user's point of view as to what the FMS consists of and how it will be used. However, the following represent a collection of FMS definitions, some traceable and some not traceable to their originating source.

(1) United States Government: A series of automatic machine tools or items of fabrication equipment linked together with an automatic material handling system, a common hierarchical digital preprogrammed computer control, and provision for random fabrication of parts or assemblies that fall within predetermined families.

(2) Kearney and Trecker: A FMS is a group of NC machine tolls that can randomly process a group of parts, having automated material handling and central computer control to dynamically balance resource utilization so that the system can adapt automatically to changes in parts production, mixes, and levels of output.

(3) FMS is a randomly loaded automated system based on group technology manufacturing linking integrated computer control and a group of machines to automatically produce and handle (move) parts for continuous serial processing.

(4) FMS combines microelectronics and mechanical engineering to bring the economics of scale to batch work. A central on-line computer controls the machine tools, other workstations, and the transfer of components and tooting. The computer also provides monitoring and information control. This combination of flexibility and overall control makes possible the production of a wide range of products in small numbers.

(5) A process under control to produce varieties of components or products within its stated capability and to a predetermined schedule.

(6) A technology which will help achieve leaner factories with better response times, lower unit costs, and higher quality under an improved level of management and capital control.

Regardless of how broadly or narrowly FMS is defined, several key items emerge as critical to a general definition of FMS, and repeat themselves through a cross-section of standard definitions. Words like NC machine tools, automatic material handling system, central computer controlled, randomly loaded, linked together and flexible all serve to help define a very general description and definition of FMS.

Flexible manufacturing affords users the opportunity to react quickly to changing product types, mixes, and volumes while providing increased utilization and predictable control over hard assets. Although FMS provides users with many benefits they are not easy to justify. Limitations and alternatives must be weighed and compared to determine if FMS is the best or even the right approach to productivity and profitability improvements.

Basically, an FMS is made up of hardware and software elements. Hardware, elements are visible and tangible such as CNC machine tools pallet queuing carrousels (part parking lots), material handling equipment (robots or automatic guided vehicles), central chip removal and coolant systems, tooling systems, coordinate measuring machines (CMMs), part cleaning stations and computer hardware equipment. Software elements are invisible and intangible such as NC programs traffic management software tooling information. CMM program work order files, and sophisticated FMS software. A typical FMS layout and its major identifiable components can be seen in Fig. 15-5.

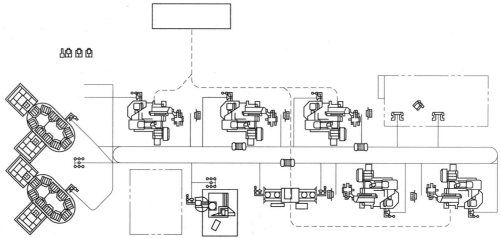

Fig. 15-5 Typical FMS and its major identifiable components.
(Courtesy of Cincinnati Milacron)

Automated Storage and Retrieval Systems

In the 1950s, a revolutionary concept in material handling was pioneered in the United States called automated storage and retrieval. At the time, this concept of high-rise, high-density storage and retrieval was considered a radical change in inventory management and control, rather than a revolutionary breakthrough.

Automated storage and retrieval systems, commonly referred to as ASRSs, are automated inventory-handling systems designed to replace manual and remote-control systems. Typically, they contain tall, vertical storage racks, narrow aisles, and stacker cranes and are coupled with some type of computer control. For the most part, ASRSs are strictly warehouse tools that track incoming material and components, store parts, tools, and fixtures, and retrieve them when necessary.

The goal of an automated storage and retrieval system is to deliver the right material to the right place at the right time. Material is held in storage and then issued to the point of use as close to the time of use as possible.

Automated storage and retrieval systems store standard-sized pallets of material, and they have aisles that divide the storage racks. In each aisle is an arm or crane, sometimes known as a stacker crane. The crane picks up a load from an input station, stores it in a computer-assigned location, and delivers it to an output station, as seen in Fig. 15-6.

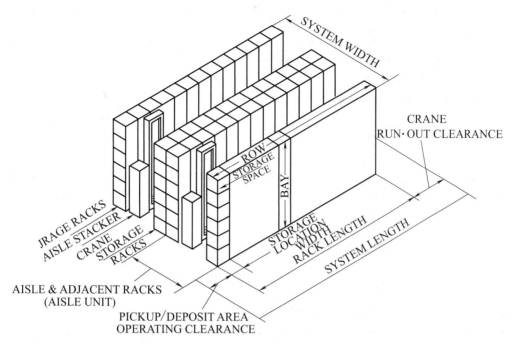

Fig. 15-6 Automatic storage and retrieval hardware

Stacker cranes are rated in terms of vertical and horizontal movement in feet per second. Cranes are capable of simultaneous vertical and horizontal movement. Loads must be presented for crane movement within size, weight, and stability limits. Even if a load is within size and weight limits, an off-center load, for example, can still jam the crane.

The principal benefits of automated storage and retrieval systems are:
(1) Improved inventory management and control.
(2) Reliable and immediate delivery.
(3) Space efficiency.
(4) Simplified and faster inventory response.
(5) Ability to operate in adverse environments.
(6) Closed storage area to reduce pilferage.
(7) Reduced lost or misplaced parts, tools, and fixtures.
(8) Design flexibility to accommodate a wide range of loads.
① Five CNC machining centers, 90 tools each.
② Five tool interchange stations, one per machine, accepting tool delivery via cart.
③ Three computer-controlled carts with wireguided path.
④ Cart maintenance station.
⑤ Two automatic workchangers, 10 pallets each, with dual load/unload positions with 90° tilt, 360° rotation.
⑥ Two material review stands, for on-demand part inspection.
⑦ Inspection module, with horizontal arm coordinate measuring machine.
⑧ Automatic part washing station.
⑨ Tool chain load/unload tool gage, and calibration gage stands.
⑩ Elevated computer room, with DEC VAX 8200 central computer.
⑪ Centralized chip/coolant collection/recovery system, with dual flume.

······Flume path

(9) Reduced labor costs.

(10) Accurate inventory and load location.

(11) Inventory reductions (as a result of improved accuracy).

(12) Increased utilization potential.

(13) Reduced scrap and rework (resulting from manual part movement damage).

Over the past several years, many companies have focused their attention on automated storage and retrieval systems as a means to solve existing warehouse problems. In many cases, implementing an ASRS and other material movement systems have successfully reduced operating costs and gained control over the storage and retrieval process. However, business conditions and objectives determine the need for an ASRS, and a fully automated warehouse may be inappropriate for some businesses.

Overall work flow and manufacturing processes must be clearly understood and known in order to determine part, tool, and fixture movement frequency, as well as maximum and minimum load sizes. Flow to and from the areas that the ASRS is to serve should be kept clean and free of obstructions and waiting to be moved components.

Storage space is the three-dimensional space required to store a single load unit of material. A bay is a vertical stack of storage locations reaching from floor to ceiling. A row is a series of bays placed side-by-side. The aisle is the space between two rows for stacker crane operation. Storage racks are the total structural entity comprising the storage locations, bays, and rows. An aisle unit is the aisle plus adjacent racks.

Automated Guide Vehicle (AGV)

An AGV is a computer-controlled, driverless vehicle used for transporting materials from point to point in a manufacturing setting. They represent a major category of automated materials handling devices. An AGV can be used for any and all materials handling tasks from bringing in raw materials to moving finished products to the shipping dock.

In any discussion of AGVs, three key terms are heard frequently:

(1) Guide path.

(2) Routing.

(3) Traffic management.

The term guide path refers to the actual path the AGV follows in making its rounds through a manufacturing plant. The guide path can be one of two types. The first and oldest type is the embedded wire guide path. With this type, which has been in existence for over 20 years, the AGV follows a path dictated by a wire that is contained within a path that runs under the shop floor. This is why the earliest AGVs were sometimes referred to as wire-guided vehicles. The more modern AGVs are guided by optical devices.

The term routing is also used frequently in association with AGVs. Routing has to do with the AGV's ability to make decisions that allow it to select the appropriate route as it moves across the shop floor. The final term, traffic management, means exactly the same thing on the shop floor that it means on the highway. Traffic management devices such as stop signs, yield signs, caution lights, and stop lights are used to control traffic in such a way as to prevent collisions and to optimize traffic flow and traffic patterns. This is also what traffic management means when used in the context of AGVs.

1. Rationale for Using AGVs

Some manufacturing plants still use traditional materials handling systems. Some use automated storage and retrieval systems. Others use AGVs. Many use all of these together. Manufacturing technology students should understand why manufacturing firms use AGVs. Five of the most frequently stated reasons are as follows:

(1) Because they can be computer controlled, AGVs represent a flexible approach to materials handling.

(2) AGVs decrease labor costs by decreasing the amount of human involvement in materials handling.

(3) AGVs are compatible with production and storage equipment.

(4) AGVs can operate in hazardous environments.

(5) AGVs can handle and transport hazardous materials safely.

Of the various reasons frequently given for using AGVs, perhaps the two that are the most important to the future of manufacturing are flexibility and compatibility. Because they are so versatile, they can be adapted to be compatible with most production and storage equipment that might exist in a typical manufacturing setting. Their flexibility and compatibility allow AGVs to fit in with trends in the world of manufacturing, including automation and integration of manufacturing processes.

2. Types of AGVs

Automated guided vehicles are called on for use in a variety of different manufacturing settings. Consequently, there is no one type that will meet the needs of every setting. Fig. 15-7 and Fig. 15-8 show typical AGVs. In the current state of development, there are six different types of AVGs.

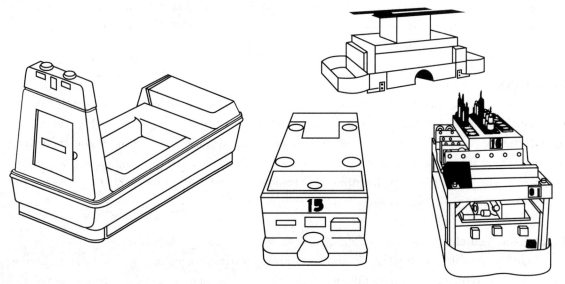

Fig. 15-7　AGV and dock　　Fig. 15-8　Sample of AGVs. Courtesy of the society of manufacturing Engineers

(1) Towing vehicles.

(2) Unit load venires.

(3) Pallet trucks.
(4) Fork trucks.
(5) Light load vehicles.
(6) Assembly line vehicles.

Towing Vehicles

These AGVs are the work horses. Towing vehicles are the most widely used type of AGVs. Their most common use is in transporting large amounts of bulky and heavy materials from the warehouse to various locations in the manufacturing plant. A popular approach is to arrange a series of vehicles into a train configuration. In such a configuration, each vehicle can be loaded with material for a specified location and the train can be programmed to move throughout the manufacturing facility, stopping at each location.

Unit Load Vehicles

Unit load vehicles represent the opposite extreme from towing vehicles. Whereas towing vehicles are used in settings requiring the movement of large amounts of material to a variety of different locations, unit load vehicles are used in settings with short guide paths, high volume, and a need for independent movement and versatility. Warehouses and distribution centers are the most likely settings for unit load vehicles. An advantage of unit load vehicles is that they can operate in an environment where there is not much room and movement is restricted.

Pallet Trucks

The pallet truck is different from other AGVs in that it can be operated manually. Pallet trucks are used most frequently for materials handling and distribution systems. They are driven along a guide path from location to location and are unloaded as they go. Because they can be operated manually pallet trucks represent a very flexible approach to materials handing.

Fork Trucks

The fork truck type AGV is to the automated manufacturing plant what the fork lift is to a traditional materials handling setting. Fork trucks are designed for use in highly automated manufacturing plants. They are used when it is necessary to pick material up at the shop floor level and move it to a location at a higher level or to pick up material at a higher level and move it down to the shop floor level. Unlike the traditional fork lift, however, fork truck type AGVs travel along a guide path.

Light Load Vehicles

Light load vehicle technology is simply the miniaturization of unit load vehicle technology. Light load vehicles, as the name suggests, are used in manufacturing settings where the material to be moved is neither heavy nor bulky.

Assembly Line Vehicles

As the name implies, assembly line vehicle type AGVs are used in conjunction with an assembly line process. Their most common use is in the assembly of automobiles. Assembly line vehicles can be used to transport major subassemblies such as automobile engines transmissions, doors, and other associated subassemblies to the proper location on an assembly line. Using such vehicles can enhance the flexibility of an automobile assembly line.

Words and Expressions

queue /kju:/	n.	对，列
	v.	排队
carrousel /kæru'sel/	n.	旋转式传送带
inventory /'inventri/	n.	（商品，货物等）清单，目录，报表；存货，库存
obstruction /əb'strʌkʃən/	n.	堵塞，障碍物
towing vehicle		小型牵引车
unit load vehicle		单载小车
pallet truck		托盘运输车
fork truck=fork lift		叉车
light load vehicle		轻载小车
assembly line vehicle		装配线运输车
bulky /'bʌlki/	adj.	大的，容量大的，体积大的
miniaturization /,miniətʃərai'ʃən/	n.	小型化

Passage Ⅴ   Computer Integrated Manufacturing System（Ⅰ）

CIM Defined

Computer-integrated manufacturing or (CIM) is the term used to describe the most modern approach to manufacturing. Although CIM encompasses many of the other advanced manufacturing technologies such as computer numerical control (CNC), computer-aided design/computer-aided manufacturing (CAD/CAM), robotics, and just-in-time delivery (JIT), it is more than a new technology or a new concept. Computer-integrated manufacturing is actually an entirely new approach to manufacturing a new way of doing business.

To understand CIM, is necessary to begin with a comparison of modern and traditional manufacturing. Modern manufacturing encompasses all of the activities and processes necessary to convert raw materials into finished products, deliver them to the market, and support them in the field. These activities include the following:

(1) Identifying a need for a product.
(2) Designing a product to meet the needs.
(3) Obtaining the raw materials needed to produce the product.
(4) Applying appropriate presses to transform the raw materials into finished products.
(5) Transporting product to the market.
(6) Maintaining the product to ensure a proper performance in the field.

This broad, modern view of manufacturing can be compared with the more limited traditional view that focuses almost entirely on the conversion processes. The old approach separates such critical preconversion elements as market analysis research, development, and design for manufacturing, as well as such after-conversion elements as product delivery and product maintenance. In other words, in the old approach to manufacturing, only those processes that take place on the shop floor are considered manufacturing. This traditional approach of separating the overall concept into numerous stand-alone specialized elements was not fundamentally changed with the advent of automation. While the separate elements themselves became automated (i. e., computer-aided drafting and design (CADD) in design and CNC in machining), they remained separate. Automation alone did not result in the integration of these islands of automation.

With CIM not only are the various elements automated, but the islands of automation are all linked together or integrated. Integration means that a system can provide complete and instantaneous sharing information. In modern manufacturing, integration is accomplished by computers. With this background, CIM can now be defined as.

The Total Integration of All Manufacturing Elements Through The Use of Computers

Fig. 15-9 is an illustration of a CIM system, which shows how the various machines and processes used in the conversion process are integrated. However, such an illustration cannot show that research, development, design, marketing, sales, shipping, receiving, management, and production personnel all have instant access to all information generated in this system. This is what makes it a CIM system.

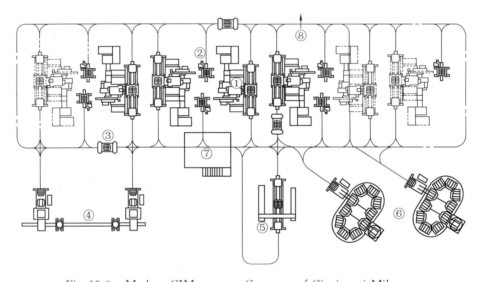

Fig. 15-9 Modern CIM system. Courtesy of Cincinnati Milacron

① Four Milacron CNC Machining Centers (Floor Space Reserved for Adding Three More).
② Four Tool Interchange Systems (One Per Machine). Computer-Controlled Tool Delivery Via Cart.
③ Three Remotely Controlled Carts With Wire-Guided Path.
④ Two Load/Unload. Clean/Orient Stations With Coolant/Chip Handling.
⑤ One Inspection Module (Coordinate Measuring Machine).
⑥ Two Automatic Workchangers (10 Pallets Each) For Part Overflow And Queue.

⑦ Raised Office (Cart Path Under).
⑧ Cart Maintenance Station.

Historical Development of CIM

The term 'computer-integrated manufacturing' was developed in 1974 by Joseph Harrington as the title of a book he wrote about tying islands of automation together through the use of computers. It has taken many years for CIM to develop as a concept, but integrated manufacturing is not really new. In fact, integration is where manufacturing actually began. Manufacturing has evolved through four distinct stages (Fig. 15-10):

(1) Manual manufacturing.
(2) Mechanization/Specialization.
(3) Automation.
(4) Integration.

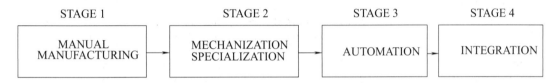

Fig. 15-10 Historical development of integrated manufacturing

1. Manual Manufacturing

Manual manufacturing using simple hand tools was actually integrated manufacturing. All information needed to design, produce, and deliver a product was readily available because it resided in the mind of the one person who performed all of the necessary tasks. The tool of integration in the earliest years of manufacturing was the human mind of the craftsman who designed, produced and delivered the product. An example of integrated manual manufacturing is the village blacksmith producing a special tool for a local farmer. The blacksmith would have in his mind all of the information needed to design, produce, and deliver the farmer's tool. In this example, all elements of manufacturing are integrated.

2. Mechanization/Specialization

With the advent of the industrial revolution, manufacturing processes became both specialized and mechanized. Instead of one person designing, producing, and delivering a product, workers and/or machines performed specialized tasks within each of these broad areas. Communication among these separate entities was achieved using drawings, specifications, job orders, process plans, and a variety of other communication aids. To ensure that the finished product matched the planned product the concept of quality control was introduced.

The positive side of the mechanization/specialization stage was that it permitted mass production interchangeability of parts, entire levels of accuracy, and uniformity. The disadvantage is that the lack of integration led to a great deal of waste.

3. Automation

Automation improved the performance and enhanced the capabilities of both people and machines within specialized manufacturing, components. For example, CADD enhanced the capability of designers and drafters; CNC enhanced the capabilities of machinists; and computer-assisted process planning (CAPP) enhanced the capabilities of industrial planners. But the improvements brought on by automation were isolated within individual components or islands. Because of this, automation did not always live up to its potential.

To understand the limitations of automation with regard to overall productivity improvement, consider the following analogy. Suppose that various subsystems of an automobile (i.e. engine, steering, brakes) were automated to make the driver's job easier. Automatic acceleration, deceleration, steering, and braking would certainly be more efficient than the manual versions. However, consider what would happen if these various automated subsystems were not tied together in a way that allowed them to communicate and share accurate, up-to-date in information instantly and continually. One system might be attempting to accelerate the automobile while another system was attempting to apply the brakes. The same limitations apply in an automated manufacturing setting. These limitations are what led to the current stage in the development of manufacturing: integration.

4. Integration

With the advent of tile computer age, manufacturing has developed full circle. It began as a totally integrated concept and, with CIM, has once again become one. However, there are major differences in the manufacturing integration of today and that of the manual era of the past. First, the instrument of integration in the manual era was the human mind. The instrument of integration in modern manufacturing is the computer. Second, processes in the modern manufacturing setting are still specialized and automated.

Another way to view the historical development of CIM is by examining the ways in which some of the individual components of CIM have developed over the years, such components as design, planning and production have evolved both as processes and in the tools and equipment used to accomplish the processes.

Design has evolved from a manual process using such tools as slide rules, triangles, pencils, scales, and erasers into an automated process known as computer-aided design (CAD). Process planning has evolved from a manual process using planning tables, diagrams, and charts into an automated process known as computer-aided process planning (CAPP). Production has evolved from a manual process involving manually controlled machines into an automated process known as computer-aided manufacturing (CAM).

These individual components of manufacturing evolved over the years into separate islands of automation. However, communication among these islands was still handled manually. This limited the level of improvement in productivity that could be accomplished in the overall manufacturing process. When these islands and other automated components of manufacturing are linked together through computer networks, these limitations can be overcome. Computer-integrated manufacturing has enormous potential for improving productivity in manufacturing, but it is not without problems.

Words and Expressions

encompass /inˈkʌmpəs/ v.　　　　　　　包括
advent /ˈædvənt/ n.　　　　　　　　　　出现，来临
reside /riˈzaid/ v.　　　　　　　　　　　居住，存放

Passage Ⅵ Computer Integrated Manufacturing System (Ⅱ)

Composition of CIM

The Computer and Automated Systems Association (CASA) of the Society of Manufacturing Engineers (SME) developed tile CIM wheel (Fig. 15-11) as a way to comprehensively, but concisely illustrate the concept of CIM. The CASA/SME developed the CIM wheel to include five distinct components:

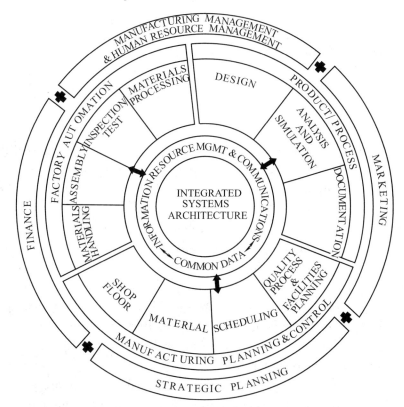

Fig. 15-11 CIM wheel. Reprinted courtesy of the Computer and Automated Systems Association (CASA) of the Society Manufacturing Engineers

(1) General business management.
(2) Product and press definition.
(3) Manufacturing planning, and control.
(4) Factory automation.
(5) Information resource management.

General Business Management

These are four principal elements of the general business management component of the CASA/SME CIM wheel. These four elements encompass all of those activities associated with doing any kind of business. They link the rest of the components of the CIM wheel to the outside world. Many of the processes within these four elements are automated. In manufacturing firms that have moved forward with automation, these four elements of the general business management component typically become individual islands of automation.

Within the finance element, it is not uncommon to have an automated payroll system, an automated accounts receivable system, and an automated accounts payable system. Such automation also exists in the other three components. However, in the typical automated manufacturing firm, these islands of automation within the general business management component are not networked for integration even within the component, much less with the other elements of the CIM wheel. For CIM to exist, every component within the CIM wheel must be networked and every individual element within components must be networked for instantaneous exchanges and updates of data.

Product and Process Definition

The product and process definition component of the CIM wheel contains three elements:
(1) Design.
(2) Analysis and simulation.
(3) Documentation.

This is the component, in which a product is engineered, designed, tested through simulation, documented through drawings, specifications, and other documentation tools such as parts lists and bills of material. Island of automation for this components of the CIM wheel have been emerging since the late 1960s.

These islands include CADD systems, modeling and simulation software including solids modeling, surface modeling, and finite-element analysis. Also within this component are such islands of automation as CAPP. Even in highly automated manufacturing plant in which all of the product and process definition systems are automated, it is rare to find effective networking and integration of the processes within this individual component, much less among the various other components of the CIM wheel. It is not uncommon, within this component of the wheel, to find incompatible hardware and software being used even in individual elements of a component such as design.

An example of this would be a company that automated its design processes early by purchasing hardware and software from supplier A. Later as technology continued to evolve, supplier B produced a better system and the company purchased it. However, due to financial limitations, the company was not able to purchase as many stations of the new system as it needed. As a result, some engineers and designers continue to work on the old automated system while others work at new stations. Because of differences in the hardware and software produced by the two suppliers, the old and new systems are incompatible. As a result, not only can this company not network its design functions with other components on the CIM wheel, it cannot even network within the product and process definition component. This type of incompatibly is more often the rule rather than the exception. It represents the principal obstacle to the full development of CIM.

Manufacturing Planning and Control

The manufacturing planning and control component includes such elements as facilities planning, scheduling, material planning and control, and shop floor planning and control. Hardware and software are available to automate each of the individual elements within this component. However as with the previous group, there is rarely integration of the elements within this component, much less outside of it. The chief problem here is also incompatibility.

Factory Automation

The factory automation component contains those elements normally associated with producing the product: materials handling assembly, inspection and testing, and materials processing. Much of the research and development in the area of automated manufacturing has focused on this group. Such automated manufacturing concepts as CNC, distributed numerical control (DNC), industrial robots, and automated malarias handling systems such as automated guided vehicles (AGVs) have been available for over 20 years. During this time, they have continually improved in performance. However, very little progress has been made in successfully networking the elements within this group with those outside of it. Some progress is being made through the concept of CAD/CAM in which the product and process definition islands of automation are networked with the factory automation elements. However, incompatibility remains the key <u>inhibitor</u> to full integration.

Information Resource Management

The importation resource management component of the CIM wheel is located in the center of Fig. 15-11. This is an appropriate position for this component because it represents the <u>nucleus</u> of CIM. Information, updated continually and shared instantaneously, is what CIM is all about. To integrate the various elements within the various components of the CIM wheel, all of the information generated by the various components must be effectively managed. One of the major goals of this component is to overcome the barriers that prevent the complete sharing of information between and among components in the CIM wheel.

There are two basic elements within this component: the information being managed and the hardware and software used to manage that information. The technology used to manage information within this component can be divided into four <u>categories</u> by function:

(1) Communications technology.
(2) Network transaction technology.
(3) Data management technology.
(4) User technology.

Each of these elements represents a different layer of computer technology. Achieving full integration of all elements and all components of the CIM wheel involves successfully horizontal and vertical networking at all four of these levels.

Benefits of CIM

In spite of the obstacles, progress is being made toward the eventual full realization of CIM in manufacturing. When this is accomplished, fully integrated manufacturing firms will realize a number of benefits from CIM:

(1) Product quality increases.
(2) Lead times are reduced.

(3) Direct labor costs are reduced.
(4) Product development times are reduced.
(5) Inventories are reduced.
(6) Overall productivity increases.
(7) Design quality increases.

Words and Expressions

payroll /ˈpeirəul/ n.	工资单
integration /ˌintiˈgreiʃən/ n.	综合，一体化，积分
instantaneous /ˌinstənˈteinjəs/ adj.	即时发生的
specification /ˌspesifiˈkeiʃən/ n.	规格
inhibitor /inˈhibitə/ n.	绊脚石
nucleus /ˈnjuːkliəs/ n.	核心
category /ˈkætigəri/ n.	种类，类别，等级，部门

Part 4 Assembly

Unit 16 Assembly

Passage I Introduction to Assembly

The increasing need for finished goods in large quantities has, in the past, led engineers to search for and to develop new methods of the production. Many individual developments in the various branches of manufacturing technology have been made and have allowed the increased production of improved finished goods at lower cost. One of the most important manufacturing processes is the assembly process. This process is required when two or more component parts are to be brought together to produce the finished product.

The early history of assembly process development is closely related to the history of the development of mass-production methods. Thus, the pioneers of mass production are also the pioneers of the modern assembly process. Their new ideas and concepts have brought significant improvements in the assembly methods employed in large-volume production.

However, although some branches of manufacturing engineering, such as metal cutting and metal forming processes, have recently been developing very rapidly, the technology of the basic assembly process has failed to keep pace, in the United States the percentage of the total labor force involved in the assembly process varies form about 20% for the manufacture of farm machinery to almost 60% for the manufacture of telephone and telegraph equipment. Because of this, assembly costs often account for more than 50% of the total manufacturing costs. Statistical surveys show that these figures are increasing every year.

In the past few years, certain efforts have been made to reduce assembly costs by the application of automation and modern techniques, such as ultrasonic welding and die-casting. However, success has been very limited and many assembly operators are still using the same basic tools as those employed at the time of the Industrial Revolution.

Choice of Assembly Method

When considering the assembly of a product, a manufacturer has to take into account the many factors that affect the choice of assembly system. For a new product, the following considerations are generally important:

  1. Cost of assembly.

2. Production rate required.
3. Availability of labor.
4. Market life of the product.

If an attempt is to be made to justify the automation of an existing operator assembly line, consideration has to be given to the redeployment of those operators who would become redundant. If labor is plentiful, the degree of automation depends on the reduction in cost of assembly and the increase in production rate brought about by the automation of the assembly line. However, it must be remembered that, in general, the capital investment in automatic machinery has to be amortized over the market life of the product unless the machinery may be adapted to assemble a new product. It is clear that if this is not the case and the market life of the product is short, automation is generally not justifiable.

A shortage of labor may often lead a manufacturer to consider automatic assembly when in fact it can be shown that operator assembly would be cheaper. Conversely, a manufacturer may be unable to automate because suitable employment cannot be found for the operators who would become redundant. Another reason for considering automation in a situation where operator assembly would be more economical is on a research basis, to gain experience in the field.

Advantages of Automatic Assembly

Following are some of the advantages of automation:
1. Reduction in the cost of assembly.
2. Increased productivity.
3. A more consistent product.
4. Removal of operators from hazardous operations.

A reduction in costs is often the main consideration and, except for the special circumstances listed above, it could be expected that automation would not be carried out if it was not expected to produce a reduction in costs.

Productivity in an advanced industrial society is an important measure of operating efficiency. Increased productivity, although not directly beneficial to a manufacturer unless labor is scarce, is necessary to an expanding economy because it releases personnel for other tasks. It is clear that when put into effect, automation of assembly lines generally reduces the number of operators required and hence increases productivity.

Some of the assembly tasks that an operator can perform easily are extremely difficult to duplicate on even the most sophisticated automatic workhead. An operator can often carry out a visual inspection of the part to be assembled, and parts that are obviously defective can be discarded. Sometimes a very elaborate inspection system is required to detect even the most obviously defective part. If an attempt is made to assemble a part that appears to be acceptable but is in fact defective, an operator, after unsuccessfully trying to complete the assembly, can reject the very quickly without a significant loss in production. In automatic assembly, however, unless the part has been rejected by the feeding device, an automatic workhead will probably stop and time then be wasted locating and eliminating the fault. If a part has only a minor defect, an operator may be able to complete the assembly, but the resulting product may not be completely satisfactory. It is often suggested that one of the advantages of automatic assembly is that it ensures a product of consistently high quality because the machine faults if the parts do not conform to the required specification.

In some situations, assembly by operators would be hazardous due to high temperatures and the presence of toxic substances and other materials. Under these circumstances, assembly by mechanical means is obviously advantageous.

An automatic assembly machine usually consists of a transfer system for moving the assemblies from workstation to workstation, automatic workheads to perform the simple assembly operations, vacant workstations for operators to carry out the more complicated assembly operations, and inspection stations to check that the various operations have been completed successfully. The automatic workheads are either fed manually with individual or magazine-stored component parts or are supplied with parts from an automatic <u>feeder</u> through a <u>feed track</u>. The workheads themselves usually consist of either a fastening device or a <u>parts-placing mechanism</u>. Examples of these workheads are nut and screw running heads, welding heads, riveting heads, soldering heads, push and guide placing mechanisms, and pick and place mechanisms.

Words and Expressions

keep pace (with)	与…同步，并驾齐驱
account for	说明，证明，是…的原因
redeployment /ˌriːdɪˈplɔɪmənt/ n.	调动，调配，重新部署
redundant /rɪˈdʌndənt/ adj.	多余的，过剩的
amortize /əˈmɔːtaɪz/ vt.	分期清偿
justifiable /ˈdʒʌstɪfaɪəbl/ adj.	言之有理的，无可非议的
workhead /ˈwəːkhed/ n.	工作台
defective /dɪˈfektɪv/ n.	次品，有缺陷的物品
adj.	有缺陷的
unsuccessfully /ˌʌnsəkˈsesfuli/ adv.	失败地，无用地
feeder /ˈfiːdə/ n.	进料器
feed track	输送道
parts-placing mechanism	元件分配装置

Exercises

Decide whether the following statements are true or false (T/F) according to the information for the text.

(　　) 1. The assembly process is used to bring two or more component parts together and produce the finished product.

(　　) 2. The assembly process is closely related to mass-production.

(　　) 3. The technology of the basic assembly process has been keeping pace with manufacturing engineering.

(　　) 4. In the past few years assembly costs have been successfully controlled at a low level.

(　　) 5. The degree of automation depends on the reduction in cost of assembly and the

increase in production rate in any case.
( ) 6. The shorter the market life of the product, the less justifiable the automation.
( ) 7. The cost of assembly is the main factor that should be considered in the carrying out automation.
( ) 8. If a part has only a minor defect, the final product may be satisfactory sometimes.
( ) 9. Assembly by mechanical means is safer than assembly operators.
( ) 10. An automatic assembly machine is usually composed of a transfer system, automatic work-heads, vacant work-stations and inspections stations.

Passage Ⅱ   Types of Manual Assembly Methods

Part acquisition time is highly dependent on the nature of the layout of the assembly area and the method of assembly. For small parts placed within easy reach of the assembly worker, the handling times are adequate if bench assembly (Fig. 16-1) or multistation assembly (Fig. 16-2) are employed. It is assumed in both cases that major body motions by the assembly worker are not required.

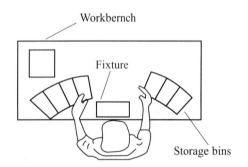

Fig. 16-1   Bench assembly

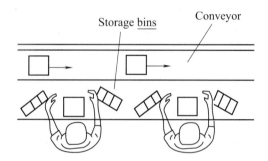

Fig. 16-2   Multistation assembly

For volumes that do not justify transfer systems and if the assembly contains several parts that weigh more than about 5 lb or that are over 12 in. in size, it will not be possible to place an adequate supply of parts within easy arm reach of the assembly worker. In this case, provided the largest part is less than 35 in. in size and no part weighs more than 30 lb, the modular assembly center might be used. This is an arrangement of workbench and storage shelves where the parts are situated as conveniently for the assembly worker as possible. However, because turning, bending or walking may be necessary for acquisition of some of the parts, the handling times will be increased. It is convenient to identify three modular work centers to accommodate assemblies falling within three size categories where the largest part in the assembly is less than 15 in., form 15 to 25 in., and from 25 to 35 in. in size, respectively.

For products with even larger parts, the custom assembly layout can be used. Here the product is assembled on a worktable or on the floor and the various storage shelves and auxiliary equipment are arranged suitably around the periphery of the assembly area. The total working area is larger than that for the modular assembly center and depends on the size category of the largest parts in the assembly. Three subcategories of the custom assembly layout are employed: for assemblies whose largest parts are from 35 to 50 in., from 50 to 65 in., and larger than 65 in.

Also, for large products, a more flexible arrangement can be used; this is called the flexible assembly layout. The layout (Fig. 16-3) would be similar in size to the custom assembly layout and the same three subcategories would be employed according to the size of the largest part. However, the use of mobile storage carts and tool carts can make assembly more efficient.

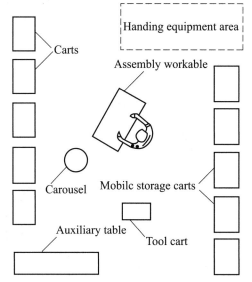

Fig. 16-3 Flexible assembly layout

In both the custom assembly layout and the flexible assembly layout, the possibility arises that mechanical assistance in the form of cranes or hand trunks might be needed. In these cases, the working areas may need to be increased in order to accommodate the additional equipment.

For high volume assembly of products containing large parts (such as in the automobile industry) transfer lines moving past manual assembly stations would be employed.

Two other manual assembly situations exist, the first assembly of small products with very low volumes-perhaps in a clean room. This would include the assembly of intricate and sensitive devices such as the fuel control valves for an aircraft where instructions must be read for each step and where the worker is near the beginning of the learning curve. The second is where assembly of large products is mainly carried out on site. This type of assembly is usually termed installation and an example would be the assembly and installation of a passenger elevator in a multistory building.

In any assembly situation, special equipment may be needed. For example, a positioning device is sometimes needed for positioning and aligning the part-especially prior to welding operations. In these cases, the device must be brought from storage within the assembly area then returned after the part has been positioned and perhaps secured. Thus, the total handling time for the device will be roughly twice the handling time for the part and must be taken into account if the volume to be produced is small.

Fig. 16-4 summarizes the basic types of manual assembly methods described above where it can be seen that the first three methods assume only small parts are being assembled. In these cases it can be assumed that the parts are all placed close to hand and will be acquired one-at-a-time. Therefore if, say, six screws are to be inserted, there is no advantage in collecting the six screws simultaneously. However, with the assembly of products containing large parts where the small items such as fasteners may not be located within easy reach or where the assembly worker must move to the various locations for the small items, there may be considerable advantage in acquiring multiple parts when needed.

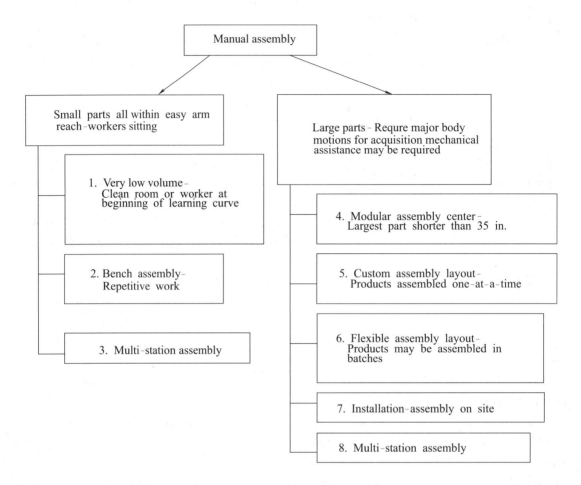

Fig. 16-4　Manual assembly methods

Words and Expressions

bin /bin/ n.　　　　　　　　　　储存斗，料箱
workbench /'wə:kbentʃ/ n.　　　工作台，手工台
situate /'sitjueit/ vt.　　　　　　使位于，使处于
subcategory /'sʌb,kætigəri/ n.　子类，子范畴
one-at-a-time /'wʌnætə'taim/ adv.　一次一个

Passage Ⅲ　Automated Assembly

Assembly in the manufacturing process consists of putting together all the component parts and sub-assemblies of a given product, fastening, performing inspections and <u>functional tests</u>, <u>labeling</u>, separating good assemblies from bad, and <u>packaging</u> and or preparing them for final use. Assembly is unique compared to the methods of manufacturing such as machining, grinding, and welding in that most of these processes involve only a few disciplines and possibly only one. Most of these nonassembly operations cannot be performed without the aid of equipment; thus the development of automatic methods has been necessary rather than optional. Assembly, on the other hand, may involve in one machine many of the fastening methods, such as riveting, welding, screwdriving, and adhesive application, as well as automatic parts selection, probing, gaging, functional testing, labeling, and packaging. The state of the art in assembly operations has not reached the level of standardization; much manual work is still being performed in this area.

Assembly has traditionally been one of the highest areas of direct labor costs. In some cases, assembly accounts for 50% or more of manufacturing costs and typically 20%~50%. However, closer cooperation between design and manufacturing engineers has resulted in reducing and in a few cases eliminating altogether the need for assembly. When assembly is required, improved design or redesign of products has simplified automated (semiautomatic or automatic) assembly.

Considerations for Automated Assembly

Before automated assembly is adopted, several factors should be considered. These include practicality of the process for automation, simulation for economic considerations and justification, management involvement, and labor relations.

Determining the practicality of automated assembly requires careful evaluation of the following:
- The number of parts in assembly.
- Design of the parts with respect to producibility, assemblability, automatic handling, and testability (materials, forms, sizes, dimensional tolerances, and weights).
- Quality of parts to be assembled. Out-of-tolerance or defective parts can cause production losses and increased costs because of stoppages.
- Availability of qualified, technically competent personnel to be responsible for equipment operation.
- Total production and production-rate requirements.
- Product variations and frequency of design changes.
- Joining methods required.
- Assembly times and costs.
- Assembly line or system configuration, using simulation, including material handling.

The best candidates for successful and economical automated assembly are generally simple, small products having a fairly stable design life. Such products are usually required in relatively large volumes and have a high labor content and/or a high reject rate because of their manual assembly. However, the development of flexible, programmable and robotic assembly systems can decrease production and product-life requirements.

Product Design for Automated Assembly

Optimum design or redesign of a product and its components is essential for successful, efficient, and economical automatic assembly. Considerable amounts of money are often spent to automate the assembly of existing product designs when it would be much more economical to redesign the products to facilitate automate assembly. Design for assembly (DFA) is being increasingly practiced because of the realization of potential production savings and better quality and improved reliability in the product.

Close cooperation is required between design and manufacturing engineers in evaluating a product design for improved assembly. The inherent capabilities and limitations of assembly operations should be considered during the early design or redesign stages. At the earliest possible design stages, it is also best to assess the parts for the ease with which they can be supplied and oriented. Assembly of various designs should be evaluated and compared.

Design for Simplification

The optimum product design is one that eliminates the need for assembly or reduces the number of parts to be assembled to a minimum. One simple example is illustrated in Fig. 16-5, which shows a single stamping that replaces a two-part assembly. Such designs usually reduce total product and assembly costs.

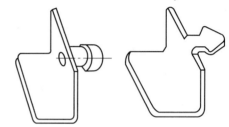

Fig. 16-5 Two-part assembly (left) replaced by a

When single-component products are impossible or uneconomical, the number of parts required should generally be kept as low as possible, and their complexity should be minimized. There are rare occasions, however, where it may be more economical to manufacture two or more pieces to replace one. The reason for minimizing the number of parts is to improve the remaining, more functional parts and to eliminate nonfunctional ones. To determine if a part can be eliminated, the following three questions should be answered:

1. Does the part move with respect to other parts?
2. Is the part made from a different material than the other parts?
3. Will the part require removal for product servicing?

An affirmative answer to any of these questions generally indicates that the part is required. Negative answers to all three questions indicate the part may not be necessary and any function it performs may be able to be transferred to a more essential component.

Design for Ease of Automatic Assembly

Parts to be assembled automatically should be designed for ease of handling, feeding, orienting, positioning, and joining. Part configurations that can be easily oriented include the following:

1. Completely symmetrical parts such as spheres, cylinders, pins, and rods. In general, the lengths of cylindrical parts should be at least 25% longer or shorter than their diameters to facilitate feeding.

2. Substantially disproportionate parts, either with respect to weight or with respect to dimensions, such as headed screws, bolts, and rivets. The center of gravity should be near one end of each part to produce a tendency to naturally feed in one specific orientation. If this nature orientation is not the desired position, it is relatively easy to rotate the parts to the proper position.

Words and Expressions

functional test	功能测试，功能试验
label /'leibl/ *vt.*	作标记
packaging /'pækidʒiŋ/ *n.*	包装，封装
nonassembly /'nɔnə'sembli/ *n.*	非装配，非组装
screwdriving /'skru:,draiviŋ/ *n.*	上螺钉
probe /prəub/ *vt.*	测探，探测
gage /geidʒ/ *vt.*	测量，测定
testability /'testəbiliti/ *n.*	可测试性，易测性
stoppage /'stɔpidʒ/ *n.*	中断，填塞
design for assembly	组装设计
single-component /,siglkəm'pəunənt/ *n.*	单个零件
nonfunctional /'nɔn'fʌŋkʃənl/ *adj.*	非功能的
affirmative /ə'fe:mətiv/ *adj.*	肯定的

Passage Ⅳ Assembly Machines and Systems

A broad variety of machines and systems is available for automated assembly. A general outline of some of the concepts is shown in Fig. 16-6. In addition, combinations of these basic systems and flexible and robotic assembly systems are discussed in this passage.

Single-Station Assembly

Machines having a single workstation are used most extensively when a specific operation has to be performed many times on one or a few parts. Assembling many parts into a single unit, like inserting blades or buckets into turbine or compressor wheels, is a common application. These machines may also be used when a number of different operations have to be performed, if the required tooling is not too complicated. These machines are also incorporated into multistation assembly systems.

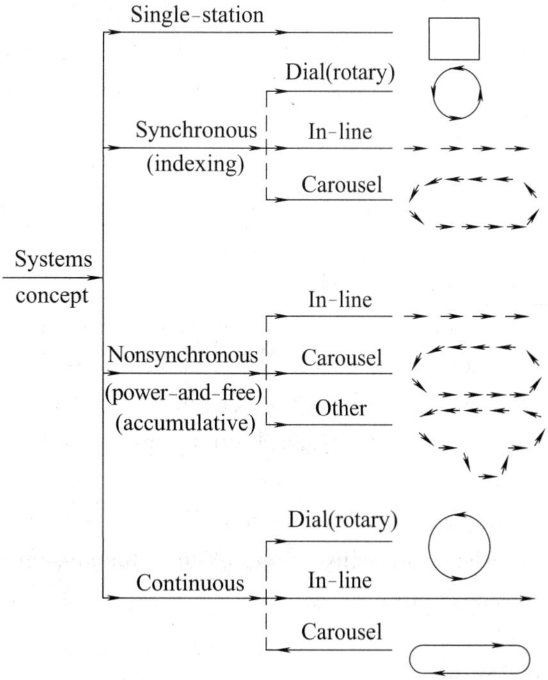

Synchronous Assembly Systems

Synchronous (indexing) assembly systems are available in dial (rotary), in-line, and carousel varieties. With these systems, all pallets or workpieces are moved at the same time and for the same distance. Because indexing intervals are determined by the

Fig. 16-6 Basic conceptions for automated assembly systems

slowest operation to be performed at any of the stations, operation time is the determining factor affecting production rate. Operators cannot vary the production rate, and a breakdown at any station causes the whole line to stop. By proper consideration to line balancing and parallel assembly operations, such downtime problems can be minimized.

Nonsynchronous assembly Systems

Nonsynchronous transfer (accumulative or power-and-free type) assembly systems, with free or floating pallets or workpieces and independently operated individual stations, are being widely used where the times required to perform different operations vary greatly and for larger products having many components. Such machines have slower cycle rates than synchronous machines, but slower stations can be double or triple tooled to boost production. One major advantage of these so-called power-and-free systems is increased versatility. The individually actuated, independent stations operate only when a pallet, supplied on demand, is present and when manual and automatic operations can easily be combined. Different methods can be used to meet line balancing needs. For example, multiple loading, joining, or testing stations can be banked or sent down multiple tracks for longer operations, while shorter operations are done on a one-at-a-time basis. Nonsyn-chronous machines often have a lower initial cost, but require more controls (a set at each station) and generally require more space.

Continuous-Motion systems

With Continuous-motion systems assembly operations are performed while the workpieces or pallets move at a constant speed and the workheads reciprocate. High production rates are possible because indexing time is eliminated. However, the cost and complexity of these systems are high because the workheads have to synchronize and move with the product being assembled. Applications for continuous-motion automated assembly are limited except for high-production uses in the packaging and bottling industries. The systems are, however, used for the manual assembly of large and heavy products, such as automobiles and refrigerators, with the operators moving with the products while performing their functions.

Dial (Rotary) Assembly

Dial or rotary index machines of synchronous design, one of the first types used for assembly, are still used for many applications. Workstations and tooling can be mounted on a central column or around the periphery of the indexing table. These machines are generally limited to smaller medium-size lightweight assemblies requiring a relatively of number of operations that are not too complex; as the table diameter increases, its mass and complexity can become impractical. Another possible disadvantage is limited accessibility to the workheads and tooling. Also, servicing the indexing table and mechanism, as well as the controls, is difficult with center-column designs.

In-Line systems

In-line assembly machines are used in synchronous, nonsynchronous, and continuous designs. In-line indexing assembly machines can be of the wraparound (circumferential) or over-and-under type or of the conventional transfer-machine type. In the over-and-under type, workholding pallets or platens move horizontally in a straight path and when empty return to the loading station on a conveyor under the machine. In the wraparound type, the work moves around the periphery of the machine in an oval, rectangular, or square path.

Carousel Machines

Similar to the synchronous in-line assembly systems just discussed, carousel machines consist of a series of fixtures or holding devices attached to a roller chain, precision chain, or steel belts or moved by fingers from one workstation to another. However, the carousel machine moves the work in a horizontal plane through a rectangular path, or some variation of the same, returning the pallets to their starting point. All parts are indexed at the same time for the same distance on either a timed or an on-demand basis.

Flexible Assembly Systems

Greater flexibility from automated assembly systems is essential because of continuing increases in product differences resulting from market demands and reductions in product life-cycles. Requirements for high-volume, long-running production are decreasing.

Considerable development work has been done and is continuing with respect to more flexible assembly systems for handing smaller lot sizes and a wider variety of products. The objectives of such systems include increased cost-effectiveness and reduced obsolescence of capital equipment expenditures.

One developing concept is the use of automatic guided vehicles (AGVs), which are currently being applied to low-volume large assemblies such as automotive and appliance products. The vehicles are usually self-powered electrically or by compressed air. They electrically follow cables buried in the floor and are computer controlled for any required paths to various assembly stations. The cost of AGVs and their control systems limit their application to large assemblies required in low volumes. Combining AGVs with programmable workstations offers considerable flexibility.

Two major classifications of flexible assembly systems are programmable and adaptable. Programmable and adaptable systems include those using industrial robots, which are discussed next in this section.

Robotic Assembly Systems

Industrial robots are programmable manipulators that perform a variety of tasks. An effective robotic assembly system requires careful consideration of the delivery of components to the workstations, component feeding and orienting, robot end effectors, sensing requirements, and system controls.

Robot characteristics that are especially suited for assembly applications include the following:
- High accuracy and repeatability in both point-to-point and path conformance.
- Reliability, flexibility, and dexterity.
- Capability for a large number of inputs and outputs.
- Sensory communications and system communications capability.
- Off-line programmability with adaptability to a high-level language.

- Memory capacity for program storage.

Words and Expressions

robotic /ˈrəubɔtik/ adj.	机器人的，机器人式的
bucket /ˈbʌkit/ n.	叶片
nonsynchronous /nɔnˈsiŋkrənəs/ adj.	非同步的（异步的，不同期的）
accumulative /əˈkjuːmjulətiv/ adj.	累积的，积累的，堆积的
power-and-free /ˈpauəˈəndˈfriː/ adj.	动力自由式的
continuous-motion /kənˈtinjujuəsˌməuʃən/ n.	连续运动
dial assembly	转盘式组装
center-column /ˈsentəˈkɔləm/ n.	中柱式
wraparound /ˈræpəraund/ n.	绕回，环绕式处理
over-and-under type /ˈəuvəˈændˌʌndətaip/ n.	升降式
platen /ˈplætən/ n.	压盘，滚筒
long-running /ˈlɔŋˈrʌniŋ/ n.	长期运行
cost-effectiveness /ˈkɔstiˈfektivnis/ n.	成本效益分析
dexterity /deksˈteriti/ n.	灵巧，机敏
programmability /ˌprəugræɡəˈbiliti/ n.	可编程序性

Exercises

Ⅰ. Select the best word to complete the following sentences and change the form where necessary.

1. justify，identify
   (1) Nothing _____ murdering another human being.
   (2) The first task is to _____ local crime problems.
2. multiple，multi-story，multi-station
   (1) Baxter was rushed to the hospital with _____ stab wounds.
   (2) A _____ building has many levels or floors.
   (3) _____ assemblies have been employed in the factory.
3. optional，optimum
   (1) Wood work was an _____ subject at our school.
   (2) Make sure the fridge is kept at the _____ temperature.
4. accommodate，assess，assemble，assume
   (1) It is difficult to _____ the effect of the new legislation just yet.
   (2) The hall can only _____ 200 people.
   (3) Over the years we've _____ a huge collection of old books.
   (4) I think we can safely _____ that interest rates will go up again soon.
5. inherent，intricate
   (1) I'm afraid the problems are _____ in the system.
   (2) Our factory imported an _____ piece of machinery last year.

Ⅱ. Fill in the blanks with proper words with the help of the first letters given in the sentences.

1. Part a _____ time is dependent on the nature of the layout of the a _____ area and

the method of assembly.

2. Various storage shelves and a _____ equipment are arranged suitably around the periphery of the assembly area.
3. A positioning device is needed for positioning and a _____ the part especially p _____ to welding operation.
4. Several factors should be taken into account before a _____ automated assembly.
5. Assembly is u _____ compared to the methods of manufacturing.
6. The continuous-motion system, the work-heads have to s _____ and move with the product.
7. The number of parts should be m _____ .
8. Several questions should be answered before you determine if a part can be e _____ .
9. Completely symmetrical parts can be easily o _____ .
10. There is no advantage in collecting the six screws s _____ if six screws are to be inserted.

Ⅲ. Translate the following expressions into Chinese.

1. bench assembly
2. multi-station assembly
3. automated assembly
4. manual assembly
5. optimum design
6. singe-component product
7. symmetrical part
8. continuous-motion system
9. synchronous assembly system
10. robotic assembly system

Part5 Machinery for Agriculture

Unit17   Engine and Tractor

Passage I   How the Engine Works

An engine that <u>converts</u> heat energy into mechanical work is called a heat engine, and the car engine is one type of heat engine. It <u>derives</u> heat from the <u>burning</u>, or '<u>combustion</u>', of a fuel and converts this heat into useful work for driving the car.

The fuel used in <u>the vast majority</u> of car engine is <u>petrol</u>, which is one of the many products obtained from crude oil found in the earth. Petrol, when mixed with the right amount of air, will burn when a <u>flame</u> or <u>spark</u> is applied to it.

In the car engine, air mixed with petrol is taken into a <u>confined</u> space and <u>compressed</u>. The mixed is then <u>ignited</u> and it burns. In burning it heats the air, which <u>expands</u>, and the force of expansion is then converted into a <u>rotary</u> movement to drive the wheels the car.

To be able to use this energy effectively we have to control the burning or combustion process and the force of expansion. Firstly, we need a tube, or <u>cylinder</u>, closed at one end, in which to compress and burn the petrol and air <u>mixture</u>. Then we need a <u>piston</u> which can slide freely in the cylinder, and which can be driven <u>outwards</u> by the force of expansion. To convert the outward movement of the piston into a rotary movement we must join it by a <u>connecting rod</u> to a <u>crankshaft</u>. We need one passage for the <u>entry</u> of the mixture into the cylinder and another to let out the used gasses. To control the entry of the mixture and the exhaust of the gases we need <u>valves</u>, and these are called the inlet and <u>exhaust</u> valves. Finally, we need some means of igniting the mixture in the top of the cylinder, the part called the combustion chamber, and for this we use a <u>sparking plug</u>.

By <u>timing</u> the opening and closing of the valves and by timing the arrival of the spark we can control the whole <u>sequence</u> of event and make the piston move in and out over and over again.

Motor-car engines may have four, six, or eight cylinders. Look at Fig. 17-1. These cylinders are usually mounted in a <u>cylinder block</u> on top of the engine. Beneath the cylinder block is the <u>crankcase</u>, which contains two shafts, the crankshaft and the <u>camshaft</u>. As you have read, the crankshaft is revolved by the outward movement of the pistons in the cylinders. This rotary movement of the crankshaft <u>transmits</u> the power developed by the engine through the gearbox to driving wheels and sets the car in motion.

When the crankshaft <u>rotates</u> it also causes the <u>rotation</u> of the camshaft, which lies <u>alongside</u> it in the crankcase. As the camshaft rotates, it pushes up rods alongside each cylinder to

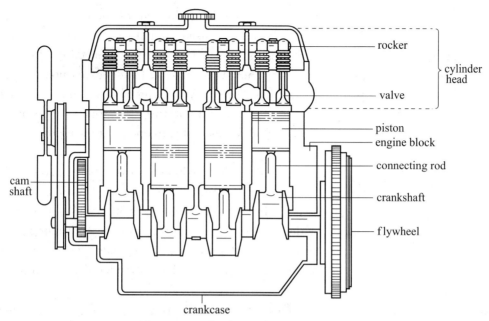

Fig. 17-1 The four-cylinder IC engine

open and shut the valves at the top of the cylinder.

There are two valves to each cylinder. The inlet valve lets air and petrol into the combustion chamber of the cylinder when it is opened. When the exhaust valve is opened the gases formed after the combustion in the chamber are allowed to escape. These gases are led away from the car through an exhaust pipe.

Let us examine the action of the cylinders in more detail. Look at Fig. 17-2. In (a) the piston is near the top of the cylinder with the inlet valve open and the exhaust valve closed. If the crankshaft is turned, either by hand or by the starter motor, the piston is drawn down by the connecting rod and a charge of petrol-air mixture <u>rushes</u> in. When the piston reaches the bottom of its stroke the inlet valve is closed by the action of a spring. This stroke is called the '<u>induction</u>' stroke.

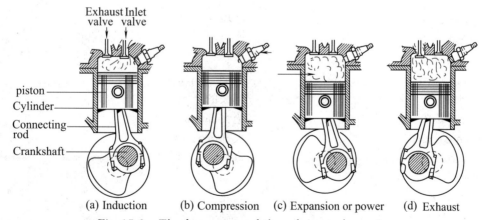

Fig. 17-2 The four stages of the a four-stroke engine

In (b) both valves are closed and the crankshaft forces the piston up to compress the mixture in the top of the cylinder. This, then, is called the '<u>compression</u>' stroke. Towards the end of the compression stroke a spark from the sparking plug causes the mixture to ignite.

In (c) we see that the heat of combustion has caused a rapid rise in pressure in the combustion chamber and this has forced the piston down. Through the connecting rod the piston causes the crankshaft to continue to rotate. This stroke is called the 'expansion' or 'power' stroke and we can say now that the engine has 'fired'. At the end of this stroke, as the crankshaft rotates, causing the camshaft alongside it to continue to rotate, one of the cams on the camshaft pushes up the rod, which causes the exhaust valve to open, allowing the exhaust gases to escape.

In (d) we see the fourth and final stroke, the 'exhaust' stroke. The exhaust valve has been forced open by the rotation of the camshaft, and the crankshaft, continuing to rotate, drives the piston back up the cylinder, forcing out the exhaust gases. At the end of this stroke the exhaust valve is closed by the action of spring, and the camshaft, continuing to rotate, pushes up a second rod to force the inlet valve open. Now the cylinder will receive another charge of petrol-air mixture, and the sequence of four strokes, 'induction', 'compression', 'expansion' or 'power', and 'exhaust', will start again.

Because there is a four-stroke sequence, or 'cycle', in this type of internal combustion engine it is a four-stroke engine. There are also two-stroke engines used, for example, for motor scooters, and for some motor cycles.

Let us think of a car with four cylinders. Remember that it is only on the expansion stroke that power is transmitted to make the crankshaft rotate. Let us number the cylinders: 1, 2, 3, 4. They may transmit power in this order: 1, 2, 4, 3. This means that when number 1 cylinder is on the expansion stroke, number 2 is on the compression stroke, number 4 is on the induction stroke, and number 3 cylinder is on the exhaust stroke. The four pistons, moving up and down inside their cylinders in this order, push down rods connected to the crankshaft at different times and at different points along its shaft. This keeps the crankshaft revolving and the crankshaft, when the gears are engaged, keeps the car moving.

Words and Expressions

convert /kən'və:t/ v.	转换
derive /di'raiv/ v.	取得
burning /'bə:niŋ/ n.	燃烧
combustion /kəm'bʌstʃən/ n.	燃烧
vast /vɑ:st/ a.	巨大的
the vast majority	绝大部分的
majority /mə'dʒɔriti/ n.	大部分
petrol /'petrəl/ n.	汽油
flame /fleim/ n.	火焰
spark /spɑ:k/ n.	火花
confine /'kɔnfain/ v.	限制
compress /kəm'pres/ v.	压缩
ignite /ig'nait/ v.	点火
ignition /ig'niʃən/ n.	点火

expand /iks'pænd/v.		膨胀
expansion /iks'pænʃən/n.		膨胀
rotary /'rəutəri/a.		旋转的
cylinder /'silində/n.		汽缸，油缸
mixture /'mikstʃə/n.		混合物，混合气
piston /'pistən/n.		活塞
outwards /'autwədz/adv.		向外
connecting rod		连杆
crankshaft /'kræŋkʃɑ:ft/n.		曲杆
entry /'entri/n.		进入
valve /vælv/n.		气门
exhaust /ig'zɔ:st/v.		排出
sparking plug		火花塞
timing /'taimiŋ/n.		定时
sequences /'si:kwəns/n.		顺序
cylinder block		汽缸体
crankcase /'kræŋkkeis/n.		曲轴箱
cam /kæm/n.		凸轮
camshaft /'kæmʃɑ:ft/n.		凸轮轴
transmit /trænz'mit/v.		传递
rotate /rəu'teit/v.		旋转
rotation /rəu'teiʃən/n.		旋转
alongside /ə'lɔŋ'said/prep.		靠…旁边
rush /rʌʃ/v.		急流
induction /in'dʌkʃən/n.		吸入
compression /kəm'preʃ(ə)n/n.		压缩
stroke /strəuk/n.		冲程
scooter /'sku:tə/n.		小型摩托车
revolve /ri'vɔlv/v.		旋转
engage /in'geidʒ/v.		接合

Terminology Practice

1. Induction stroke or intake stroke: the during which the working fluid is brought into the cylinder.
   How much gas was brought in during the induction stroke?
   The inlet value will open during the intake stroke.
2. Compression stroke: the stroke during which the gas mixture is compressed.
   Both values are closed during the compression stroke.
   Towards the end of the compression stroke a spark causes the mixture to ignite.
   Did you calculate the final pressure of compression stroke?
3. Power stroke or expansion stroke:
   The stroke during which combustion occurs and is produced.

Power is obtained only during the power stroke.

The maximum pressure occurs at the power stroke.

4. Exhaust stroke or stroke: during the burnt gases are forced out.

   The exhaust value is open during the exhaust stroke.

   What is the pressure during the exhaust stroke?

5. Timing: arrangement the time of.

   By timing the opening and closing of the valves the whole sequence of events can be controlled.

   The arrival of the spark must be timed.

6. Charge: the things that put into some devices, the quantity of fuel-air mixture supplied in the cylinder.

   There is a loss of power from pumping the charge in and out of the cylinder.

   It's important to control the mixture of the charge.

   The charge will be the fired at the proper time.

7. Ignition: the process of firing the gas mixture.

   The ignition occurs slightly before TDC.

   The ignition is caused by a spark from the sparking plug.

   The function of the ignition system is to provide the spark.

8. Combustion: process of burning.

   Internal combustion engines are heat engines.

   We have to control the combustion process.

   The combustion chamber is in the top of the cylinder.

9. Convert: change from one from into another.

   Water is converted into steam in a boiler.

   A heat engine converts heat energy into mechanical work.

   Any form of engine can be converted into any other form.

10. Piston: round plate or short cylinder of metal, fitting closely inside anther cylinder in which it moves up and down or backwards and forwards.

    The closed upper end of the piston is called the crown.

    There are several grooves in the piston walls near the top.

11. Cycle: a completed series of actions with a return to the original condition or a sequence of events which happens again and again and again in speaking of engines, cycle means stroke.

    The mechanical engineer deals which two-and four cycle engines. The two-cycle engine fires once each time the engine turns over.

12. Connection rod:

    The connecting rod is a linkage which joins the piston to the crankshaft.

    The piston is drawn down by the connecting rob on the induction stroke.

    The connecting rod is 300 mm long.

13. Sparking plug:

    What is the function of the sparking plug?

    A spark from the sparking plug causes the mixture to ignite.

    The metal part of the sparking plug is screwed into the combustion chamber.

Each cylinder of a engine has a sparking plug.
14. Camshaft:
    The crankcase contains a crankshaft and a camshaft.
    The function of the camshaft is to open and shut the value at the values at the right moment.
    The rotation of the camshaft is caused by the crankshaft.
15. Spring:
    The value is closed by the action of a spring.
    The spring is a device of coiled wire which tends to return to its original position.

Exercises

I. Reading Comprehension

Study the following statements carefully and write down whether they are true (T) or not true (N) according to the text.

1. Petrol is used in all car engines. (   )
2. Petrol, when mixed with the right amount of air, will burn. (   )
3. To convert the outward movement of the piston into a rotary movement a connecting rod must be used to join it to a crankshaft. (   )
4. To control the entry of the mixture and the exhaust of the gases the inlet and exhaust values are needed. (   )
5. To ignite the mixture in the combustion chamber a sparking plug is used. (   )
6. The cylinder block is the crankcase. (   )
7. When the piston is drawn and a charge of petrol-air mixture rushes in, this stroke is called the induction stroke. (   )
8. When both valves are closed and the crankshaft forces the piston up to compress the mixture, we call this the compression stroke. (   )
9. The expansion stroke is the power stroke. (   )
10. If we number the cylinder 1, 2, 3, 4 they may transmit power in this order 1, 2, 3, 4. (   )

II. Use these words to complete the following sentences: camshaft, charge, converted, crankcase, ignited, petrol, pistons, pressure, two-stroke, valve, gases.

1. In a car engine heat is _____ into useful work.
2. The fuel used in a car engine is _____.
3. The _____ slide up and down inside the cylinders.
4. The mixture in the combustion chamber is _____ by a sparking plug.
5. There are two shafts inside the _____.
6. The valves at the top of the cylinder are opened and shut by the action of the _____.
7. During the induction stroke a _____ of petrol-air mixture enters the combustion chamber.
8. The piston is forced down by a rapid rise in _____ during the expansion stroke.
9. When the exhaust _____ is forced open the _____ caused by combustion are allowed to escape.

10. Motor scooters used a _____ engine.

Ⅲ. **Answer these questions.**

1. What three things are required to make the combustion in the combustion chamber?
2. What are the two valves at the top of each cylinder called?
3. How is the downward movement of the pitons converted into a rotary movement?
4. What does the crankcase contain?
5. What makes the camshaft revolve?
6. What function of the camshaft is mentioned in the passage?
7. What happens in a cylinder during the induction stroke?
8. What forces the piston down the cylinder?
9. When do we say that the engine has fired?
10. What stroke follows the induction stroke in a four-stroke engine?
11. How is the power developed by the engine transmitted to the driving wheels of the car?
12. What happens when the exhaust valve in the cylinder is forced open?

Passage Ⅱ   The patrol Engine

In the internal combustion engine, heat is generated by the combustion of an inflammable charge inside a cylinder, and the heat energy is immediately converted into mechanical energy. Engines used in motor-cars are petrol engines, the charge is a mixture of petrol and air, and is ignited by a spark from the distributor.

When the mixture is ignited, the products of combustion expand down the cylinder, which is fitted with a reciprocating piston. The downward movement of piston is converted into a rotational movement of the crankshaft by means of a connecting rod. As the crankshaft rotates, the piston is driven upwards again, and the exhaust gases are expelled through the exhaust valve in the cylinder head. When the piston nears the top of this stroke, the inlet valve is opened and the exhaust valve closed. The piston then descends on the induction stroke, and draws a fresh charge into the cylinder. As the piston rises again on the compression stroke, the charge is compressed and ignited, and the cycle begins again. This is the four-stroke cycle which is in common use. An alternative cycle is the two-stroke cycle, which combines the exhaust and compression stroke into one.

The combustion of the mixture does not take place instantaneously, the spark is therefore timed to occur before the piston reaches top dead center, otherwise maximum pressure would not be reached in time. By the time the piston is at top dead center, combustion is well under way and the expansion of the gases is beginning. Once combustion starts, it should be carried through the mixture very rapidly, and this is assisted by making the clearance space above the piston as small as possible, and by careful design of the cylinder head. Rapid propagation of the flame through the compressed gas is also assisted by creating turbulence in the gas.

The torque is liable to be uneven in any case when the engine is running slowly, and a flywheel is fitted to the crankshaft to damp out these variations.

It is essential for the inlet and exhaust valves to open and close at exactly the appropriate moment in relation to the position of the piston. Therefore they are actuated by a camshaft running in phase with the crankshaft.

Words and Expressions

inflammable /in'flæməbl/ adj.　　易燃的
reciprocate /ri'siprəkeit/ v.　　来回，往复
expel /iks'pel/ v.　　驱逐
instantaneously /ˌinstə'teiniəsli/ adj.　　瞬间
propagation /ˌprɔpə'geiʃən/ n.　　传播
damp /dæmp/ vt.　　衰减，减弱
appropriate /ə'prəupriit/ adj.　　恰当的
phase /feiz/ n.　　与…同步

Passage Ⅲ　　Diesel Engines

The term 'diesel' is applied to a variety of types of engine which run without the necessity of an electric spark to cause ignition of the fuel. Fig. 17-3 shows a diesel engine.

The cycle of a typical modern four-stroke diesel engine is as follows:

1. On the induction stroke pure air is drawn into the cylinder.

2. On the compression stroke this air is compressed at a high compression-ratio, so that the temperature is raised to a high value.

3. Towards the end of the compression stroke the fuel is injected into the combustion chamber in the form of a fine spray. The temperature of the air in the combustion chamber is sufficiently high to ignite the fuel as it enters, and combustion of the mixture of fuel and air produces the working stroke.

4. As the piston moves upwards on the final stroke the exhaust gases are expelled from the cylinder in the usual way.

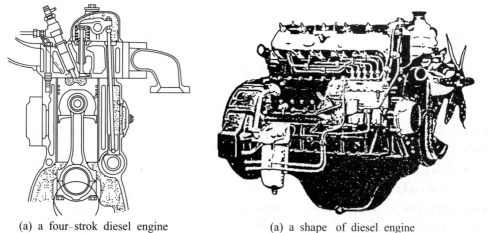

(a) a four-strok diesel engine　　(a) a shape of diesel engine
Fig. 17-3　A diesel engine

The diesel cycle thus differs in many important respects from the Otto cycle. The compression of pure air instead of a mixture of fuel and air makes it possible to employ high compression pressures without any danger of detonation. Thus, whereas the usual compression-rations employed in petrol engines are not more than 8∶1 or 9∶1, the compression-ratios employed in CI diesels range up over 16∶1 and result in compression pressure of up to 5000 kN/m². The temperature of the compressed air at the moment of fuel injection is generally about 750℃.

The injection of the fuel takes place over a period equivalent to about 15° to 30°of rotation of the crankshaft. Injection usually commences from 10° to 20° before the piston reaches top centre, but both the point of commencement of injection and the duration are variable. The fuel is injected at pressures ranging from about 5500 to 20000kN/m². The gradual combustion of the fuel and expansion of the gases give an impulse to the piston that is more sustained than that produced in the petrol or paraffin engine, and the higher compression-ratio makes high efficiency possible.

Modern diesels employ solid or airless injection, achieved by use of the fuel pump and injection nozzle. Many types of pump and nozzle are now obtainable.

One type of fuel pump comprises a hardened steel barrel and plunger, ground to a very high degree of accuracy. The plunger is operated by a cam and it forces fuel, which enters the barrel through ports in the sides, through a springloaded delivery valve situated in the upper end of barrel, and thence along steel tubing to the injection nozzle. When the plunger is at the bottom of its stroke the inlet ports are uncovered, and the barrel is filled with fuel. As the plunger rises on the delivery stroke the fuel is at first forced back through the inlet ports, until these are entirely covered, after which it is force through the delivery valve. So long as the ports are kept closed by the plunger, injection of the fuel continues, but before the plunger reaches the top of its stroke the helical edge of the annular groove may partly uncover one of the ports, and as soon as this occurs the fuel above the plunger is free to flow down through the vertical channel and annular groove, back through the inlet ports.

Words and Expressions

Diesel /ˈdiːzəl/ n.	狄赛尔
Diesel＝Diesel engine	柴油机
compression-ratio	压缩比
inject /inˈdʒekt/ v.	喷射
sufficiently /səˈfəntli/ adv.	充足地，充分地
expel /iksˈpel/ v.	驱逐，逸出
Otto cycle	奥托循环
detonation /ˌdetəuˈneiʃən/ n.	爆震，爆燃
CI(compression ignition)	压缩，点火
kN(kilonewton)	千牛顿
equivalent /iˈkwivələnt/ a.	相等的，等效的
injection /inˈdʒkʃən/ n.	喷射
commence /kəˈmens/ v.	开始
top centre(top dead centre)	上止点，上死点
bottom centre(bottom dead centre)	下止点，下死点
commencement /kəˈmensmənt/ n.	开始
duration /djuəˈreiʃn/ n.	持续，期间
range from…to…	范围从…到…

gradual /'grædjuəl/ a.	逐渐的，平缓的
sustained /səs'teind/ a.	被支持的，持续的
paraffin /'pærəfin/ n.	煤油
nozzle /'nɔzl/ n.	喷嘴
obtainable /əb'teinəb(ə)l/ a.	可得到的，能达到的
comprise kəm'praiz/ vt.	包括，由…组成
harden /'hɑ:dn/ v.	变硬，淬火
hardened steel	淬火钢
plunger /'plʌndʒə/ n.	柱塞
accuracy /'ækurəsi/ n.	精密（度），准确（性）
barrel /'bærəl/ n.	套筒
port /pɔ:t/ n.	孔，口
springloaded	弹簧加载的
delivery valve	输送阀
thence /ðens/ adv.	从那里（起），从那时起
tubing /'tju:biŋ/ n.	管，管道
uncover /ʌn'kʌvə/ v.	打开，使露出
helical /'helikəl/ n.	螺线
a.	螺线形的
annular /'ænjulə/ a.	环形的，有螺纹的
groove /gru:v/ n.	槽，油槽
vertical /'və:tikəl/ a.	垂直的

Exercises

Ⅰ. Reading Comprehension and write the letter T if the sentence is true, and N if it is not true according to the text.

1. 'Diesel' is a variety of types of engine which run which the help of an electric spark to cause ignition of the fuel. （　　）
2. On the intake stroke the air is compressed at a high compression ratio in the cylinder. （　　）
3. The stroke on which the piston moves upwards and the exhaust gases are expelled is called the exhaust stroke. （　　）
4. In the petrol engines the usual compression-ratio range up to over 16∶1 and result in compression pressures of up to $50000kN/m^2$. （　　）
5. Injection of the fuel begins 10℃ to 20℃ before the piston reaches top center. （　　）
6. One type of fuel pump consists of a hardened steel barrel and plunger, which are ground to a very high degree of accuracy. （　　）

Ⅱ. Choose the right answer according to the text.
    1. On _____ the pure air is compressed at a high compression ratio.
        a. the intake stroke
        b. the compression stoke
        c. the working stroke

2. The usual compression-ratios of the CI diesel engine range _____ .
   a. from 8∶1 to 9∶1
   b. upto 8 or 9∶1
   c. upto over 16∶1
3. So long as the ports are kept closed by the plunger, injection of the fuel _____ .
   a. continues
   b. stops
   c. decreases

Ⅲ. **Answer the following questions according to the text.**
  1. What are the four strokes of the diesel engine?
  2. When does the injection of the fuel take place?
  3. Where is the springloaded delivery valve situated?
  4. What happens when the plunger is at the bottom of its stroke?
  5. What makes it possible to employ high compression pressures?

Ⅳ. **Fill in the blanks with suitable words according to the text.**
  1. Towards the end of the _____ stroke the fuel is injected into the combustion chamber.
  2. As the piston moves upwards on the final stroke the _____ gases are expelled.
  3. The diesel cycle differs in many respects from the _____ .
  4. The injection of the fuel takes place over a period equivalent to about 15° to 30° of rotation of the _____ .
  5. The fuel is injected at pressures _____ from about 5500 to 20000 kN/m².
  6. One type of fuel pump comprises a _____ steel barrel and plunger.

Passage Ⅳ   The tractor

The tractor, more than any other piece of equipment, has made possible the introduction of many machines on the farm. It is the farmer's maid-of-all-work, the one basic machine from which nearly all the others can be worked. It can tow a trailer laden with hay or animal feed and, by means of a power take-off, operate equipment pulled or carried behind it in the field or standing in the yard. Its special design enables it to travel over rough or soft ground so that there are very few occasions when it is not able to work.

Many different types and sizes of tractors are in use today, depending on the type and size of farm and the particular jobs the machines are called upon to do. However, the principles on which they are the same and the descriptions which following apply to all.

All farm tractors manufactured today have diesel engines, and though they are more expensive to buy than those built with petrol and vaporizing oil (paraffin) engines a few years ago, they stand up better to the rough, slogging work that tractors have to do. Fig. 17-4 shows the major components of a tractor.

Engine Governors

All tractor engines are fitted with a governor. Its purpose is to keep the engine running at an even speed and so save the driver having to make throttle adjustments every time there is a change of ground conditions. For instance, when the tractor is pulling a plough it might go

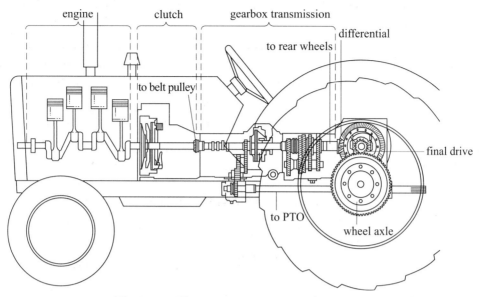

Fig. 17-4 The major components of a tractor

over a patch of soft earth. The plough cuts through it more easily. Without a governor the engine would speed up making the tractor to go faster. In hard ground the plough would meet with greater resistance, slowing down the engine and the tractor. By allowing less fuel into the engine over the easy portions of ground, and increasing the supply when the going is difficult, the governor acts as an automatic throttle adjuster to keep the tractor running at a constant speed whatever the state of the ground.

Transmission, Wheels and Tracks

Power from the engine is transmitted to the big driving wheel of the tractor by means of the transmission system. This consists of the clutch, gearbox and rear-axle differential unit. Briefly, the clutch allows the drive from the engine to the gearbox to be disconnected so that various gears can be engaged. The gearbox contains several pairs of gears, and by selecting certain combinations the driver can match the speed and pulling power of the tractor to the work it has to do. A slow speed with high engine revs. (Low gear) is required for working farm implements in rough ground, while faster speeds with lower engine revs. (High gear) is needed for towing light trailers and generally running about the farm. Finally, the differential unit transmits the drive to the rear wheels and allows each wheel to rotate at different speeds so that the tractor can turn corners.

Because tractor have to work in crops sown in rows, the distance, or track, between the front and rear pairs of wheels can be widened or narrowed so that they run between the rows and over the crops.

Power Take-off

Tractors were originally designed and produced to take the place of horses on the farm, and until recent years, were used most frequently as machines for towing. As the need for farm mechanization grew, a whole new range of machinery was developed and the tractor has now also become a source of auxiliary power from which many other machines can be driven, using a Power Take-off device, or P. T. O.

The power take-off is driven from the engine via the gearbox and a shaft which extends rearward to the back of the tractor. From there it can be coupled to the machinery to be driven. The power take-off works independently of the tractor's normal transmission system, so that machinery can be operated whilst it is being towed across a field as well as in the standing position.

Because the driven machinery cannot always be in direct line behind the tractor and because the ground is often rough, the P. T. O. shaft has universal joints to allow for variations in the driving angle.

Words and Expressions

maid-of-all-work	全能助手
tow /təu/ v.	牵引
vaporize /ˈveipəraiz/ v.	蒸发
vaporizing /ˈveipəraiŋ/ a.	蒸发的
paraffin /ˈpærəfin, ˈpærəfiːn/ n.	煤油
slogging /ˈslɔgiŋ/ a.	艰难的
governor /ˈgʌvənə/ n.	调速器
patch /pætʃ/ n.	小块田
speed up	加速
plough /plau/ n.	犁
driving wheel	驱动轮
transmission /trænsˈmiʃən/ n.	传动装置
differential unit	差速器
revs. (revolutions)	转速
turn corners	转弯
sow(sowed, sown/sowed) /sau/ v.	播种
track /træk/ n.	轮距
mechanization /ˌmekənaiˈzeiʃən/ a.	机械化
auxiliary /ɔːgˈziljəri/ a.	辅助的
P.T.O. (Power take-off)	动力输出轴
via /ˈvaiə, ˈviːə/ prep.	通过…
rearward /ˈriəwəd/ adv.	向后部
couple /ˈkʌpl/ v.	连接
standing position	停车状态
driven machinery	被驱动的机器
universal joint	万向节

Exercises

I. Answer these questions:

1. Why do all farm tractors manufactured today have diesel engines?

2. What is the purpose that tractor engines are fitted with a governor?

3. What is the function of the deferential unit?

4. What is the function of the universal joints?

II. **Translate the following passage into Chinese.**

The tractor, more than any other piece of equipment, has made possible the introduction of many machines on the farm. It is the farmer's maid-of-all-work, the one basic machine from which nearly all the others can be worked. It can tow a trailer laden with hay or animal feed and, by means of a power take-off, operate equipment pulled or carried behind it in the field or standing in the yard. Its special design enables it to travel over rough or soft ground so that there are very few occasions when it is not able to work.

III. **Use each of the following words in a sentence.**

1. engine   2. transmit   3. high gear   4. P. T. O.   5. turn corners
6. transmission   7. governor   8. widen

Glossary

A

abrasion /əˈbreiʒən/ n.	磨损，磨蚀
abrasive cloth	砂布
abrasive disk	砂轮，磨盘
AC=Adaptive Control	自适应控制
acceleration /æk,seləˈreiʃən/ n.	加速度
accessory /ækˈsesəri/ n.	附件，零件
adj.	附属的，补充的
accommodate /əˈkɔmədeit/ vt.	使适应，调节
account for	说明，证明，是…的原因
accumulative /əˈkju:mjulətiv/ adj.	累积的，积累的，堆积的
accuracy /ˈækurəsi/ n.	精密（度），准确（性）
acetal /ˈæsitæl/ n.	乙缩醛
acicular /əˈsikjulə/ adj.	针状的，针尖状的
acrylic /əˈkrilik/ n.	丙烯酸
adhesive /ədˈhi:siv/ n.	黏合剂；
adj.	带黏性的，胶黏
advent /ˈædvənt/ n.	到来，出现，来临
affirmative /əˈfə:mətiv/ adj.	肯定的
agitate /ˈædʒiteit/ v.	摇晃，搅动
airfoil /ˈɛəfɔil/ n.	机翼，螺旋桨
align /əˈlain/ v.	排成一线
alongside /əˈlɔŋsaid/ prep.	靠…旁边
alphanumeric /ˌælfənju:ˈmerik/ adj.	字母数字混合编制的
alumina /əˈlu:minə/ n.	矾土
alumina silicate	水合硅酸铝
American National Standards Institute	美国国家标准协会
ammonia /əˈmounjə/ n.	氨水
amorphous /əˈmɔ:fəs/ adj.	无定形的，非晶体的
amortize /əˈmɔ:taiz/ vt.	分期清偿
analogy /əˈnælədʒi/ n.	模拟
analysis /əˈnælisis/ n.	分析，分解；[数]解析；验定
analytical mechanics	分析力学
animate /ˈænimeit/ vt.	动画制作
annealing /æˈni:liŋ/ n.	退火
annular /ˈænjulə/ adj.	环形的，环状的，有螺纹的

anodic coating　　　　　　　　　　　　　　阳极镀层，阳极保护层
antifriction bearing　　　　　　　　　　　　滚动轴承，减摩轴承
appropriate /əˈprəupriit/ adj.　　　　　　　恰当的
APT＝Automatically Programming Tools　　自动编程工具
aqueous /ˈeikwiəs/ adj.　　　　　　　　　　水的，含水的
arbor /ˈɑːbə/ n.　　　　　　　　　　　　　柄轴，心轴
articulated /ɑːˈtikjuleitid/ adj.　　　　　　铰接的
artwork /ˈɑːtwəːk/ n.　　　　　　　　　　工艺图；照相原图图纸
asbestos /æzˈbestɔs/ n.　　　　　　　　　石棉
assemblage /əˈsemblidʒ/ n.　　　　　　　　集合
assembly line vehicle　　　　　　　　　　　装配线运输车
assembly drawing　　　　　　　　　　　　总图，装配图，组装图
atomization /ˌætəmaiˈzeiʃən/ n.　　　　　　雾化，粉化
attachment /əˈtætʃmənt/ n.　　　　　　　　附件，附加装置
augment /ɔːgˈment/ vt. & vi.　　　　　　　增大，增加
authentic /ɔːˈθentik/ adj.　　　　　　　　真实的，确凿的
automatic tool changer　　　　　　　　　　自动换刀装置
autoshade /ˈɔːtouʃeid/ n.　　　　　　　　　自动遮蔽
auxiliary /ɔːgˈziljəri/ a.　　　　　　　　　辅助的
axle /ˈæksl/ n.　　　　　　　　　　　　　车轴，轮轴

B

backlash /ˈbæklæʃ/ n.　　　　　　　　　　间隙，齿间隙
back up　　　　　　　　　　　　　　　　支持，倒退
bakelite /ˈbeikəlait/ n.　　　　　　　　　　酚醛塑料，胶木
balance /ˈbæləns/ n.　　　　　　　　　　　平衡
ball bearing　　　　　　　　　　　　　　　滚珠轴承
band saw　　　　　　　　　　　　　　　　带锯
band sawing　　　　　　　　　　　　　　　带锯法
barrel /ˈbærəl/ n.　　　　　　　　　　　　套筒
barrier /ˈbæriə/ n.　　　　　　　　　　　障碍
base /beis/ n.　　　　　　　　　　　　　基座，底座
batch /bætʃ/ adj.　　　　　　　　　　　　分批的，间歇式的
bed /bed/ n.　　　　　　　　　　　　　　床身
bending strength　　　　　　　　　　　　抗弯强度，抗扳强度
bevel gear　　　　　　　　　　　　　　　伞齿轮
bin /bin/ n.　　　　　　　　　　　　　　储存斗，料箱
bioengineering /ˌbaiəuˌendʒiˈniəriŋ/ n.　　生物工程学
blasting /ˈblɑːstiŋ/ n.　　　　　　　　　　喷丸处理，喷砂处理
blind riser　　　　　　　　　　　　　　　暗冒口
blind rivet　　　　　　　　　　　　　　　埋头铆钉，盲铆钉，空心铆钉
block /blɔk/ n.　　　　　　　　　　　　　滑轮，阻滞

	vt.	阻碍，阻塞
blueprint /ˈbluːprint/	*n.*	蓝图，设计图
	vt.	制成蓝图
bolt /boult/	*n.*	螺栓，螺钉
Boolean rule		布尔定律
bore /bɔː/	*n.*	孔径
boring /ˈbɔːriŋ/	*n.*	镗孔，镗削
boring bar		镗杆，钻杆
boring mill		镗床
bottleneck /ˈbɔtlnek/	*n.*	瓶颈，薄弱环节；影响生产流程的因素
bottom centre (bottom dead centre)		下止点，下死点
bowling pin		保龄球棒
boxy /ˈbɔksi/	*adj.*	箱状的，四四方方的
brainstorming /ˈbreinˌstɔːmiŋ/	*n.*	头脑风暴法
brake /breik/	*n.*	刹车，压弯机
brazier head		扁头
brine /brain/	*n.*	盐水
brittleness /ˈbritlnis/	*n.*	脆度
broach /brəutʃ/	*n.*	拉刀
	v.	拉削
broaching /ˈbrəutʃiŋ/	*n.*	拉削
broaching machine		拉床
broken section		局部剖视
bucket /ˈbʌkit/	*n.*	叶片
bucking bar		打钉杆，铆钉顶棒
buffing /ˈbʌfiŋ/	*n.*	擦光，磨光
bulky /ˈbʌlki/	*adj.*	大的，容量大的，体积大的
bulk density		松装密度，散装密度
burning /ˈbəːniŋ/	*n. & a.*	燃烧
bushing /ˈbuʃiŋ/	*n.*	轴衬
butyl /ˈbjuːtil/	*n.*	丁基合成橡胶

C

cadmium /ˈkædmiəm/	*n.*	镉
cam /kæm/	*n.*	凸轮
cam-lock /ˈkæmˈlɔk/	*n.*	偏心夹
camshaft /ˈkæmʃɑːft/	*n.*	凸轮轴
capital cost		基建费，投资费
cap screw		帽螺钉
carbide /ˈkɑːbaid/	*n.*	碳化物，硬质合金
carbon soot		炭黑
carburetor /ˈkɑːbjuretə/	*n.*	化油器

carburizing /ˈkɑːbjuraiziŋ/ n.	渗碳，碳化
carousel /ˌkærəˈsel/ n.	圆盘传送带
carriage /ˈkæridʒ/ n.	（机床的）拖板
carrousel /ˌkæruˈzel/ n.	回转车
carrousel /ˌkæruˈsel/ n.	旋转式传送带
Cartesian /kɑːˈtizjən/ n.	笛卡儿的，笛卡儿坐标系
case hardening	表面淬火，表面硬化
casting /ˈkɑːstiŋ/ n.	铸造；铸件
category /ˈkætigəri/ n.	种类，类别，等级，部门
cavity /ˈkæviti/ n.	空腔，模槽
center-column /ˈsentəˈkɔləm/ n.	中柱式
center drilling	打中心孔
centrifugal /senˈtrifjugəl/ adj.	离心的
ceramic /siˈræmik/ adj.	陶瓷的，陶器的
n.	陶瓷制品
ceramic molding	陶瓷造型
chamfered /ˈtʃæmfəd/ adj.	倒角的
channel /ˈtʃænl/ n.	槽钢
charcoal /ˈtʃɑːkoul/ n.	木炭
chatter /ˈtʃætə/ n.	振动，颤动
chip /tʃip/ n.	碎片
chip conveyor	切屑输送机
chip-making /ˈtʃipˈmeikiŋ/ adj.	制造切屑的
chisel /ˈtʃizl/ n.	凿子
chisel edge	横刃，凿锋
chromium /ˈkroumjəm/ n.	铬
chromizing /ˈkroumaiziŋ/ n.	渗铬，铬化
chuck /tʃʌk/ n.	卡盘
chucking reamer	机用铰刀
CI(compression ignition)	压缩，点火
clamping /ˈklæmpiŋ/ n.	固定，卡紧
clearance /ˈkliərəns/ n.	间隙，游隙
clearance angle	后角，间隙角
clearness /ˈkliənis/ n.	清晰度，明白
clutch /klʌtʃ/ n.	离合器，联轴器
CNC＝Computerized numerical Control	计算机数控
coefficient of friction	摩擦系数
coke /kouk/ n.	焦炭
cold-drawing /ˌkouldˈdrɔːiŋ/ n.	冷拔，冷拉
cold forming	冷成形，冷态成形，冷作成形
collaborate /kəˈlæbəreit/ vi.	合作，协作
collet /ˈkɔlit/ n.	夹头，有缝夹套
colloidal /kəˈlɔidl/ adj.	胶态的，胶体的

columbium /kəˈlʌmbiəm/ n.	铌
column /ˈkɔləm/ n.	立柱
combustion /kəmˈbʌstʃən/ n.	燃烧
commence /kəˈmens/ v.	开始
commencement /kəˈmensmənt/ n.	开始
compatible /kəmˈpætəbl/ adj.	兼容的，协调的，相容的
composite /ˈkɔmpəzit/ n.	复合材料
compress /kəmˈpres/ v.	压缩
compression /kəmˈpreʃ(ə)n/ n.	压缩
compression-ratio	压缩比
compressive strength	抗压强度，耐压强度
compressor /kəmˈpresə/ n.	压气机，压缩器
comprise /kəmˈpraiz/ vt.	包括，由…组成
computer-aided design	计算机辅助设计
computer-aided engineering	计算机辅助工程
computer-aided manufacturing	计算机辅助制造
computer modeling	计算机模拟
concentrated /ˈkɑːnsntreitid/ adj.	集中的
concentric /kɔnˈsentrik/ adj.	同心的，同轴的
concentricity /ˌkɔnsenˈtrisiti/ n.	同心，同心度
conceptual /kənˈseptjuəl/ adj.	概念上的
conceptualize /kənˈseptjuəlaiz/ vt.	构思；使概念化
conductive /kənˈdʌktiv/ adj.	传导的，导电的
configuration /kənˌfigjuˈreiʃən/ n.	构造，结构；配置；
confine /ˈkɔnfain/ v.	限制
conical /ˈkɔnikəl/ adj.	圆锥的，圆锥形的
conjointly /ˈkɔndʒɔintli/ adv.	相连地，结合地
conjugate /ˈkɔndʒugeit/ adj.	成对的，共轭的
connecting rod	连杆
constraint /kənˈstreint/ n.	限制，约束
contaminant /kənˈtæminənt/ n.	污染物，杂质
continuous-motion /kənˈtinjujuəsˌmouʃən/ n.	连续运动
contour /ˈkɔntuə/ n.	轮廓，形状；断面
contour /ˈkɔntuə/ vt.	曲面仿形
contour sawing	仿形锯法
control cabinet	操纵台，控制柜
convert /kənˈvəːt/ v.	转换
conveyor /kənˈveiə/ n.	输送机；运输装置，传送器
coolant /ˈkuːlənt/ n.	冷却剂，冷却液
coordinator /kəuˈɔːdineitə/ n.	协调者
cope /kəup/ n.	上箱
coplanar /kəuˈpleinə/ adj.	共面的，同一平面的
cost-effectiveness /ˈkɔstiˈfektivnis/ n.	成本效益分析

cotter pin	开口销，扁销，开尾销
counterbore /ˈkauntəˌbɔː/ n.	镗孔，沉孔
counterboring /ˌkauntəˈbɔːriŋ/ n.	镗孔，锪孔
countershaft /ˈkauntəʃɑːft/ n.	（机械中的）副轴，间轴
countersink /ˈkauntəˌsiŋk/ vt.	钻孔装埋，打埋头孔
n.	埋头孔，锥形扩孔
couple /ˈkʌpl/ v.	连接
coupling /ˈkʌpliŋ/ n.	连接；连接器
crankcase /ˈkræŋkkeis/ n.	曲轴箱
crankpin /ˈkræŋkpin/ n.	曲柄销
crankshaft /ˈkræŋkʃɑːft/ n.	曲柄轴，曲杆
crossfeed /ˈkrɔsfiːd/ n.	横向送进，横进给
crosshair /ˈkrɔshɛə/ n.	横标线，十字线
cross-hatching /ˈkrɔsˈhætʃiŋ/ n.	交叉影线；用交叉线画成的阴影
crossed-axis /ˈkrɔstˈæksis/ adj.	轴交叉的
cross-linking /ˈkrɔsˈliŋkiŋ/ n.	交联
cross slide	横向滑板，横向架，横拖板
cryogenic /ˌkraiəˈdʒenik/ adj.	低温学的
crystalline /ˈkristəlain/ adj.	水晶的，结晶的，水晶般的
cumbersome /ˈkʌmbəsəm/ adj.	笨重的
cure /kjuə/ v.	硬化
cutter /ˈkʌtə/ n.	刀具
cyanide /ˈsaiənaid/ n.	氰化物
cyaniding /ˈsaiənaidiŋ/ n.	氰化法，氰化处理
cylinder /ˈsilində/ n.	汽缸，油缸
cylinder block	汽缸体
cylindrical /ˈsilindrikəl/ adj.	圆筒形的，圆柱的
cylindrical grinding	外圆磨削
cylindrical grinding machine	外圆磨床

D

damp /dæmp/ vt.	衰减，减弱
data base	数据库
debug /diːˈbʌg/ v.	调试，排出程序中的错误
decimal point	小数点
deformable /diˈfɔːməbəl/ adj.	可变形的
decomposition /ˌdiːkɔmpəˈziʃən/ n.	分解，腐烂
deep drawing	拉伸
defective /diˈfektiv/ n.	次品，有缺陷的物品
adj.	有缺陷的
deflect /diˈflekt/ v.	（使）偏斜，（使）偏转
deflection /diˈflekʃən/ n.	偏移，挠度

deflection /diflekʃən/ n. 偏转，偏差，偏斜，挠度
deformation /ˌdiːfɔːˈmeiʃen/ n. 变形，形变
delivery valve 输送阀
dendritic /denˈdritik/ adj. 树枝状的；多枝的
deposition /ˌdepəˈziʃn/ n. 沉积，淀积
derive /diˈraiv/ v. 取得
design for assembly 组装设计
detail drawing 细部图
detonation /ˌdetəuˈneiʃən/ n. 爆震，爆燃
detrimental /ˌdetriˈmentl/ adj. 有害的
deviation /ˌdiːviˈeiʃən/ n. 偏差，偏移
dexterity /deksˈteriti/ n. 灵巧，机敏
diagrammatically /ˌdaiəgrəˈmætikəli/ adv. 用图解法
dial assembly 转盘式组装
dialogue box 对话框
diazo /daiˈæzəu/ adj. 重氨基的
die /dai/ n. 模，冲模
Diesel /ˈdiːzəl/ n. 狄赛尔
Diesel＝Diesel engine 柴油机
differential unit 差速器
dilute /daiˈljuːt/ v. 冲淡，变淡，变弱，稀释
dimensional /diˈmɛnʃənl/ n. & adj. 维的；尺寸的
disclose /disˈkləuz/ v. 揭露，披露，泄露
dispersement /disˈpəːsmənt/ n. 分散
displacement /disˈpleismənt/ n. 位移，移动
distortion /disˈtɔːʃən/ n. 扭曲，变形
distributed /diˈstrɪbjuːtid/ adj. 分散的
DNC＝Distributed numerical Control 直接数控
dog /ˈdɔg/ n. 销，卡箍
double curvature 双曲面；双曲率
double-ended /ˈdʌblˌendid/ adj. 双端的
draftsman /ˈdrɑːftsmən/ n. 制图员
drag /dræg/ n. 下箱
drastically /ˈdræstikəli/ adv. 严重的，猛烈的，严格的
drill /dril/ vt. 钻
              n. 钻头
drilling machine 钻床，钻机
drill-press /ˈdrilˌpres/ n. 钻床，压钻机
drive /draiv/ vt. 驱动，传动
              n. 驱动，传动
driven machinery 被驱动的机器
drive screw 传动螺杆

driving wheel	驱动轮
droplet /ˈdrɔpliːt/ n.	小滴，液滴
ductile /ˈdʌktail/ adj.	可延展的，易于塑造的
ductility /dʌkˈtiliti/ n.	延展性；顺从
duration /djuəˈreiʃn/ n.	持续，期间
dynamics /daiˈnæmiks/ n.	力学，动力学

E

eccentric /ikˈsentrik/ adj.	偏心的
n.	偏心轮
elastomer /iˈlæstəmə/ n.	弹性体，合成橡胶
electrolyte /iˈlektrəulait/ n.	电解液，电解质
electrolytic /i,lektrəuˈlitik/ adj.	电解的，由电解产生的
electromechanical /iˈlektrəumiˈkænikəl/ adj.	机电式的
electroplating /iˈlektrəupleitiŋ/ n.	电镀，电镀法
elevate /ˈeliveit/ vt.	升高，增加
elongation /,iːlɔŋˈgeiʃən/ n.	伸长，拉伸
enamelling /iˈnæməliŋ/ n.	上珐琅，上釉
encompass /inˈkʌmpəs/ v.	包括，围绕，拥有
end-effector	端（立）铣刀
end for end	两端的位置颠倒过来，反过来
engage /inˈgeidʒ/ v.	接合
engineering drawing	工程制图，工程图
engineering mechanics	工程力学
engine lathe	普通车床
entry /ˈentri/ n.	进入
envelope = envelop /ˈenviləup/ n.	包络（线、面），信封
envision /inˈviʒən/ vt.	想象，预见
epoxy /eˈpɔksi/ n.	环氧树脂
adj.	环氧的
equilibrium /,ikwiˈlibriəm/ n.	平衡
equivalent /iˈkwivələnt/ a.	相等的，等效的
etched-circuit /ˈetʃidˈsəːkit/ n.	腐蚀印制电路
ethyl /ˈeθil/ n.	乙基
exhaust /igˈzɔːst/ v.	排出
exotherm /,eksəuˈθəːm/ n.	放热量
expand /iksˈpænd/ v.	膨胀
expander sleeve	膨胀套
expansion /iksˈpænʃən/ n.	膨胀
expedient /iksˈpiːdjənt/ adj.	有利的
n.	权宜之计
expel /iksˈpel/ v.	驱逐，逸出

exponential /ˌekspəu'nenʃəl/	*n.*	指数
	adj.	指数的，幂数的
external view		外视图
extrude /eks'tru:d/	*vt.*	挤压，模压
extrusion /eks'tru:ʒən/	*n.*	挤压加工，挤压件

F

fabricate /'fæbrikeit/	*vt.*	构成，制作
fabricated steel		预制钢
face milling		铣面
faceplate /'feispleit/	*n.*	卡盘，面板，花盘
facilitate /fə'siliteit/	*v.*	使容易，促进，提供
facilitated /fə'siliteitd/	*v.*	使容易，促进
facing /'faisiŋ/	*n.*	端面车削，刮削
family-of-part /'fæmiliəv'pɑ:t/	*n.*	成族零件
fastener /'fɑ:snə/	*n.*	固定器，紧固零件
fatigue strength		疲劳强度
feed /fi:d/	*vt.*	供给，进给，走刀
feeder /'fi:də/	*n.*	进料器
feed track		输送道
ferrophosphorus /ˌferəu'fɔsfərəs/	*n.*	铁磷合金
ferrosilicon /ˌferəu'silikən/	*n.*	硅铁
filament /'filəmənt/	*n.*	细丝，丝状体
fillet /'filit/	*n.*	圆角，倒角
film /film/	*n.*	薄膜
finite-element /'fainait'elimənt/	*n.*	有限元
fit into		适合
fitting /'fitiŋ/	*n.*	安装，装配
fixture /'fikstʃə/	*n.*	装置，夹具，卡具，定位器
flame /fleim/	*n.*	火焰
flash /flæʃ/	*n.*	飞边
flashless /'flæʃlis/	*adj.*	无飞边的
flat-die forging		无模锻造，自由锻造
flawlessly /'flɔ:lisli/	*adv.*	无缺点的
flip /flip/	*vi.*	交换；翻页
floating holder		浮动刀夹
flow-line /fləu'lain/	*n.*	流线
flute /flu:t/	*n.*	沟槽
fluid dynamics		流体动力学
flywheel /'flaihwi:l/	*n.*	飞轮
follower /'fɔləuə/	*n.*	从动机构；从动轮
forging /'fɔ:dʒiŋ/	*n.*	锻造，锻件

fork truck=fork lift	叉车
formidable /ˈfɔːmidəbl/ adj.	强大的；可怕的；艰难的
forming /ˈfɔːmiŋ/ n.	成型，成形；定型
four-bar linkage	四连杆机构
fraction /ˈfrækʃən/ n.	分数，分式
fracture /ˈfræktʃə/ n.	断裂
friction-cut /ˈfrikʃənˈkʌt/ v.	摩擦切割
full section	全剖面
full-size /ˌfulˈsaiz/ n.	实际大小
functional test	功能测试，功能试验

G

gage /geidʒ/ vt.	测量，测定
gang milling	组合铣削
gantry /ˈgæntri/ n.	（起重机）门形框架，台架
gap /gæp/ n.	缺口，裂口，间隙，缝隙，差距
gauge /geidʒ/ n.	直径；（金属板的）厚度；量具
gearshaft /ˈgiəʃɑːft/ n.	齿轮轴
geometrical /dʒiəˈmetrikəl/ adj.	几何的，几何学的
gib-head key	弯头键
governor /ˈgʌvənə/ n.	调速器
gradual /ˈgrædjuəl/ a.	逐渐的，平缓的
grain /grein/ n.	晶粒
graphics /ˈgræfiks/ n.	图解计算法，图形法
graphics terminal	图形终端
graphite /ˈgræfait/ n.	石墨
grinding machine	磨床
grinding wheel	砂轮
grit /grit/ n.	磨料粒，小砂粒
groove /gruːv/ n.	凹槽，槽沟
gullet /ˈgʌlit/ n.	锯齿间空隙
gun barrel	枪筒，炮筒

H

hacksaw /ˈhæksɔː/ n.	弓锯
hacksawing /ˈhækˈsɔːiŋ/ n.	弓锯法
half section	半剖面
hand reamer	手铰刀，手用铰刀
harden /ˈhɑːdn/ v.	变硬，淬火
hardened steel	淬火钢
hardening /ˈhɑːdəniŋ/ n.	淬火，硬化

head /hed/ n.	（动力）头，颈部
headstock /'hed'stɔk/ n.	机头座，车［刨］床头座，床头座，床头箱，主轴箱
heat treatment	热处理
helical /'helikəl/ n.	螺线
a.	螺线形的
helical gear	斜齿轮，螺旋齿轮
helix /'hiːliks/ n.	螺旋线
helix angle	螺旋角
herein /ˌhiər'in/ adv.	于此，在这里
herringbone /'heriŋbəun/ n.	人字形；交叉缝式
hexagonal /hek'sægənəl/ adj.	六边形的，六角形的
hidden line	隐线，虚线
hierarchical /ˌhaiə'rɑːkikəl/ adj.	分层次的，体系的，等级的，层次的，分级的
high-performance /ˌhaipə'fɔːməns/ n.	高性能
hinge /hindʒ/ n.	铰接，铰链
hobbing /'hɔbiŋ/ n.	滚铣，滚齿
hoist /hɔist/ n.	起重机，卷扬机
honing /'həuniŋ/ n.	搪磨，珩磨
horsepower /'hɔːsˌpauə/ n.	马力，输出功率
hot forming	热成形
hot-rolling /ˌhɔt'rəuliŋ/ n.	热轧，加热压光
hot working	热加工，热处理
hub /hʌb/ n.	轮毂
hybrid /'haibrid/ adj.	混合的
hypoid gear	偏轴伞齿轮
hypothetical /ˌhaipəu'θətikəl/ adj.	假设的，假定的

I

Ignite /ig'nait/ v.	点火
ignition /ig'niʃən/ n.	点火
impart /im'pɑːt/ vt.	给予
impetus /'impitəs/ n.	推动力，动力
impression-die forging	压印模锻造
impurity /im'pjuəriti/ n.	不纯；杂质
incandescent /ˌinkæn'desnt/ adj.	遇热发光的，白炽的
ingenuity /ˌindʒi'njuː(ː)iti/ n.	机灵，独创性
impact strength	冲击强度，冲击韧性
impinge /im'pindʒ/ n.	碰撞，冲击；
v.	撞击
implement /'implimənt/ n.	工具，器具

inability /ˌinəˈbiliti/ n.	无能，无力
incorporate /inˈkɔːpəreit/ vt.	结合，收编，合并
increment /ˈinkrimənt/ n.	增加
incremental forging	步进锻造
induction /inˈdʌkʃən/ n.	吸入
infeed /inˈfiːd/ n.	横进给，横向进磨，横切
inflammable /inˈflæməbl/ adj.	易燃的
ingot /ˈiŋɔt/ n.	锭，钢锭
ingot casting	铸锭，模铸锭
inherently /inˈhiərəntli/ adv.	本能的，自然的，本质上的
inhibitor /inˈhibitə/ n.	绊脚石
inject /inˈdʒekt/ v.	喷射
injection /inˈdʒkʃən/ n.	喷射
inquiry /inˈkwaiəri/ n.	查询
iterative /ˈitərətiv/ adj.	重复的，反复的
insert /ˈinsəːt/ n.	嵌入，插入，嵌入物
inside caliper	内卡钳，内径卡
instantaneous /ˌinstənˈteinjəs/ adj.	瞬间的
instantaneously /ˌinstəˈteiniəsli/ adj.	瞬间
interactive graphics	交互式图形学
interchangeability /ˌintəːˌtʃeindʒəˈbiliti/ n.	互换性
intercrystalline /ˌintəːˈkristəlain/ adj.	晶（粒）间的，沿晶界的
interference fit	干涉配合，过盈配合
integration /ˌintiˈgreiʃən/ n.	综合，一体化，积分
intermittent /ˌintə(ː)ˈmitənt/ adj.	间歇的，断断续续的
interpolation /intəːpəuˈleiʃn/ n.	插补
intrinsic /inˈtrinsik/ adj.	固有的，本质的
inventory /ˈinventri/ n.	（商品，货物等）清单，目录，报表；存货，库存
inversion /inˈvəːʃən/ n.	颠倒，转换
investment casting	熔模铸造法，蜡模铸造法
involute /ˈinvəluːt/ n.	渐开线，切展线
isothermal forging	等温锻造

J

jackshaft /ˈdʒækʃɑːft/ n.	中间轴
jerk /dʒəːk/ n.	急拉，急推，弯扭
jig /dʒig/ n.	夹具，钻模
joint-interpolated	联合插补
journal bearing	滑动轴承
joy-stick /ˈdʒɔiˌstik/ n.	操纵杆
judicious /dʒuˈdiʃəs/ adj.	明智的，有见识的；审慎的

justifiable /ˈdʒʌstifaiəbl/ adj.　　　言之有理的，无可非议的

K

kaolin /ˈkeiəlin/ n.	高岭土
keep pace (with)	与……同步，并驾齐驱
kerf /kə:f/ n.	切口，截口，锯痕
key /ki:/ n.	键，楔
adj.	主要的，关键的
key-pad=keyboard　n.	键盘
keyway /ˈki:wei/ n.	键沟；扁形钥孔
kinematics /ˌkainiˈmætiks/ n.	运动学
kinetics /kaiˈnetiks/ n.	动力学
kN (kilonewton)	千牛顿
knee /ni:/ n.	升降台
knurl /nə:l/ n.	刻痕，滚花

L

label /ˈleibl/ vt.	作标记
laminated /ˈlæmineitid/ adj.	薄板状的，层压的
lanolin /ˈlænəlin/ n.	羊毛脂
lapping /ˈlæpiŋ/ n.	研磨，抛光
laser gage	激光测厚仪
lathe /leið/ n.	车床
vt.	用车床加工
layer /ˈleiə/ n.	层
layout drawing	布置图，轮廓图
legibility　n.	易解（读），清晰度
lever /ˈli:və/ n.	手柄
liability /ˌlaiəˈbiliti/ n.	易用性，倾向性，责任
lighten /ˈlaitn/ v.	减轻，（使）轻松，使发亮
light load vehicle	轻载小车
linkage /ˈliŋkidʒ/ n.	连杆机构，连接
line shafting	轴系
lip relief angle	钻缘后角
lithography /liˈɵɔgrəfi/ n.	平版印刷术
load-carrying capacity	负荷能力，承载能力
locknut /ˈlɔknʌt/ n.	防松螺母
lock washer	锁紧垫圈，止动垫圈，防松垫圈
longitudinal section	纵剖面
long-running /ˈlɔŋˌrʌniŋ/ n.	长期运行
lubricate /ˈlju:brikeit/ vt.	加润滑剂，使润滑

M

machinability /məʃi:nə'biliti/ n.	机械加工性，切削性
machine center	加工中心
machine-finishing n.	机械精加工，机械抛光
machined surface	加工面
magazine /ˌmægə'zi:n/ n.	仓库
magnesia /mæg'ni:ʃə/ n.	氧化镁
magnitude /'mægnitu:d/ n.	量级；巨大，广大；重大，重要
maid-of-all-work	全能助手
main spindle	主轴
majority /mə'dʒɔriti/ n.	大部分
malfunction /mæl'fʌŋkʃən/ n.	故障、工作不正常
malleability /ˌmæliə'biliti/ n.	有延展性，柔顺
malleable /'mæliəbl/ adj.	有延展性的，可锻的
manganese /'mæŋgəni:z/ n.	锰
management /'mænidʒmənt/ n.	操纵，处理
management information system	管理信息系统
manila /mə'nilə/ n.	马尼拉麻
manipulate /mə'nipjuleit/ vt.	操作
manipulator /mə'nipjuleitə/ n.	操作手，机械手
margin /'mɑ:dʒin/ n.	钻缘
mechanical drawing	机械图，机械制图
mechanical engineering	机械工程（学）
mechanics /mi'kæniks/ n.	力学
mechanization /ˌmekənai'zeiʃən/ a.	机械化
member /'membə/ n.	组成部分，构件
messy /'mesi/ adj.	凌乱的
metallurgical /metə'lə:dʒikəl/ adj.	冶金学的，冶金的
metallurgist /me'tælədʒist/ n.	冶金家
metallurgy /me'tælədʒi/ n.	冶金学，冶金术
metalworking /'metlwə:kiŋ/ n.	金属加工
adj.	金属制造的
metrology /mi'trɔlədʒi/ n.	度量衡学，度量衡
mica /'maikə/ n.	云母
microinch /'maikrəuintʃ/ n.	百万分之一英寸，微英寸
milling /'miliŋ/ n.	铣削
milling cutter	铣刀
milling machine	铣削机，铣床
miniaturization /ˌminiətʃərai'ʃən/ n.	小型化
minicell /'minisel/ n.	微单元
misalignment /ˌmisə'lainmənt/ n.	未对准；位移；角度误差；失调

misnomer /mis'nəumə/ n.	误称
mixer /'miksə/ n.	混合器，搅拌机
mixture /'mikstʃə/ n.	混合物，混合气
mock-up /'mɔkʌp/ n.	实体模型
molecular /mə'lekjulə/ adj.	分子的
modification /mɔdifi'keiʃən/ n.	改进了的形式
module /'mɔdju:l/ n.	组件，模块
modulus /'mɔdjuləs/ n.	模数，模量
molding /'məuldiŋ/ n.	翻砂；制模，压模
molybdenum /mə'libdinəm/ n.	钼
moment of inertia	转动惯量
Monel metal	蒙乃尔合金，铜镍合金
multitooth /'mʌltitu:θ/ n.	多齿
adj.	多齿的
Mylar /'mailɑ:(r)/ n.	聚酯薄膜
Mylar film	聚酯薄膜

N

near-net-shaped /,niənet'ʃeipt/ adj.	近净形的
nebulous /'nebjuləs/ adj.	模糊的，朦胧的
necessitate /ni'sesiteit/ vt.	使需要，使成为必需
needle bearing	滚针轴承
negative /'negətiv/ n.	负片，底片
neoprene /'ni:əupri:n/ n.	氯丁橡胶
net result	最终结果
net-shaped /'netʃeipt/ adj.	净形的
nickel /'nikl/ n.	镍
nickel-cobalt-base /'nikl,kəubɔ:lt'beis/ n.	镍钴基
niobium /nai'əubiəm/ n.	铌
nodular iron	球墨铸铁
nominal /'nɔminl/ adj.	公称的，标称的，额定的
nomography /nəu'mɔgrəfi/ n.	图解构成术
nonassembly /'nɔnə'sembli/ n.	非装配，非组装
nonferrous /,nɔn'ferəs/ adj.	有色的；非铁或钢的
nonfunctional /'nɔn'fʌŋkʃənl/ adj.	非功能的
noninterference /'nɔn,intə'fiərəns/ n.	不互相干扰
nonparallelism /'nɔn'pærəlelizm/ n.	不平行度
nonsynchronous /'nɔn'siŋkrənəs/ adj.	非同步的（异步的，不同期的）
nonvalue-added /'nɔn'vælju:æ'did/ adj.	没有附加值的，不增值的
normal distribution	正态分布
nozzle /'nɔzl/ n.	喷嘴
nucleus /'nju:kliəs/ n.	核心
numerical control	数字控制

O

oblique /əˈbliːk/ adj.	倾斜的；间接的
obstruction /əbˈstrʌkʃən/ n.	堵塞，障碍物
obtainable /əbˈteɪnəb(ə)l/ a.	可得到的，能达到的
off-center /ˈɔ(ː)fˈsentə/ adj.	偏离中心的
adv.	偏离中心地
offsetting /ˈɔːfsetɪŋ/ n.	偏心距，位移，偏移
one-at-a-time /ˈwʌnætəˈtaɪm/ adv.	一次一个
one-way /ˈwʌnˈweɪ/ adj.	单向的
open-die /ˈəupəndaɪ/ n.	开式模具
open-die forging	开式模锻造；开式锻模
operations research	运筹学
option /ˈɔpʃən/ n.	可选品，选择，备选件
orbital forging	轨形锻造
orient /ˈɔːrɪənt/ vt.	定……的方向
orientation /ˌɔːrɪenˈteɪʃən/ n.	方向，方位，定位，倾斜性
orifice /ˈɔrɪfɪs/ n.	孔，节流孔
orthographic representation	正视表示法
Otto cycle	奥托循环
outwards /ˈautwədz/ adv.	向外
oval /ˈəuvəl/ adj.	卵形的，椭圆的
n.	椭圆形
overall /ˈəuvərɔːl/ adv.	大体上
over-and-under type /ˈəuvəˈænd,ʌndətaɪp/ n.	升降式
overfill /ˌəuvəˈfɪl/ vt.	使满溢，过度填充
overhang /ˈəuvəˌhæŋ/ n.	伸出物，伸出量
oxide /ˈɔksaɪd/ n.	氧化物

P

PABLA	逻辑法问题分析
package /ˈpækɪdʒ/ n.	程序包；组件；成套设备
packaging /ˈpækɪdʒɪŋ/ n.	包装，封装
pallet /ˈpælɪt/ n.	托盘，货盘
pallet elevator	托盘升降机
pallet truck	托盘运输车
paraffin /ˈpærəfɪn/ n.	石蜡，烷烃，煤油
parts-placing mechanism	元件分配装置
patch /pætʃ/ n.	小块田
payroll /ˈpeɪrəul/ n.	工资单
pendant /ˈpendənt/ n.	控制板，悬挂式操纵台
perception /pəˈsepʃən/ n.	理解，理会

permeability /ˌpəːmiəˈbiliti/ n.	渗透性
perpendicularity /ˌpəːpənˌdikjuˈlæriti/ n.	垂直，垂直度
perplexing /pəˈpleksiŋ/ adj.	复杂的，令人困惑的
petrol /ˈpetrəl/ n.	汽油
phase /feiz/ n.	与……同步
phenolic /fiˈnɔlik/ n.	酚醛
phenomena /fiˈnɔmənə/ n.	现象
phenolic resin	酚醛树脂
phonograph /ˈfəunəɡrɑːf/ n.	留声机，电唱机
phosphate /ˈfɔsfeit/ n.	磷酸盐，磷酸酯
phosphoric acid	磷酸
phosphorus /ˈfɔsfərəs/ n.	磷
photosensitize /ˌfəutəˈsensitaiz/ vt.	使感光；使具有感光性
pictorial view	插图，示图
piece-handing time	工件装卸时间
pinion /ˈpinjən/ n.	小齿轮
piston /ˈpistən/ n.	活塞，柱塞
pitch /pitʃ/ n.	节距
pitch diameter	节径，节圆直径，中径
pivot /ˈpivət/ n.	枢轴，支点
planar /ˈpleinə/ adj.	平面的，二维的
planer /ˈpleinə/ n.	龙门刨床
planing /ˈpleiniŋ/ n.	刨削，刨工
plaster molding	石膏造型
plate cam	平板凹轮
platen /ˈplætən/ n.	压盘，滚筒
plating /ˈpleitiŋ/ n.	镀件
plot /plɔt/ n.	曲线；图表
plough /plau/ n.	犁
plumbing /ˈplʌmiŋ/ n.	铅管系统，水管装置
plunger /ˈplʌndʒə/ n.	柱塞
pneumatic /njuːˈmætik/ adj.	气动的，气体的，气体力学的
pneumatically adv.	气动地
pocket /ˈpɔkit/ n.	槽
point angle	顶角
polishing /ˈpɔliʃiŋ/ n.	磨光，抛光
pollutant /pəˈljuːtənt/ n.	污染物，污染物质
polymer /ˈpɔlimə/ n.	聚合物
polymerize /ˈpɔliməraiz/ v.	（使）聚合
polyester /ˈpɔlistə/ n.	聚酯
porcelain /ˈpɔːslin/ adj.	瓷制的，精美的
n.	瓷器
porcelain enamel	搪瓷
porosity /pɔːˈrɔsiti/ n.	多孔性，有孔性

port /pɔːt/ n.	孔，口
potential /pəˈtenʃəl/ adj.	潜在的
pouring basin	浇口杯，外浇杯
pouring gate	浇口，注口，直浇口
powder metallurgy	粉末冶金，粉末冶金学
power-and-free /ˈpauəˈəndˈfriː/ adj.	动力自由式的
power plant	发电厂，动力装置
prealloy /priˈæloi/ n.	预合金
predominantly /priˈdɔminəntli/ adv.	主要地，显著地
prematurely /ˌpreməˈtjuəli/ adv.	过早地，早熟地
primary axis	主坐标轴
prismatic pair	棱形副
principle /ˈprinsəpəl/ n.	原则，准则
probe /prəub/ vt.	测探，探测
process planning	工艺规程设计
product design specification	产品设计说明书
programmability /ˌprəugrægəˈbiliti/ n.	可编程序性
projection /prəˈdʒekʃən/ n.	投影，投射
promote /prəˈməut/ vt.	提倡，鼓励
propagation /ˌprɔpəˈgeiʃən/ n.	传播
prototype /ˈprəutətaip/ n.	样机，原型
protuberance /prəˈtjuːbərəns/ n.	凸起，隆起
prudent /ˈpruːdənt/ adj.	谨慎的，精明的，节俭的
P. T. O.（Power take-off）	动力输出轴
pulldown /ˈpulˈdaun/ n.	下拉
pulley /ˈpuli/ n.	滑轮
pullup /ˈpulˈʌp/ n.	拉起，吸起
punch /pʌntʃ/ n.	冲头，冲压机
vt.	穿孔
pushdown /ˈpuʃˈdaun/ n.	下推
pushup /ˈpuʃˈʌp/ n.	上推
pyrometer /paiˈrɔmitə/ n.	高温计

Q

quality control	质量管理，质量控制
quenching /ˈkwentʃiŋ/ n.	淬火，骤冷
queue /kjuː/ n.	对，列
v.	排队

R

raceway /ˈreiswei/ n.	滚道
rack-and-pinion /rækˈəndˈpinjən/ n.	齿条与齿轮

reaction /ri'ækʃən/ n.	反应；反作用力
radial /'reidjəl/ adj.	径向的，（沿）半径的
range from…to…	范围从…到…
ream /ri:m/ vt.	铰大（…的）口径
reaming /'ri:miŋ/ n.	铰孔，扩孔，清除毛边，铰削作业
rearward /'riəwəd/ adv.	向后部
recess /ri'ses/ n.	凹进部分，退刀槽
reciprocate /ri'siprəkeit/ v.	来回，往复
reciprocating /ri'siprəkeitiŋ/ adj.	往复的
record strip	记录员
recrystallization /ˌri:ˌkristəlai'zeiʃən/ n.	再结晶
redeployment /ˌri:di'plɔimənt/ n.	调动，调配，重新部署
red-hot /ˌred'hɔt/ adj.	炽热的，最新的
reduced instruction set processor	简化指令集处理器
reduction /ri'dʌkʃən/ n.	还原
redundant /ri'dʌndənt/ adj.	多余地，重复地
reel /ri:l/ n.	卷盘，磁带盘
refractory /ri'frʌktəri/ adj.	耐熔的；耐火的；
n.	耐火材料
reiterative /ri:'itərətiv/ adj.	反复的
removal /ri'mu:vəl/ n.	移去，除去
reservoir /'rezəvwɑ:/ n.	油箱
resharpen /ˌri:'ʃɑ:pən/ v.	尖刃修磨
reside /ri'zaid/ v.	居住，存放
resilience /ri'ziliəns/ n.	弹性，弹力
resin /'rezin/ n.	树脂
resistance /ri'zistəns/ n.	阻力；抵抗；抗力
resolver /ri'zɔvə/ n.	解析器，解算装置
resultant /ri'zʌltənt/ adj.	合成的；作为结果而发生的
retaining ring	挡圈，卡环，固定环
retrieval /ri'tri:vəl/ n.	（可）取回，（可）恢复
retrieve /ri'tri:v/ v.	检索
retrofit /'retrəˌfit/ v.	改进，改造
revolve /ri'vɔlv/ v.	旋转
revs. (revolutions)	转速
rheocasting /'ri:əkʌstiŋ/ n.	流变铸造
ridge /ridʒ/ n.	脊，螺脊
rifle /'raifl/ n.	在（枪膛）内制来复线
rim /rim/ n.	边缘；轮缘
ring rolling	环锻
rivet /'rivit/ n.	铆钉；
vt.	铆；铆接
rivnut /'raivnʌt/ n.	螺纹铆钉

robotic /'rəubɔtik/ adj.	机器人的，机器人式的
robotics /'rəubɔtiks/ n.	机器人学
roller /'rəulə/ n.	滚柱，辊
roll forging	滚锻，轧锻
roller bearing	滚柱轴承
root mean square	均方根
rotary /'rəutəri/ a.	旋转的
rotate /rəu'teit/ v.	旋转
rotation /rəu'teiʃən/ n.	旋转
roughing /'rʌfiŋ/ n.	粗加工
roughing cut	粗切削
routinely /ruː'tiːnli/ adv.	例行公事地
rubber band	橡胶圈，橡皮筋
rudimentary /ˌruːdi'mentəri/ adj.	初步的，基本的
rule of thumb	经验法则
running accuracy	旋转精度
runout /'rʌnaut/ n.	跳动，径向跳动
rupture /'rʌptʃə/ n.	断裂，破裂
rush /rʌʃ/ v.	急流

S

saddle /'sædl/ n.	滑板，座板
sag /sæg/ n.	下垂，垂度
schematic drawing	简图，示意图
scooter /'skuːtə/ n.	小型摩托车
scrap /skræp/ vt.	扔弃
n.	废料，废金属
scratch /skrætʃ/ n.	刻痕，划痕
screwdriving /'skruːˌdraiviŋ/ n.	上螺钉
screw pair	螺旋副
scrutiny /'skruːtini/ n.	研究，推敲
sectional view	剖视图，截面图
section-lining /'sekʃənlainiŋ/ n.	剖面线法
segregation /ˌsegri'geiʃən/ n.	偏析，分离
self-aligning /ˌselfə'lainiŋ/ adj.	自动对准的；
n.	自动定心，自动调心
self-locking nut	自锁螺母，防松螺母
self-piercing /ˌself'piəsiŋ/ adj.	自开孔的
self-tapping /ˌself'tæpiŋ/ adj.	自动攻螺纹的
semi-continuous /ˌsemikən'tinjuəs/ adj.	半连续的，断断续续的
sensitive drilling	手压钻削
sequences /'siːkwəns/ n.	顺序

serration /seˈreiʃən/ n.	锯齿，细齿
servomotor /ˈsəːvəuˌməutə/ n.	伺服电机
servosystem /ˈsəːvəuˌsistəm/ n.	伺服系统
setscrew /ˈsetskruː/ n.	固定螺钉，止动螺钉，定位螺钉
shafting /ˈʃɑːftiŋ/ n.	传动轴，轴系
shank /ʃæŋk/ n.	柄，刀柄，钎尾
shaped /ʃeipt/ adj.	成形的，仿形的
shaper /ˈʃeipə/ n.	牛头刨床
shaping /ˈʃeipiŋ/ n.	牛头刨削
share /ʃɛə/ n.	份，均分
shear strength	抗剪强度
shear stress	切向应力
shellac /ʃəˈlæk/ n.	虫胶
sherardizing /ˈʃerədaiziŋ/ n.	渗锌法
shop floor	车间，工场
shot /ʃɔt/ n.	丸，砂
shot blasting	喷砂清理
shoulder /ˈʃəuldə/ n.	肩，凹肩
shrinkage /ˈʃriŋkidʒ/ n.	收缩
silica /ˈsilikʒ/ n.	硅石，硅土
silicon /ˈsilikən/ n.	硅；硅元素
single-component /ˌsiŋlkəmˈpəunənt/ n.	单个零件
situate /ˈsitjueit/ vt.	使位于，使处于
sketch /sketʃ/ vi.	绘略图；素描
slab /slæb/ n.	板坯，扁坯
slab milling	平面铣刀
sleeve bearing	滑动轴承，套筒轴承
slider-crank /ˌslaidəˈkræŋk/ n.	滑块曲柄
slider-crank mechanism	滑块曲柄机构
sliding /ˈslaidiŋ/ adj.	滑行的，变化的
slogging /ˈslɔgiŋ/ a.	艰难的
slotted nut	有槽螺母，开槽螺母
slurry /ˈsləːri/ n.	泥浆，浆
snugly /ˈsnʌgli/ adv.	贴身地；隐藏地；尚可地
Society of Automotive Engineers	汽车工程师协会
socket /ˈsɔkit/ n.	承物的凹处
Solidification /səˌlidifiˈkeiʃən/ n.	凝固，固化体（作用）
solid modeling	实体造型
sow (sowed, sown/sowed) /sau/ v.	播种
sparingly /ˈspɛəriŋli/ adv.	节俭地，保守地
spark /spɑːk/ n.	火花
sparking plug	火花塞
spatial /ˈspeiʃəl/ adj.	空间的，立体的

specification /ˌspesifiˈkeiʃən/ n.	规格
specimen /ˈspesimin/ n.	范例，标本，样品，样本，待试验物
spectrum /ˈspektrəm/ n.	光谱，波谱
speed up	加速
spherical /ˈsferikəl/ adj.	球面的；球形的
spigot /ˈspigət/ n.	插销，塞子；阀门
spindle /ˈspindl/ n.	轴，主轴
spiral /ˈspaiərəl/ adj. n.	螺旋形的；螺旋形，螺旋，螺线
spline /splain/ n.	花键，止转楔
split rivet	开口铆钉
spot-facing /ˌspɔtˈfeisiŋ/ n.	锪孔，锪端面
springloaded	弹簧加载的
sprue /spru:/ n.	浇入口
spur gear	正齿轮
stack /stæk/ n.	堆；堆栈
staggering /ˈstægəriŋ/ adj.	交错的，摇摆的
standing position	停车状态
statistically /stəˈtistikəli/ adv.	统计上地，统计
stereotomy /ˌstiəriˈɔtəmi/ n.	实体物切割术（切石法）
stickout /ˈstikaut/ n.	悬臂
stiffness /ˈstifnis/ n.	刚度，刚性
stimulant /ˈstimjulənt/ n.	兴奋剂
stock /stɔk/ n.	原料，备料
stop /stɔp/ n.	挡块
stoppage /ˈstɔpidʒ/ n.	中断，填塞
storage matrix	存储矩阵
straddle /ˈstrædl/ adj.	跨式的
straddle-milling /ˈstrædlˈmiliŋ/ n.	跨铣法
strain hardening	应变硬化，加工硬化，冷作硬化
stress /stres/ n.	应力，应力状态
stress-reversal /ˈstresriˈvə:səl/ n.	应力反向
stroke /strəuk/ n.	冲程，行程；一笔，一画
structural drawing	结构图，构造图
stub /stʌb/ n.	轴端
stylus /ˈstailəs/ n.	唱针，铁笔
subcategory /ˈsʌbˌkætigəri/ n.	子类，子范畴
succession /səkˈseʃən/ n.	自然演替；一系列，接连
sufficiently /səˈfəntli/ adv.	充足地，充分地
sulphur /ˈsʌlfə/ n.	硫，硫磺
superalloy /ˌsju:pəˈælɔi/ n.	超合金，超耐热合金
superfinishing /ˌsju:pəˈfiniʃiŋ/ n.	超精加工
supersede /ˌsju:pəˈsi:d/ vt.	代替，紧接着……而到来

superstructure /ˈsjuːpəˌstrʌktʃə/ n.	上部结构
supplemental /ˌsʌpliˈmentl/ adj.	辅助的
surface finish	表面粗糙度
surface treatment	表面处理
susceptible /səˈseptəbl/ adj.	易受影响的，易感动的
susceptibility /səˌseptəˈbiliti/ n.	敏感度，灵敏度
sustained /səsˈteind/ a.	被支持的，持续的
swage /sweidʒ/ vt.	锻造，顶锻
sweep /swiːp/ n.	扫描，摇杆
symmetrical /siˈmetrikəl/ adj.	对称的；均匀的
synectics /siˈnektiks/ n.	协力创新法；协同学

T

table-top /ˈteiblˈtɔp/ adj.	台式的
tabular /ˈtæbjulə/ adj.	制成表的，表格式的
tabulation /ˌtæbjuˈleiʃən/ n.	制表，造册
tail stock /ˈteilˈstɔk/ n.	[机] 尾架，尾座，顶针座
tang /tæŋ/ n.	柄舌
tangential /tænˈdʒenʃel/ adj.	相切的，切线的
tantalum /ˈtæntələm/ n.	钽
taper /ˈteipə/ n.	锥形，锥度
v.	逐渐变细，逐渐减少
tapered /ˈteipəd/ adj.	带梢的；有锥度的
tapered key	锥形键
taper turning	锥体车削
tapping /ˈtæpiŋ/ n.	攻螺纹
tear /tɛə/ n.；v.	扯裂，撕裂
temper /ˈtempə/ v.	回火，调和，调节
tempering /ˈtempəriŋ/ n.	回火
template /ˈtempleit/ n.	样板，模板
temporary /ˈtempərəri/ adj.	暂时的，临时的
tensile strength	抗拉强度，抗张强度
terminology /təːrməˈnɑːlədʒi/ n.	专门名词；术语，术语学；用辞
testability /ˈtestəbiliti/ n.	可测试性，易测性
thence /ðens/ adv.	从那里（起），从那时起
thermal /ˈθəːməl/ n.	热；
adj.	热的，热量的
thermal stability	热稳定性，耐热性
thermodynamics /ˈθəːməudaiˈnæmiks/ n.	热力学
thermoplastic /ˈθəːməuˈplæstik/ n.	热塑性塑料
adj.	热塑性的
thermoset /ˈθəːməuset/ n.	热固性塑料；
adj.	热固性的

thermosetting /ˌθəːməuˈsetiŋ/ n.	热硬化，加热固化
the vast majority	绝大部分的
thread /θrəd/ n.	螺纹；线
three-shift /ˈθriːʃift/ n.	三班制
threshold /ˈθreʃhəuld/ n.	门槛，界限
through-feed /ˈθruːˈfiːd/ n.	贯穿进给，贯穿进刀
time-phased /taimˈfeizd/ adj.	分时的
timing /ˈtaimiŋ/ n.	定时
tin /tin/ n.	锡，马口铁
tinner /ˈtinə/ n.	白铁工，锡工
titanium /taiˈteinjəm/ n.	钛
tolerance /ˈtɔlərəns/ n.	公差
vt.	给（机器部件等）规定公差
tone arm	唱臂，拾音器臂
tong /tɔŋ/ n.	夹钳，抓手
tool-and-die /ˈtuːlənˈdai/ n.	工具和模具
tool changer	换刀器，换刀装置
toolchanging /ˈtuːlˈtʃeindʒiŋ/ n.	刀具更换
top centre (top dead centre)	上止点，上死点
torque /tɔːk/ n.	扭矩，转矩
torsional strength	抗扭强度
tow /təu/ v.	牵引
towing vehicle	小型牵引车
tracer /ˈtreisə/ n.	描图员
tracing paper	描图纸，透明纸
track /træk/ n.	轮距
transference /ˈtrænsfərəns/ n.	移动，转送
transient surface	过渡面
translatory /ˈtrænslətəri/ adj.	平移的，平动的
transmission /trænsˈmiʃən/ n.	传动装置
transmit /trænzˈmit/ v.	传递
trial and error	试错法
trial-cut /ˈtraiəlˈkʌt/ n.	试切，试切割
troubleshoot /ˈtrʌblʃuːt/ v.	故障检修
n.	排除故障
truncated cone	截头圆锥体，截体
tubing /ˈtjuːbiŋ/ n.	管，管材
tubular /ˈtjuː(ː)bjulə/ adj.	管状的，空心的
tungsten /ˈtʌŋstn/ n.	钨
turn corners	转弯
turret /ˈtʌrit/ n.	转刀架，转塔
turret drill	六角机床
twist drill	［机］麻花钻，螺旋钻
two-way /ˈtuːˈwei/ adj.	双向的，两路的

U

unclamp /ˌʌnˈklæmp/ vt.	松开……的夹钳
uncover /ʌnˈkʌvə/ v.	打开，使露出
uniform /ˈjuːnifɔːrm/ adj.	一样的；规格一致的
unit load vehicle	单载小车
unit strain	单位应变
universal joint	万向节
unobstructed /ˌʌnəbˈstrʌktid/ adj.	无阻碍的，没有阻挡的，自由的
unorthodox /ʌnˈɔːθədɔks/ adj.	非正式的，不正统的
unscrew	拧松螺丝，拆卸
unsuccessfully /ˌʌnsəkˈsesfuli/ adv.	失败地，无用地
upsetting /ʌpˈsetiŋ/ n.	镦锻，镦粗
urethane /ˈjuəriˌθein/ n.	氨基甲酸乙酯

V

validate /ˈvælideit/ vt.	使生效，确认
value-added /ˌvæljuːˈædid/ adj.	有附加值的，增值的
value engineering	价值工程，工程经济学
valve /vælv/ n.	气门
vanadium /vəˈneidjəm/ n.	钒
vaporize /ˈveipəraiz/ v.	蒸发
vaporizing adj.	蒸发的
variant /ˈvɛəriənt/ n.	变量
variation /ˌvɛəriˈeiʃən/ n.	偏差
vast /vɑːst/ a.	巨大的
vertical /ˈvəːtikəl/ a.	垂直的
vessel /ˈvesəl/ n.	容器；船，飞船；血管
via /ˈvaiə, ˈviːə/ prep.	通过……
vibration /vaiˈbreiʃən/ n.	振动，摆动，摇动
vibration amplitude	振幅
vitreous /ˈvitriəs/ adj.	玻璃状的，透明的
vitreous enamel	釉瓷，搪瓷
vitrified /ˈvitrifaid/ adj.	陶瓷的，玻璃化的
vitrified clay	玻化焦

W

warping /ˈwɔːpiŋ/ n.	翘曲，歪扭变形
washer /ˈwɔʃə/ n.	垫圈
water-cooled /ˈwɔːtəkuːld/ adj.	水冷的
web /web/ n.	腹部，缩颈

wedge rolling	楔形滚轧，楔形轧制
wedge-shaped /ˈwedʒˈʃeipt/ adj.	楔形的
weld bead	焊缝
welding /ˈweldiŋ/ n.	焊接
welded-steel /ˈweldidˈsti:l/ n.	焊接钢
woodruff key	半圆键，半月键
workbench /ˈwə:kbentʃ/ n.	工作台，手工台
worktable /ˈwə:kˈteibl/ n.	工作台
worm gear	蜗轮，蜗杆与蜗轮
worn-out /ˌwɔ:nˈaut/ adj.	不能再用的，磨破的
wraparound /ˈræpəraund/ n.	绕回，环绕式处理
wrought /rɔ:t/ adj.	可锻的
wrought iron	熟铁

Y

yaw /jɔ:/ n.	侧滑角
yield stress	屈服应力

参考文献

[1] 卜玉坤. 大学专业英语机械英语 [M]. 北京:外语教学与研究出版社,2001.

[2] 陈统坚. 机械工程英语 [M]. 北京:机械工业出版社,1999.

[3] 李鹏飞,朱小燕等. 高等学校专业英语阅读教程 [M]. 北京:北京理工大学出版社,2001.

[4] 贺自强. 高等学校教学用书——机械工程专业英语 [M]. 北京:北京理工大学出版社,1989.

[5] Wright R T. Processes of Manufacturing [M]. The Coodheart-Willcox Company Inc,1987.

[6] Amstead B H, Oswald Phillip E. Begeman Myron L. Manufacturing processes [M]. John Wiley & sons,1987.

[7] Wakil Sherif D El. Processes and Design for Manufacturing [M]. Prentice Hall,1989.

[8] Chemov N. Machine Tools. Mir Publishers,1984.

[9] Lindberg R A. Processes and Materials of Manufacture [M]. Ally and Bacon/A Division of Simon & Schuster. Inc,1990.

[10] George Rzevski. On conceptual design of intelligent mechatronic systems [J]. Mechatronics,2003,(13):1029-1044.

[11] A. Gharbi, J.-P. Kenné. Maintenance scheduling and production control of multiple-machine manufacturing systems [J]. Computers & Industrial Engineering,2005,48 (4):693-707.

[12] Hédi Chtourou, Wassim Masmoudi, Aref Maalej. An expert system for manufacturing systems machine selection [J]. Expert Systems with Applications,2005,28 (3):461-467.

[13] K. L. Edwards. Manufacturing technologies for machines of the future:21st century technologies Dashchenko, A. I., (Ed.) [M]. New York:Springer-Verlag,2003.

[14] Chulho Chung, Qingjin Peng. The selection of tools and machines on web-based manufacturing environments [J]. International Journal of Machine Tools and Manufacture,2004,44 (2-3):317-326.

[15] D. M. Kennedy, J. Vahey, D. Hanney. Micro shot blasting of machine tools for improving surface finish and reducing cutting forces in manufacturing [J]. Materials & Design,2005,26 (3):203-208.

[16] Raúl Suárez, Jan Rosell. Feeding sequence selection in a manufacturing cell with four parallel machines [J]. Robotics and Computer-Integrated Manufacturing,2005,21 (3):185-195.